25 BOOKS

EVERY CHRISTIAN

SHOULD READ

Also by Renovaré

Connecting with God
by Lynda L. Graybeal and Julia L. Roller

Contemplative Compassion
by Sarah Butler Berlin

Devotional Classics
co-edited by Richard J. Foster and James Bryan Smith

Embracing the Love of God
by James Bryan Smith

Learning from Jesus
by Lynda L. Graybeal and Julia L. Roller

Life with God
by Richard J. Foster with Kathryn A. Helmers

The Life with God Bible
edited by Richard J. Foster and others

Living the Mission
by Lynda L. Graybeal and Julia L. Roller

Prayer and Worship
by Lynda L. Graybeal and Julia L. Roller

Spiritual Classics
co-edited by Richard J. Foster and Emilie Griffin

A Spiritual Formation Workbook
by James Bryan Smith with Lynda L. Graybeal

Streams of Living Water
by Richard J. Foster

Wilderness Time
by Emilie Griffin

A Year with God
compiled by Julia L. Roller

RENOVARÉ

25 BOOKS

EVERY CHRISTIAN

SHOULD READ

A Guide to
the Essential
Spiritual
Classics

Edited by Julia L. Roller

SELECTED BY:

Gayle Beebe • James Catford • Richard J. Foster
Emilie Griffin • Frederica Mathewes-Green • Michael G. Maudlin
Richard Rohr • Lyle SmithGraybeal • Phyllis Tickle
Chris Webb • Dallas Willard • John Wilson

HarperOne
An Imprint of HarperCollinsPublishers

HarperOne

25 BOOKS EVERY CHRISTIAN SHOULD READ: *A Guide to the Essential Spiritual Classics.*
Copyright © 2011 by Renovaré, Inc. All rights reserved. Printed in the United States of
America. No part of this book may be used or reproduced in any manner whatsoever
without written permission except in the case of brief quotations embodied in critical
articles and reviews. For information address HarperCollins Publishers, 10 East 53rd
Street, New York, NY 10022.

HarperCollins books may be purchased for educational, business, or sales promotional
use. For information please write: Special Markets Department, HarperCollins
Publishers, 10 East 53rd Street, New York, NY 10022.

HarperCollins website: http://www.harpercollins.com

HarperCollins®, ■ ®, and HarperOne™ are trademarks of HarperCollins Publishers

FIRST EDITION

Library of Congress Cataloging-in-Publication Data is available upon request.

ISBN 978-0-06-084143-0

11 12 13 14 15   RRD(H)   10 9 8 7 6 5 4 3 2 1

Contents

Foreword

25 Books Every Christian Should Read. Really? That seems such a huge claim. Are there really *any* definitive books every Christian should read, other than the Bible itself?

In selecting this list of twenty-five books, the editorial board has tried to identify a handful of the most outstanding books ever written on Christian faith and the life of prayer and discipleship. These books are an extraordinary distillation of wisdom about following Jesus written by some of our greatest saints, poets, and thinkers over the last two thousand years. Although our contemporary Western culture often seems allergic to serious reading and thought, Christians cannot afford such a complacent attitude. Just as any serious philosopher should at some point wrestle with Aristotle, and every actor with Shakespeare, so anyone who seriously desires to learn what it means to follow Christ without reserve, heart and soul, *must* wrestle with these writings. This list of twenty-five books is not final, complete, or definitive. But it is representative of the very best Christians have to offer.

Our selection of books comes with a warning and an encouragement. First the warning: there are no easy reads on this list. Some are more accessible than others, of course, but every one of these books is deeply challenging. Some will bust your brains; John Calvin's *Institutes of the Christian Religion* and Blaise Pascal's *Pensées* represent some of the most profound thinking about faith in twenty centuries of Christian history. Others, like William Law's *A Serious Call to a Devout and Holy Life,* will shake down your soul, forcing you to confront the very real cost of following Christ. Yet others will call you into a deeply attractive intimacy with Jesus—books like *The Way of a Pilgrim,* or John of the Cross's *Dark Night of the Soul.* But even here we are reminded that the treasure uncovered in the field can only be bought at great cost. These writings all take very seriously what Dietrich Bonhoeffer calls *The Cost of Discipleship.*

But together with the warning comes encouragement. These books have the power to renew your soul, rekindle your spiritual passion, and transform your life. If you have ever experienced a longing for God, a desire and thirst for a richer knowledge of Christ, a yearning for a deeper life, these writers will not disappoint. These twenty-five books are challenging precisely because their authors have dug down far below the superficialities of our age and theirs in search of the foundations of reality. They have known God intimately and profoundly, and their writings are intended to draw us into their experience.

This is rich fare. These books demand slow, thoughtful, and prayerful reading. They will not yield their rewards easily, yet there is an indescribable wealth in their pages, which no serious disciple of Christ, no devoted lover of Jesus, can possibly afford to miss. *25 Books Every Christian Should Read* will not only introduce you to these writings but will act as an informed companion as you read— introducing each book and writer, setting each one in context, pointing out a roadmap through the texts for new readers, highlighting key ideas and concepts.

Reading these books has changed my life. My prayer has been shaped by the insights of *The Philokalia*. Dante has helped me understand spiritual formation more fully through the pages of *The Divine Comedy*. Hopkins has helped me see the world more clearly and fully. As you begin to journey deeply into the classical tradition of Christian spiritual writing, may you, too, find yourself opened to the surprising grace of God and so made entirely new.

—Chris Webb
President, Renovaré USA
Englewood, Colorado
Season of Pentecost 2011

Introduction

We all want to be better. Our thinking. Our acting. Our believing. But how do we really change?

Throughout the history of the Christian faith, Christians have been transformed by spiritual reading. Our primary resource is the Bible, but our life of faith has also been shaped by the writings of many Christians who were seeking to interpret the Bible, further their understanding, and live the Christian life. Such writings serve not only as lenses to reveal and clarify the biblical message but also as testimonies and guidance from Christians who have walked our path before us. We recognize that these authors have achieved Christlikeness in a way we would like to emulate, and, so, by reading their works, we, too, hope to be transformed in the ways these exemplars of the faith were transformed.

While it is helpful and important to read these many witnesses of the Great Tradition to understand the impact they have had on our faith tradition—works like Augustine's *Confessions* and Calvin's *Institutes of the Christian Religion* changed the course of Christianity as we know it—the main reason we read the Christian classics is because they are powerful instruments of change. The goal of spiritual reading is for it to affect who we are and what we do, to transform us. As Richard J. Foster writes in *Celebration of Discipline,* "Remember that the key to the Discipline of study is not reading many books, but experiencing what we do read." The resource you hold in your hands will help you make the most of your time of spiritual reading for transformation into Christlikeness.

Why These Twenty-five Books

Perhaps it is hubris to try to select twenty-five books *every* Christian should read. Yet John Wesley had an even longer list of books that he recommended for every "serious" Christian, and since his list feels a bit dated, more than two hundred years later, we felt that creating such a list for a modern audience was a worthy goal. Instead of the dozens of titles in Wesley's library, however, we decided to choose only twenty-five, a number less intimidating than Wesley's long list but containing enough substance for a lifetime of thoughtful reflection. No matter how avid a reader you are, we hope that reading these twenty-five classics will become a goal for you.

Renovaré has a tradition of promoting the devotional classics of yesteryear, and so our first step was to solicit recommendations from our community of thousands across the country who have long been supporters of the Renovaré tradition and specifically our emphasis on devotional reading. We asked people to list the top five books that impacted their lives as Christians, and we were thrilled with the outpouring of feedback. Close to four hundred titles were nominated.

Next, we at Renovaré chose an editorial board to narrow this list to just twenty-five. Because we know that God has worked through a range of traditions, we wanted an editorial board that represented that diversity. Not surprisingly, then, the final list includes books essential to the Eastern (Orthodox) tradition as well as books more familiar to those in the Western (Latin) tradition, both Protestant and Catholic. In short, in the words of Gayle Beebe, a member of our editorial board, "We invite the reader to read the books that have drawn people of all backgrounds into a deeper and richer life with God."

Next, the board had to clarify just what our list should be. This book is not the list of the best Christian books ever written or a list of the top twenty-five devotional books; it isn't even the list of the top twenty-five classics, although we believe all of the books on the list are or will be considered classics of their respective genres. The books we have chosen to include are, instead, the books that the board judged served as the best guides for living life with God. Cumulatively, these books embody a rich treasure of wisdom and counsel for how to live the Christian life.

Because God has created us with different styles of learning and writing, we also included a variety of literary genres. While the list is skewed toward what one might consider traditionally "devotional," such as, for example, *The Imitation of Christ,* there is poetry and fiction and biography and more. Some books included here explain the faith; some explain spirituality and Christian living; and some illustrate or incarnate the faith through story, biography, or imagery.

It is also interesting to note that the list of twenty-five bends toward the contemplative in nature. There are two sides of our life with God, of course: the contemplative and the active. "Ora et lab-ora," prayer and work, is shorthand for the rule of many monastic orders. Nevertheless, the centuries of the Church have yielded vastly more literature on the regular practice of prayer and the more contemplative disciplines than on daily work in the world and the active life. This imbalance led inevitably to a similar skewing in our list.

In our choosing, of course, we had to set some parameters. One of the most obvious is that we excluded all books from living authors. Our belief is that it is best for books to be in the canon for a while before we can clearly evaluate their worth and helpfulness. As C. S. Lewis pointed out in his introduction to St. Athanasius's *On the Incarnation* (one of the twenty-five books we have selected), old books have the advantage of having been tested by time. As Lewis wrote, "A new book is still on its trial and the amateur is not in a position to judge it. It has to be tested against the great body of Christian thought down the ages, and all its hidden implications (often unsuspected by the author himself) have to be brought to light. . . . The only safety is to have a standard of plain, central Christianity ('mere Christianity' as Baxter called it) which puts the controversies of the moment in their proper perspective. Such a standard can be acquired only from the old books."[1] Thus we have given preference to those books that have been tested by "the clean sea breeze of the centuries," as Lewis puts it.[2]

And finally, the board also decided to exclude the most obvious entry. The most important book in the Christian devotional life is, of course, the Bible. Indeed, as Richard Foster writes in *Life with God,* "God has given us a written revelation of who God is and of what God's purposes are for humanity. And God has chosen to accomplish this great work through the People of God on earth. This written revelation now resides as a massive fact at the heart of human history. There is, simply, no book that is remotely close to achieving the significance and influence of the Bible. It is truly The Book (*hay Biblos*)."[3] Time with the Bible, on our own and in our communities, is vital and well spent. No book can supplant its primary importance for us as Christians. The Bible is the foundational work for the reading of all of these twenty-five books, just as the foundation of a building allows for the creativity and function of the building on top of it.

How to Do Spiritual Reading

These twenty-five books represent a unique opportunity and challenge: the opportunity is that reading them can assist in the reformation of our hearts and minds into the likeness of Jesus Christ; the challenge is that reading for this purpose can be very different from the way we typically interact with written material. In short, here we are reading primarily for formation rather than for information. Our society has trained us to extract data and knowledge from what we read. In contrast, what we hope to get out of reading these heart-oriented texts is wisdom and guidance from God. So we need to adjust our approach to the books and style of reading accordingly.

First of all, these chapters do not need to be read in any order. We have listed them here chronologically according to when they were written, and they can certainly be read in that order. Or you may want to consider which book it would be good for you to read based on what you need at the time. Those seeking wisdom to chew on throughout the day might select *The Sayings of the Desert Fathers*. Those needing an affirmation of the love of God might try *Revelations of Divine Love* or *The Return of the Prodigal Son*. It may be a good idea in the beginning to use this resource you hold in your hands to become familiar with all of the twenty-five books. We have created this book so that everyone can have a basic understanding of each author and work. Here you will also find strategies for reading, an excerpt to showcase the work, and questions for individuals or groups who want to process what they have read.

Another consideration for making the most of your spiritual reading is time and space. Many of the twenty-five books require extended time for the formational nature of the writing to have an effect. While a half hour is good, an hour or more is better, even if time cannot be set aside each and every day. Time allows one the opportunity to pore over and soak in the text, to chew and savor it. So often we are inclined to blast through a book like we go through magazines or mystery novels. We can do this with these twenty-five books as well, but it is much better for our souls if we give ourselves the permission to read and reread and read yet again the same paragraph that at any given moment is speaking to the heart within us. This slower pace of reading requires time. In fact, that could almost be another way of defining the list: these are the twenty-five spiritual books that are worth reading slowly and repeatedly.

Space is another consideration. Where will you do your spiritual reading? Know that the focus that spiritual reading requires is best achieved when we are comfortable and there are few competitors for our attention.

A time-tested way for slowing our reading and focusing our attention is to keep a journal on hand while reading for thoughts and reflections. Writing in the margins of the book and underlining words and phrases that resonate can also become a type of journal, a record of reading that will both mark time and bring benefit again when the book is referenced later. As such, while we do encourage simplicity, it may be best to find your own copy of this volume or get full editions of the books so that you can make them your own, as opposed to checking them out from the library or borrowing them from a friend. Many of these books are so well known that a well-stocked used bookstore will have a number of them.

We also recommend approaching the text in a nonjudgmental fashion. Often when reading older books or books in unfamiliar genres, we focus so much on the differences between our own outlook and that of the author that we close our minds to the wisdom found in this different perspective. We must consider the distance of time between when many of the twenty-five books were written and our period. Many of these authors were also experiencing a much different style of living than our own, such as a religious community or cloistered order. And there is the matter of our post-Enlightenment outlook; for instance, some of the authors of these books thought that the sun revolved around the earth! For whichever reason, to read these books for formation, we need to allow the stories and phrases that strike us as odd and peculiar to stand, at least initially. A good strategy might be to try to suspend judgment and simply allow the author to teach whatever it is she or he has to teach even if at times it seems unrealistic or strange. Remind your inner critic that the authors of many of these books were asking much different questions than we do, and that maybe we should be asking different questions ourselves.

The results of reading these books may be that (1) your vision of the kingdom of God becomes more and more acute, and it makes you long for the potential of it for yourself and your neighbors, and (2) you become depressed because this vision is so far away from your current reality. Such reactions are inevitable. Even with all of their human limitations and imperfect knowledge, few authors in the centuries of the Church have better captured the life of the kingdom of God than these authors here in *25 Books*. Inevitably, as we read, we will be caught up into this vision as well, and we may feel discouraged as we see how our own lives fail to measure up to this ideal. Reading these books with others can help moderate such feelings of discouragement, and even add to the benefit of our study. This is why we have designed this reader so it can be used by small groups. But ultimately we are alone with our thoughts and will look to God as our solace. In so doing, we enter into the joy and sorrow of God over the life of the world and our role in it.

The Structure of *25 Books*

A word about the way *25 Books* was built is in order. The first section of each chapter offers a brief background of the author and the book and summarizes the book's major themes. Our intention is not to offer extended biography or literary criticism; you'll more than likely find such information in the introduction of the actual book. We are more concerned with briefly describing the shape of the book, in a way that we hope will be helpful as a first introduction. We then describe why we consider the book essential, from the point of view of the Christian tradition and, more important, for the individual spiritual formation of the reader.

The next section offers guidance and strategies for reading the book. Of course, whenever we read literature of a bygone era, our attention is immediately drawn to mistakes, misunderstandings, or interpretations that are no longer accepted by today's standards. We mentioned above how important it is to try to suspend judgment initially when reading older works and unfamiliar genres, but of course all of these books were written by humans and so contain errors and misunderstandings. We in no way mean to suggest that we stand by every word in every one of these books. Just because we admire these books and the authors who penned them doesn't mean that we suggest reading them with minds turned off. Indeed it is best to approach every work, especially those dealing with the spiritual life, with a sense of discernment. We have endeavored to help by listing some of these possible trouble areas in this section and also offering some strategies for reading for spiritual formation.

Finally, each chapter includes sizable key excerpts from the selected book that provide a generous sample of the full work. We also provide a study guide with questions for individuals or groups. We wrote the questions so that they could be used both for those reading the whole work or for those just reading the excerpts included here. If you feel a question is too difficult to answer based on just the materials in this reader, then feel free to skip the question.

Our hope is that you will not stop with the excerpts but instead will be inspired to read each book in its entirety. All of them are still in print in at least one translation or edition, and many are available free of charge on websites such as Christian Classics Ethereal Library (www.ccel.org), where you can read many classic books online for free or download them for a small charge.

We have also added a couple of bonus features. We asked several Christian leaders to provide their own personal list of favorite or most influential spiritual books and have sprinkled them through-out the book in no particular order. Some answered biographically and some thematically; some annotated their list and some just pro-vided their recommended list. We thought these more personal and particular lists might also lead to good recommendations and in-sights. We hope you enjoy them.

The editorial board also debated, as mentioned above, about whether to include living authors on the list. In the end, we decided not to, as we explained. But we thought readers would appreciate a list of those contemporary authors the board would point to as providing the best guidance today for living the with-God life. We did it by simple math. Each member sent their top five choices; we added the votes and determined that nine authors clearly emerged on top. You will find the list starting on page 353.

In closing, as you read and engage with these twenty-five books, we encourage you to give some thought as to the works that have spiritually formed you. We know that upon seeing such a list and probably even after reading all the books on it, you will likely not agree with all of our choices. That is part of the beauty of such an endeavor. We hope to persuade you to read some books that might otherwise never cross your desk and also to start a conversa-tion about what books are essential to our spiritual lives. As Dante writes in *The Divine Comedy,* another of the books on the list, "Di-verse voices make sweet music" (Paradise 6:124). It is our strong be-lief that the diverse voices represented here can make a tremendous difference in forming your heart to be more like that of Jesus. To that end, Godspeed!

—Julia L. Roller
Lyle SmithGraybeal
for the editorial board

25 BOOKS

EVERY CHRISTIAN

SHOULD READ

On the Incarnation

ST. ATHANASIUS

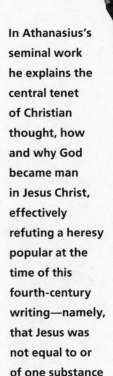

⟳ You must understand why it is that the Word of the Father, so great and so high, has been made manifest in bodily form. He has not assumed a body as proper to His own nature, far from it, for as the Word He is without body. He has been manifested in a human body for this reason only, out of the love and goodness of His Father, for the salvation of us men.

In Athanasius's seminal work he explains the central tenet of Christian thought, how and why God became man in Jesus Christ, effectively refuting a heresy popular at the time of this fourth-century writing—namely, that Jesus was not equal to or of one substance with God.

ATHANASIUS WAS BORN in Alexandria in 297. As a boy, he was taken on by the patron Alexander, the bishop of Alexandria. When, in 318, Arius of Alexandria began to communicate his views that Jesus was made by God and was thus subordinate to God, Athanasius wrote *On the Incarnation* as a refutation of Arius's ideas.

Athanasius first came to prominence in his own right at the Nicaean Council in 325, where he and Alexander successfully argued against Arius, who was later excommunicated by Alexander. When Alexander died, Athanasius succeeded him as bishop of Alexandria. His writings and his speeches at the Nicaean Council had already established him as a natural counterpoint to the Arian philosophy, and indeed his tenure as archbishop was in many ways characterized by this role. Although Arius's ideas had been refuted at the council, they continued to circulate. Influenced by one of Arius's friends, Emperor Constantine himself applied to Athanasius that Arius be readmitted to communion. Athanasius refused, leading to the first of five exiles that he underwent for his belief in Jesus' divinity.

The ideas Athanasius expresses in *On the Incarnation,* in particular the concept of Jesus Christ the God-man, were central in his refutation of Arian thought. *On the Incarnation* is a work of apologetics, hence its persuasive tone. Athanasius mentions by name various other heretical ideas that were making the rounds at the time of his writing. One was the Platonic idea that God created the earth from some kind of preexistent matter; another was the Epicurean idea that no thought or Mind was behind creation at all, that all things came about through some haphazard process of self-origination. Athanasius refutes the idea that the world and its creatures were not created by God, using logic and the Scriptures as evidence. Further, if God made the world from some preexistent matter, God would not be the creator, but simply a craftsman.

Then he describes what he calls the "divine dilemma"—namely, that once humankind broke faith with God by disobeying and eating of the tree of the knowledge of good and evil, it opened itself to the powers of evil. And then what was God to do? God could not let his creation be destroyed, writes Athanasius. After all, we are made in God's image. It would be worse than if we were never made at all. Simple repentance could not be sufficient to return us to God's grace, since God could not remain true if this were the case. Drastic measures were needed—so "the incorporeal and incorruptible and immaterial Word of God entered our world."[1] This Word had always been with us but now was with us in a new way. Moved by compassion for humans that death should have the mastery of us, the Word took on a human body and surrendered it to death for all. Such an act could only have been performed by God. As Athanasius writes, "the rescue of mankind from corruption was the proper part only of Him Who made them in the beginning."[2]

Of course, another essential reason for God becoming man was so that we could know our creator. As Athanasius writes, "For of what use is existence to the creature if it cannot know its Maker?"[3] Although we should have been able to know God through being made in God's image or by creation or by the law and prophets, we so successfully obscured these sources by falling prey to death and corruption that God had to send Jesus so that we could know God once again. Since humans were looking for God among the created things, earthly things, God came to us in this way, a simple means so that we could understand. But God could not come simply to die and then rise again. Jesus let himself be seen as a man, doing and saying things that showed clearly that he was not only man, but God. But Athanasius hastens to add that Jesus' body was not a limitation to God, but an "instrument."[4] He was in the body and at the same time in all things. Being in that body did not defile God but rather sanctified the body. Jesus' actions as described in the Bible—eating and drinking and so forth—show that he was a man, but his other actions—healing and driving out evil spirits and performing miracles—equally show that he is God. And then the miraculous, stupendous event occurred. As Athanasius writes, "The body of the Word, then, being a real human body, in spite of its having been uniquely formed from a virgin, was of itself mortal and, like other bodies, liable to death. But the indwelling of the Word loosed it from this natural liability, so that corruption could not touch it. Thus it happened that two opposite marvels took place at once: the death of all was consummated in the Lord's body; yet, because the Word was in it, death and corruption were in the same act utterly abolished."[5] So because of this death, all who believe in Christ shall no longer die, as was our lot by law.

It was important that Christ's death be public so as not to incur any doubt that he truly was dead, that it occur on the cross because he who healed could not grow sick, and that it be at the hands of others so that it could not be said that he planned his own death in some special way that enabled him to rise again. As Athanasius writes, "A marvelous and mighty paradox has thus occurred, for the death which they thought to inflict on Him as dishonor and disgrace has become the glorious monument to death's defeat."[6] For Athanasius, every part of the cross is significant, from its being viewed as cursed—adding to the symbolism of Christ's overcoming the curse of death and thus becoming a curse himself (Gal 3:13)—to its causing Christ to die with his hands outstretched, as if reaching out to both the Jews

When I first opened [*On the Incarnation*] I discovered by a very simple test that I was reading a masterpiece, for only a mastermind could have written so deeply on such a subject with such classical simplicity.

—C. S. Lewis

and the Gentiles to draw them together in him. By his death and resurrection, Christ rendered death impotent, a bound and helpless former tyrant.

Why *On the Incarnation* Is Essential

Athanasius is a key figure in Church history because of his essential contributions to the doctrine of the Trinity. Theologically speaking, he is remembered for his description of Christ as "co-equal in substance with the Father." Whether Athanasius actually originated this expression or not is unknown, but because of his eloquent expression of it in *On the Incarnation,* his name has become most closely tied with it.[7] But Athanasius's writings are notable for more than just doctrine. The ideas Athanasius expands upon in *On the Incarnation* are bedrock elements for faith. He explains just why God had to become man and why God had to die. And most important, he makes it clear that Christ had to be God; otherwise he could not effect our salvation. God created us; God called us good, so when we responded with disobedience and fell so deeply into corruption that we were held hostage by sin and death, God did the only thing possible to save us: taking form in a human body so God could die. By countering the corruption of death with Jesus' perfect incorruption, God conquered death once and for all. These points have wide-reaching implications for our spiritual formation. As editorial board member Frederica Mathewes-Green, author of *The Illumined Heart,* writes, "*On the Incarnation* gives a clear presentation of a Christian doctrine that is essential for understanding human life and the nature of salvation."

Reflecting on God's taking on a human body in order to save us teaches us about the great importance we have in the eyes of God. And it also teaches us about our bodies and the process of discipleship. We have fallen into corruption, but our bodies are not to blame. Indeed it was in a body that Christ saved and continues to save us. Our bodies are blessings, and spiritual formation itself is an embodied process, not something that is done just with our minds or even just with our hearts. Without the body's involvement we cannot be said to be practicing discipleship.

What Athanasius also helps to restore for us, which perhaps we can only find in a book as old as this one, is a renewed understanding of the jaw-dropping awe we should feel at the Incarnation. For example, in chapter 7, Refutation of the Gentiles, Athanasius takes pains to describe why God took form in a human instead of as the moon or a star. His answer is interesting—that the moon and the stars had not strayed from God's path. But perhaps something even more interesting to reflect on is that we are so used to the concept of the Incarnation that few would even think to ask such a question today. Athanasius can help renew in us some of the wonder we should feel at the radical act that is the Incarnation.

Finally, reading *On the Incarnation* makes it clear that there are no new heresies. The beliefs Athanasius takes on are still present in our world today—that God made all things out of preexisting matter, that everything originated by a haphazard method of self-creation, that Jesus was simply a man. Studying Athanasius's persuasive words can help us steer clear of any such misapprehensions about God. It can also help us understand just how dangerous such ideas are, because they can lead us to devalue our bodies, cheapen our view of God, or even question our salvation.

How to Read *On the Incarnation*

On the Incarnation is a short book written in an engaging, persuasive tone. One way to read it may be to take it in chapters, taking time after each one to reflect and make sure we have really understood his points. In *Celebration of Discipline,* Richard J. Foster outlines four steps for study: repetition, concentration, comprehension, and reflection. These four steps are applicable to our reading of *On the Incarnation* and to every other book on the list. Whether for the entire book or for a particular chapter or passage, our first step, of course, is to read through the material, repeatedly bringing our minds to the subject matter before us. At the same time, we seek to concentrate on the material, with a focused singleness of purpose, if at all possible in an environment free from other stimuli. Third, we seek to comprehend what it is that we have read. Sometimes we need outside sources such as the Bible, other books, friends, and our experiences in order to come to this place of understanding. And, finally, we reflect on what we have read. Foster describes this important fourth step as the way we determine the significance of what we are studying: "Reflection brings us to see things from God's perspective. In reflection we come to understand not only our subject matter, but ourselves."[8]

EXCERPTS FROM

On the Incarnation

CHAPTER 2: THE DIVINE DILEMMA AND ITS SOLUTION IN THE INCARNATION

6. We saw in the last chapter that, because death and corruption were gaining ever firmer hold on them, the human race was in process of destruction. Man, who was created in God's image and in his possession of reason reflected the very Word Himself, was disappearing, and the work of God was being undone. The law of death, which followed from the Transgression, prevailed upon us, and from it there was no escape. The thing that was happening was in truth both monstrous and unfitting. It would, of course, have been unthinkable that God should go back upon His word and that man, having transgressed, should not die; but it was equally monstrous that beings which once had shared the nature of the Word should perish and turn back again into non-existence through corruption. It was unworthy of the goodness of God that creatures made by Him should be

brought to nothing through the deceit wrought upon man by the devil; and it was supremely unfitting that the work of God in mankind should disappear, either through their own negligence or through the deceit of evil spirits. As, then, the creatures whom He had created reasonable, like the Word, were in fact perishing, and such noble works were on the road to ruin, what then was God, being Good, to do? Was He to let corruption and death have their way with them? In that case, what was the use of having made them in the beginning? Surely it would have been better never to have been created at all than, having been created, to be neglected and perish; and, besides that, such indifference to the ruin of His own work before His very eyes would argue not goodness in God but limitation, and that far more than if He had never created men at all. It was impossible, therefore, that God should leave man to be carried off by corruption, because it would be unfitting and unworthy of Himself.

7. Yet, true though this is, it is not the whole matter. As we have already noted, it was unthinkable that God, the Father of Truth, should go back upon His word regarding death in order to ensure our continued existence. He could not falsify Himself; what, then, was God to do? Was He to demand repentance from men for their transgression? You might say that that was worthy of God, and argue further that, as through the Transgression they became subject to corruption, so through repentance they might return to incorruption again. But repentance would not guard the Divine consistency, for, if death did not hold dominion over men, God would still remain untrue. Nor does repentance recall men from what is according to their nature; all that it does is to make them cease from sinning. Had it been a case of a trespass only, and not of a subsequent corruption, repentance would have been well enough; but when once transgression had begun men came under the power of the corruption proper to their nature and were bereft of the grace which belonged to them as creatures in the Image of God. No,

repentance could not meet the case. What—or rather Who was it that was needed for such grace and such recall as we required? Who, save the Word of God Himself, Who also in the beginning had made all things out of nothing? His part it was, and His alone, both to bring again the corruptible to incorruption and to maintain for the Father His consistency of character with all. For He alone, being Word of the Father and above all, was in consequence both able to recreate all, and worthy to suffer on behalf of all and to be an ambassador for all with the Father.

8. For this purpose, then, the incorporeal and incorruptible and immaterial Word of God entered our world. In one sense, indeed, He was not far from it before, for no part of creation had ever been without Him Who, while ever abiding in union with the Father, yet fills all things that are. But now He entered the world in a new way, stooping to our level in His love and Self-revealing to us. He saw the reasonable race, the race of men that, like Himself, expressed the Father's Mind, wasting out of existence, and death reigning over all in corruption. He saw that corruption held us all the closer, because it was the penalty for the Transgression; He saw, too, how unthinkable it would be for the law to be repealed before it was fulfilled. He saw how unseemly it was that the very things of which He Himself was the Artificer should be disappearing. He saw how the surpassing wickedness of men was mounting up against them; He saw also their universal liability to death. All this He saw and, pitying our race, moved with compassion for our limitation, unable to endure that death should have the mastery, rather than that His creatures should perish and the work of His Father for us men come to nought, He took to Himself a body, a human body even as our own. Nor did He will merely to become embodied or merely to appear; had that been so, He could have revealed His divine majesty in some other and better way. No, He took our body, and not only so, but He took it directly from a spotless, stainless virgin, without the agency of human father—

a pure body, untainted by intercourse with man. He, the Mighty One, the Artificer of all, Himself prepared this body in the virgin as a temple for Himself, and took it for His very own, as the instrument through which He was known and in which He dwelt. Thus, taking a body like our own, because all our bodies were liable to the corruption of death, He surrendered His body to death instead of all, and offered it to the Father. This He did out of sheer love for us, so that in His death all might die, and the law of death thereby be abolished because, having fulfilled

My Personal Top 5

GAYLE BEEBE

1 I first read C. S. Lewis's ***Mere Christianity*** when I was a junior in high school. It provided a reasonable, commonsense approach to the Christian faith that I found compelling then, and still do today.

2 Shortly thereafter, I read Augustine's ***Confessions***. This was such a remarkable and helpful excavation of the longing for God that lies at the heart of every honest spiritual journey.

3 Then, during my first year of seminary I read Pascal's ***Pensées***. For the first time in my life I experienced the full wealth of conviction of my Christian faith. Pascal taught me how to use the power of reason to think clearly about the Christian faith, but he also helped me recognize the limits of reason. His three orders of reality provided the thought forms I needed to see the right way to address and answer the questions that come to every honest seeker.

4 During this same time, I read John Woolman's ***Journal***. This eighteenth-century American Quaker provided one of the most profound examples of how to live for God and allow every encounter to be a sacramental moment filled with divine grace.

5 Finally, while in my doctoral studies at Claremont, I read Calvin's ***Institutes*** from cover to cover. What a remarkable discussion of how we come to knowledge of God and grow in it. In so many respects, Calvin's *Institutes* anticipated and addressed so many issues of what it means to grow in our knowledge of Christ—to live a life that exemplifies his presence in our life.

GAYLE D. BEEBE is the current president of Westmont College in Santa Barbara, California, and is the author or editor of ten books, including *Longing for God: Seven Paths of Christian Devotion*.

in His body that for which it was appointed, it was thereafter voided of its power for men. This He did that He might turn again to incorruption men who had turned back to corruption, and make them alive through death by the appropriation of His body and by the grace of His resurrection. Thus He would make death to disappear from them as utterly as straw from fire.

9. The Word perceived that corruption could not be got rid of otherwise than through death; yet He Himself, as the Word, being immortal and the Father's Son, was such as could not die. For this reason, therefore, He assumed a body capable of death, in order that it, through belonging to the Word Who is above all, might become in dying a sufficient exchange for all, and, itself remaining incorruptible through His indwelling, might thereafter put an end to corruption for all others as well, by the grace of the resurrection. It was by surrendering to death the body which He had taken, as an offering and sacrifice free from every stain, that He forthwith abolished death for His human brethren by the offering of the equivalent. For naturally, since the Word of God was above all, when He offered His own temple and bodily instrument as a substitute for the life of all, He fulfilled in death all that was required. Naturally also, through this union of the immortal Son of God with our human nature, all men were clothed with incorruption in the promise of the resurrection. For the solidarity of mankind is such that, by virtue of the Word's indwelling in a single human body, the corruption which goes with death has lost its power over all. You know how it is when some great king enters a large city and dwells in one of its houses; because of his dwelling in that single house, the whole city is honored, and enemies and robbers cease to molest it. Even so is it with the King of all; He has come into our country and dwelt in one body amidst the many, and in consequence the designs of the enemy against mankind have been foiled and the corruption of death, which formerly held them in its power, has simply ceased to be. For

the human race would have perished utterly had not the Lord and Savior of all, the Son of God, come among us to put an end to death.

10. This great work was, indeed, supremely worthy of the goodness of God. A king who has founded a city, so far from neglecting it when through the carelessness of the inhabitants it is attacked by robbers, avenges it and saves it from destruction, having regard rather to his own honor than to the people's neglect. Much more, then, the Word of the All-good Father was not unmindful of the human race that He had called to be; but rather, by the offering of His own body He abolished the death which they had incurred, and corrected their neglect by His own teaching. Thus by His own power He restored the whole nature of man. The Savior's own inspired disciples assure us of this. We read in one place: "For the love of Christ constraineth us, because we thus judge that, if One died on behalf of all, then all died, and He died for all that we should no longer live unto ourselves, but unto Him who died and rose again from the dead, even our Lord Jesus Christ." And again another says: "But we behold Him Who hath been made a little lower than the angels, even Jesus, because of the suffering of death crowned with glory and honor, that by the grace of God He should taste of death on behalf of every man." The same writer goes on to point out why it was necessary for God the Word and none other to become Man: "For it became Him, for Whom are all things and through Whom are all things, in bringing many sons unto glory, to make the Author of their salvation perfect through suffering." He means that the rescue of mankind from corruption was the proper part only of Him Who made them in the beginning. He points out also that the Word assumed a human body, expressly in order that He might offer it in sacrifice for other like bodies: "Since then the children are sharers in flesh and blood, He also Himself assumed the same, in order that through death He might bring to nought Him that hath the power of death, that is to say, the Devil, and might rescue

those who all their lives were enslaved by the fear of death." For by the sacrifice of His own body He did two things: He put an end to the law of death which barred our way; and He made a new beginning of life for us, by giving us the hope of resurrection. By man death has gained its power over men; by the Word made Man death has been destroyed and life raised up anew. That is what Paul says, that true servant of Christ: "For since by man came death, by man came also the resurrection of the dead. Just as in Adam all die, even so in Christ shall all be made alive," and so forth. Now, therefore, when we die we no longer do so as men condemned to death, but as those who are even now in process of rising we await the general resurrection of all, "which in its own times He shall show," even God Who wrought it and bestowed it on us.[9]

A Study Guide for *On the Incarnation*

1. Which heresy that Athanasius takes on do you think is most present today? The Arian idea that Jesus was subordinate to God, the Platonic idea that God created the earth from preexisting matter, or the Epicurean idea that no Mind was behind creation?

2. What is the divine dilemma? What does this dilemma say about our worth in God's eyes?

3. By coming to earth in a human body, Athanasius writes, God met us halfway. "When, then, the minds of men had fallen finally to the level of sensible things, the Word submitted to appear in a body, in order that He, as Man, might center their senses on Himself, and convince them through His human acts that He Himself is not man only but also God, the Word and Wisdom of the true God."[10] How does Jesus Christ make it easier for you to relate to God?

4. Athanasius writes, "His body was for Him not a limitation, but an instrument, so that He was both in it and in all things, and outside all things, resting in the Father alone. At one and the same time—this is the wonder—as Man He was living a human life, and as Word He was sustaining the life of the universe, and as Son He was in constant union with the Father."[11] What does Athanasius mean by saying that the Word contained all things?

5. Athanasius anticipates that some might ask why Christ had to die on the cross for all, why he could not simply die a private death of sickness or old age. His response, in part, is that if Christ had died quietly in his bed, it would have looked as if he were no more than another human; he who healed could not himself sicken and die. What do you make of his reasoning? Why do you believe Christ died on the cross?

6. According to Athanasius, although we may have found death horrible before, once we are believers in Christ, we despise death, deride it as a bound and helpless former tyrant, and indeed "go eagerly to meet it."[12] How have you manifested this in your own life?

7. Athanasius takes great pains to explain why it was fitting and necessary for God to enter a human body and also how God operated while in human form, anticipating questions such as why God did not take the form of the sun or moon or stars (his answer being that they had not deviated from their paths as humans had). Would such arguments even occur to you? Do you have questions about God's coming in human form? If so, how do Athanasius's arguments answer them, and if not, why do you think the concept of God in a human body does not feel difficult or surprising to you?

8. In the second part of his Refutation of the Gentiles, Athanasius argues for Christ with cultural examples of people in his time forsaking idols and oracles as proof of

Christ's identity and power. "But since the Word of God has been manifested in a body, and has made known to us His own Father, the fraud of the demons is stopped and made to disappear; and men, turning their eyes to the true God, Word of the Father, forsake the idols and come to know the true God. Now this is proof that Christ is God, the Word and Power of God."[13] What similar claims might a contemporary Christian make? How do you read this argument in contemporary times? Do you find any of Athanasius's arguments less than compelling? If so, why? How does the passage of time since he made them affect your answer?

9. What differences do you see between your own faith, forged after two thousand years of Christianity, and that of Athanasius, writing just a few hundred years after Christ's life?

Confessions

ST. AUGUSTINE

> *You made us for yourself and our hearts find no peace until they rest in you.*

ST. AUGUSTINE OF HIPPO was born in Thagaste, Numidia (now Algeria), in 354 to a pagan father, Patricius, and a Christian mother, Monica. His intellect and public-speaking skills led him to a profession as a teacher and speaker in first Rome and then Milan. After a long dalliance with Manicheanism, a school of thought exalting science and astrology and positing life as a struggle between the spiritual world of light and the material world of darkness, he became a Christian and was baptized at age thirty-two. Afterward he became a priest and founded his own monastic order.

Augustine wrote *Confessions* in 397 and 398, shortly after being named bishop of Hippo, as both a description of his personal journey to Christ and a statement of faith. His story, addressed to God, is as much prayer as it is autobiography. His conversational tone belies an enviable intimacy with God. Much of *Confessions* focuses on sin and grace. In fact, after some words of praise and some philosophical musings, he begins by wondering if even as a baby he was truly innocent. His mother chose not to have him baptized, ostensibly because she believed it better that he be baptized after he had gotten his inevitable sinning out of his system. Augustine writes, "It would, then, have been better if I had been healed at once and if all that I and my family could do had been done to make sure that once my soul had received its salvation, its safety should be left in your keeping, since its salvation had come from you. This would surely have been the better course. But my mother well knew how many great tides of temptation threatened me before I grew up, and she chose to let them beat upon the as yet unmoulded clay rather than upon the finished image which had received the stamp of baptism."[1]

Augustine paints a very dark picture of the great tides of temptation and describes an adolescence characterized by lust and fornication. But the pivotal moment for him is when he steals some pears and has his first real recognition of sin. This incident also introduces the idea of true, or spiritual, friendship, an important theme throughout *Confessions*. Augustine realizes that without the negative influence of his companions, he would never have stolen those pears, since he had no interest in eating them. With a group of companions, however, such an act was fun. As Augustine grew older, he continued to recognize the importance of friendship. In Book IV he writes about a close friend who dies from a fever. Despite the fact that he believes their relationship was not a true friendship since they were not both Christian, writing, "For though they cling together, no friends are true friends unless you, my God, bind them fast to one another through that love which is sown in our hearts by the Holy Ghost,"[2] his friend's death leaves Augustine feeling as though he is living with half a soul. Even as he extols the charms of friendship—talking and laughing together, discussing books, learning from each other—he also exhorts us, "If your delight is in souls, love them in God, because they too are frail and stand firm only when they cling to him."[3] For we must always be careful not to exalt above God even those good gifts *from* God: "The good things which you love are all from God, but they are good and sweet only as long as they are used to do his will."[4]

Augustine knew well the folly of exalting things above God. As a young man, despite the wishes of his devout mother, he was attracted to the Manichean religion. Because of their teachings, Augustine believed that God and evil both took material shape and that humans were small pieces broken from God, who was a "bright, unbounded body."[5] Augustine devoured and studied every book he could find, discovering inconsistencies within the Manichean teachings that no one was able to resolve for him. He took a teaching position in

Rome, and then one in Milan, where he met Ambrose, the bishop who was to have a tremendous influence on him. Through the influence of Ambrose's sermons, Augustine became more attracted to the Christian point of view. One important turning point came when he began to take some of the Old Testament passages figuratively rather than literally. He also came to understand that some things must be taken on faith, in contrast to the Manicheans, who professed to have a rational explanation for everything and then "put forward a whole system of preposterous inventions which they expected their followers to believe on trust because they could not be proved."[6] After careful and thorough study of the Platonists and then the Scriptures, Augustine found many of his intellectual issues with Christianity resolved. But he still could not bring himself to take that step of actually becoming a Christian, mostly because he feared continence, giving up the pleasures of the body. As he writes, "My lower instincts, which had taken firm hold of me, were stronger than the higher, which were untried. And the closer I came to the moment which was to mark the great change in me, the more I shrank from it in horror."[7] In misery over this internal conflict, Augustine flees to the garden behind his house, where he hears a child repeating in a singsong voice, "Take it and read. Take it and read." So encouraged, Augustine returns to the Bible he has left near his friend Alypius and opens it to this passage: *"Not in revelling and drunkenness, not in lust and wantonness, not in quarrels and rivalries. Rather, arm yourselves with the Lord Jesus Christ; spend no more thought on nature and nature's appetites"* (Rom 13:13, 14).[8] After reading these words, both Augustine and Alypius decide to become Christian, to Augustine's mother's great joy.

At this point Augustine tells us that he has shared his confession with us so that other people may see that they, too, can be forgiven in God's great mercy, grace, and love. But then he goes on to describe his life after believing in Christ, in addition to what his life was before he became a Christian. He shares his continued temptations to give in to his physical appetites, to ask for signs and wonders, and to desire being feared or loved by others. "My life is full of such faults," he writes, "and my only hope is in your boundless mercy."[9]

We find in [Augustine's] delineation of the essence of religion and of the deepest problems of morality, such striking depth and truth of observation, that we must still honour him as our master, and that his memory is still able in some measure, even to-day, to unite Protestant and Catholic.

—Adolf von Harnack

Why *Confessions* Is Essential

It is close to impossible to overestimate the influence of Augustine and his *Confessions*. *Confessions* was the first spiritual autobiography, a genre without which we can hardly imagine modern Christianity. *Confessions* established Augustine as *the* Christian apologist, after the apostles themselves. For better or for worse, Christianity as we know it has been interpreted through Augustine's lens. Virtually every book that follows *Confessions* on our list was influenced by Augustine in some way—by his theology, his literary style, or both. Augustine broke away from the intellectual tradition he had been steeped in to write a book that focused on his feelings; he broke away from Christian tradition to write about the sinful person he was before and the temptations that continued after his conversion, in contrast to the biographies of his own day that focused on their subjects' great piety or the circumstances leading up to their martyrdom. Instead, Augustine describes his personal journey toward Christian faith, the longings of his restless heart for God, and all the steps on his path to baptism. There is much in his journey for any Christian to relate to, up to and including the dramatic story of his final decision. Yet as is true for all of us, the story does not end there. Instead, baptism represents another beginning; the journey continues. Nor does becoming a Christian represent the end of Augustine's temptations. In fact, the very same things continue to tempt him. The difference is that he now has Jesus to help him, and God's grace and mercy to trust in when he falls prey to sin.

Augustine's story is notable for the power of its narrative, which so many others have sought to emulate. Like all the stories in the Bible, Augustine's story is a story of God's love for and pursuit of us. From the very first words of his story, we see that Augustine is addressing God. His story is also a prayer. This literary device is entirely appropriate because the Lord is a constant presence for Augustine. Even before he was baptized, God was seeking Augustine every step of the way.

For Augustine, as for so many of us, his decision to become a Christian is a multitiered process. Perhaps it is because he has the benefit of hindsight, but he seems to know in his heart the truth of Christianity long before he admits it to himself. The first step for him is intellectual. Interestingly, it is reading the works of famous pagans such as Plato that starts Augustine along the path toward baptism. Friends and mentors play a role as well. Ambrose and Alypius both heavily influence Augustine. But even after he is convinced of Christianity's truth, the conversion of the mind, Augustine still resists taking that final step toward baptism, the conversion of the heart, because, he tells us, he does not want to give up his pleasure-seeking lifestyle. It takes that famous moment in the garden, with the child's chanting and the eerily appropriate Bible verse, to finally convince Augustine to be baptized. Reading his story allows us space to assess our own process of conversion to Christianity, and our ongoing journey today. It also affords us the opportunity to reflect on the meaning and power of baptism. Augustine considered it probably the most significant decision and event of his life.

Confessions is also famous, or perhaps notorious, for Augustine's harsh depiction of his own sinfulness. This is intentional. One reason Augustine wrote *Confessions* was to combat the idea that, after his years as the well-known and respected leader of his monastic community, he was pure and free from the temptation to sin. The title of his book is no mistake; Augustine's entire story is an example of the spiritual discipline of confession. Augustine had the courage to confess to everyone in this most public way the sins in which he had engaged and even his present temptations. Augustine recounts and mourns all the occasions he gave in to vice, in everything from sexual temptations to frivolous entertainment, all those years before he was baptized. Even after he is baptized, these temptations continue to plague him, but the central point, for Augustine and for us, is not the blackness of our sin, but the great power of God's grace to overcome it all. No sin is too great for Jesus' death to cover. God's grace and mercy is enough for us all. As Richard J. Foster writes, "Augustine's life and writings make it clear that the Gordian knots of sin can be severed." And so Augustine's story provides a noteworthy example of the workings of the process of sanctification. Step by step, he describes the story of the Holy Spirit's having its way with him, transforming him into holiness.

How to Read *Confessions*

Confessions is an extremely famous work, and its reputation and the fact that it was written more than fifteen hundred years ago may feel intimidating. It is a fairly long book and not one that we should expect to devour in one sitting. *Confessions* also differs from most modern-day spiritual autobiographies in that it is peppered with long philosophical discourses. The last two books are almost entirely theological rather than autobiographical. But despite this difference, what is astonishing about Augustine's story is just how engaging and relevant it still feels today. When we read other people's stories, we ourselves join them on their journeys, and Augustine's story is no exception. As we read about Augustine's steps toward faith, we can feel our own spiritual formation at stake. In all those places in the book where we identify with his story, we relate it to our own experiences and evaluate our own journeys in the light of grace. His temptations become our temptations; his prayers, our prayers; the grace he receives, the grace we receive.

EXCERPTS FROM

Confessions

BOOK II

4. It is certain, O Lord, that theft is punished by your law, the law that is written in men's hearts and cannot be erased however sinful they are. For no thief can bear that another thief

should steal from him, even if he is rich and the other is driven to it by want. Yet I was willing to steal, and steal I did, although I was not compelled by any lack, unless it were the lack of a sense of justice or a distaste for what was right and a greedy love of doing wrong. For of what I stole I already had plenty, and much better at that, and I had no wish to enjoy the things I coveted by stealing, but only to enjoy the theft itself and the sin. There was a pear-tree near our vineyard, loaded with fruit that was attractive neither to look at nor to taste. Late one night a band of ruffians, myself included, went off to shake down the fruit and carry it away, for we had continued our games out of doors until well after dark, as was our pernicious habit. We took away an enormous quantity of pears, not to eat them ourselves, but simply to throw them to the pigs. Perhaps we ate some of them, but our real pleasure consisted in doing something that was forbidden.

Look into my heart, O God, the same heart on which you took pity when it was in the depths of the abyss. Let my heart now tell you what prompted me to do wrong for no purpose, and why it was only my own love of mischief that made me do it. The evil in me was foul, but I loved it. I loved my own perdition and my own faults, not the things for which I committed wrong, but the wrong itself. My soul was vicious and broke away from your safe keeping to seek its own destruction, looking for no profit in disgrace but only for disgrace itself....

6. If the crime of theft which I committed that night as a boy of sixteen were a living thing, I could speak to it and ask what it was that, to my shame, I loved in it. I [sic] had no beauty because it was a robbery. It is true that the pears which we stole had beauty, because they were created by you, the good God, who are the most beautiful of all beings and the Creator of all things, the supreme Good and my own true Good. But it was not the pears that my unhappy soul desired. I had plenty of my own, better than those, and I only picked them so that I might steal. For no sooner had I picked them than I threw them away,

and tasted nothing in them but my own sin, which I relished and enjoyed. If any part of one of those pears passed my lips, it was the sin that gave it flavour.

And now, O Lord my God, now that I ask what pleasure I had in that theft, I find that it had no beauty to attract me. I do not mean beauty of the sort that justice and prudence possess, nor the beauty that is in man's mind and in his memory and in the life that animates him, nor the beauty of the stars in their allotted places or of the earth and sea, teeming with new life born to replace the old as it passes away. It did not even have the shadowy, deceptive beauty which makes vice attractive—pride, for instance, which is a pretence of superiority, imitating yours, for you alone are God, supreme over all; or ambition, which is only a craving for honour and glory, when you alone are to be honoured before all and you alone are glorious for ever. Cruelty is the weapon of the powerful, used to make others fear them: yet no one is to be feared by God alone, from whose power nothing can be snatched away or stolen by any man at any time or place or by any means. The lustful use caresses to win the love they crave for, yet no caress is sweeter than your charity and no love is more rewarding than the love of your truth, which shines in beauty above all else. Inquisitiveness has all the appearance of a thirst for knowledge, yet you have supreme knowledge of all things. Ignorance, too, and stupidity choose to go under the mask of simplicity and innocence, because you are simplicity itself and no innocence is greater than yours. You are innocent even of the harm which overtakes the wicked, for it is the result of their own actions. Sloth poses as the love of peace: yet what certain peace is there besides the Lord? Extravagance masquerades as fullness and abundance: but you are the full, unfailing store of never-dying sweetness. The spendthrift makes a pretence of liberality: but you are the most generous dispenser of all good. The covetous want many possessions for themselves: you possess all. The envious struggle for preferment: but what is to be preferred before you? Anger demands revenge: but what vengeance is as just as yours? Fear shrinks from any sudden, unwonted danger which threatens the things that it loves, for its only care is safety: but to you nothing is strange, nothing unforeseen. No one can part you from the things that you love, and safety is assured nowhere but in you. Grief eats away its heart for the loss of things which it took pleasure in desiring, because it wants to be like you, from whom nothing can be taken away.

My Personal Top 5

JAMES CATFORD

These are my top five books addressing social justice issues.

1 *The Poverty & Justice Bible* (CEV). Over 2,000 verses of the Bible explicitly speak about the poor. Rick Warren once reflected, "How could I have missed them?" How come so many Christian leaders have missed them, too?

2 *The Riches of Simplicity: Selected Writings of Francis and Clare*. The theme of simplicity is central to becoming more like Jesus, and this book is one of the original classics. Short, sharp, and straightforward, it acts as a striking counterpoint to the conspicuous consumption of today and valuing everything only in econometric terms.

3 *The Journal of John Woolman*. America's William Wilberforce, John Woolman spoke out gracefully on the conditions of slaves and risked his life to live with American Indians. Powerful in its simplicity, Woolman listened deeply to the marginalized and said "I love to hear where words come from."

4 *The Politics of Jesus*, John Howard Yoder. Yoder's classic on engagement with society includes teaching on government, the state, and the poor. This book has become a set text for all who are looking for meaningful ways to connect Christ with culture.

5 *Bias to the Poor*, David Sheppard. This book caused a sensation when it challenged the British establishment of Margaret Thatcher. The late bishop of Liverpool, the industrial port from where so many settlers in America left Europe, outlines God's heart for the poor.

JAMES CATFORD is vice-chair of Renovaré USA and chair of Renovaré Britain and Ireland. He is group chief executive of Bible Society, England and Wales (BFBS), and was formerly publishing director at HodderHeadline and HarperCollins.

So the soul defiles itself with unchaste love when it turns away from you and looks elsewhere for things which it cannot find pure and unsullied except by returning to you. All who desert you and set themselves up against you merely copy you in a perverse way; but by this very act of imitation they only show that you are the Creator of all nature and, consequently, that there is no place whatever where man may hide away from you.

What was it, then, that pleased me in that act of theft? Which of my Lord's powers did I imitate in a perverse and wicked way? Since I had no real power to break his law, was it that I enjoyed at least the pretence of doing so, like a prisoner who creates for himself the illusion of liberty by doing something wrong, when he has no fear of punishment, under a feeble hallucination of power? Here was the slave who ran away from his master and chased a shadow instead! What an abomination! What a parody of life! What abysmal death! Could I enjoy doing something wrong for no other reason than that it was wrong?

7. *What return shall I make to the Lord* (Pss 115:12; 116:12) for my ability to recall these things with no fear in my soul? I will love you, Lord, and thank you, and praise your name, because you have forgiven me such great sins and such wicked deeds. I acknowledge that it was by your grace and mercy that you melted away my sins like ice. I acknowledge, too, that by your grace I was preserved from whatever sins I did not commit, for there was no knowing what I might have done, since I loved evil even if it served no purpose. I avow that you have forgiven me all, both the sins which I committed of my own accord and those which by your guidance I was spared from committing.

What man who reflects upon his own weakness can dare to claim that his own efforts have made him chaste and free from sin, as though this entitled him to love you the less, on the ground that he had less need of the mercy by which you forgive the sins of the penitent? There are some who have been called by you and because they have listened to your voice they have avoided the sins which I here record and confess for them to read. But let them not deride me for having been cured by the same Doctor who preserved them from sickness, or at least from such grave sickness as mine. Let them love you just as much, or even more, than I do, for they can see that the same healing hand which rid me of the great fever of my sins protects them from falling sick of the same disease.

8. It brought me no happiness, for *what harvest did I reap from acts which now make me blush* (Rom 6:21), particularly from that act of theft? I loved nothing in it except the thieving, though I cannot truly speak of that as a 'thing' that I could love, and I was only the more miserable because of it. And yet, as I recall my feelings at the time, I am quite sure that I would not have done it on my own. Was it then that I also enjoyed the company of those with whom I committed the crime? If this is so, there was something else I loved besides the act of theft; but I cannot call it 'something else,' because companionship, like theft, is not a thing at all.

No one can tell me the truth of it except my God, who enlightens my mind and dispels its shadows. What conclusion am I trying to reach from these questions and this discussion? It is true that if the pears which I stole had been to my taste, and if I had wanted to get them for myself, I might have committed the crime on my own if I had needed to do no more than to win myself the pleasure. I should have had no need to kindle my glowing desire by rubbing shoulders with a gang of accomplices. But as it was not the fruit that gave me pleasure, I must have got it from the crime itself, from the thrill of having partners in sin.

9. How can I explain my mood? It was certainly a very vile frame of mind and one from which I suffered; but how can I account for it? *Who knows his own frailties?* (Pss 18:13; 19:12).

We were tickled to laughter by the prank we had played, because no one suspected us of it although the owners were furious. Why was it, then, that I thought it fun not to have been the only culprit? Perhaps it was because we do not laugh easily when we are alone. True enough: but even when a man is all by himself and quite alone, sometimes he cannot help laughing if he thinks or hears or sees something especially funny. All the same, I am quite sure that I would never have done this thing on my own.

My God, I lay all this before you, for it is still alive in my memory. By myself I would not have committed that robbery. It was not the takings that attracted me but the raid itself, and yet to do it by myself would have been no fun and I should not have done it. This was friendship of a most unfriendly sort, bewitching my mind in an inexplicable way. For the sake of a laugh, a little sport, I was glad to do harm and anxious to damage another; and that without thought of profit for myself or retaliation for injuries received! And all because we are ashamed to hold back when others say 'Come on! Let's do it!'

10. Can anyone untangle this twisted tangle of knots? I shudder to look at it or to think of such abomination. I long instead for innocence and justice, graceful and splendid in eyes whose sight is undefiled. My longing fills me and yet it cannot cloy. With them is certain peace and life that cannot be disturbed. The man who enters their domain goes to *share the joy of his Lord* (Matt 25:21). He shall know no fear and shall lack no good. In him that is goodness itself he shall find his own best way of life. But I deserted you, my God. In my youth I wandered away, too far from your sustaining hand, and created of myself a barren waste.[10]

A Study Guide for *Confessions*

1. Many famous Christians have noted the profound impact reading *Confessions* had on their lives. How does *Confessions* affect your view of what it means to be a Christian?

2. Why does Augustine conclude that it would have been better for him to have been baptized as an infant? What does he tell us is Monica's rationale for not doing so? Do you find her reasons compelling? Why or why not?

3. His theft from the pear trees is Augustine's first realization of his own sin. Not only does he take what isn't his, he revels in the wrong of it. His friend Alypius later has a similar experience when his friends drag him to a gladiator show. Do you have a similar memory of the first time you did wrong and recognized it? What kinds of sins were you prone to as an adolescent? How was peer pressure a factor in your behavior?

4. From the beginning, Augustine is impressed with the effect his friends have on him. In the case of the theft of the pears it is a negative effect, but he also learns of the positive effects others can have, when the friendship is from God. When have friends or companions influenced you negatively? What friendships do you have that are blessed by the Holy Spirit, as Augustine describes?

5. The first time Augustine read the Scriptures as a young man, he recounts that he "had too much conceit to accept their simplicity and not enough insight to penetrate their depths."[11] How does his experience compare to your first remembered encounter with the Scriptures? How have you experienced them as being both simple and containing great depth?

6. Augustine regrets his attachment to the "low things" such as theater and secular books, but even those things that are "higher," the good things in life that God has given us, are only of use insofar as we view them as blessings from God and subordinate to God. What are some of the "low things" you have been tempted by or attached to? What are some of the "higher" things that you have misused or grown too attached to?

7. Augustine describes his pre-Christian beliefs as a "huge fable which I loved instead of [God]" and a "long-drawn lie."[12] For him those beliefs were Manicheanism. What fables and lies of the culture have you been tempted to believe?

8. In struggling with Christian beliefs, Augustine initially has trouble with the idea that some things have to be taken on faith without being proved, but upon reflection he realizes that he believes countless things on trust, whether they are historical events or facts about places and things he has never seen. He is also troubled by materialism—not being able to understand God outside of a physical body or physical presence. What similar struggles have you had? Does Augustine's rationale about taking things on trust make sense to you? Explain.

9. Even once he has made up his mind to become a Christian, Augustine finds himself engaged in an internal battle, between his higher self and his lower self, that which loved pleasure. From adolescence he had fought this war, famously asking of God, "Give me chastity and continence, but not yet."[13] How have you experienced such a battle within yourself? Did such a conflict hold you back from committing yourself to Christ?

The Sayings of the Desert Fathers

VARIOUS

A collection of sayings and stories from the third-, fourth-, and fifth-century hermits and monks who renounced the world for a life of humility, charity, and extreme discipline.

Someone questioned Abba Biare in these words, "What shall I do to be saved?" He replied, "Go, reduce your appetite and your manual work, dwell without care in your cell and you will be saved."

IN THE FOURTH CENTURY a remarkable number of Christians, men and a few women, too, fled to the desert—in Egypt, Syria, Palestine, and other places—to live lives marked by asceticism and single-minded focus on God. Their extreme commitment to Christ earned these desert fathers and mothers a great deal of respect, and they were often consulted on religious and even political matters. Their sayings and anecdotes were passed along orally and later written down so all could learn from them, now comprising the collection we know as *The Sayings of the Desert Fathers.*

The desert fathers and mothers withdrew in order to be closer to God. In the desert, they lived both alone and in various groups, some organized and some not. But each had his or her cell, usually a simple hut, into which each could escape from all the distractions of the outside world and meet God. As Anthony the Great said, "Just as fish die if they stay too long out of water, so the monks who loiter outside their cells or pass their time with men of the world lose the intensity of inner peace. So like a fish going towards the sea, we must hurry to reach our cell, for fear that if we delay outside we will lose our interior watchfulness."[1] For the monks did not see the desert as a place to avoid temptation. Far from it, just as Jesus did, they expected to meet temptation and demons in the desert and to strengthen their souls from the resulting inner warfare. The desert was a place of particular spiritual power, a place not only of temptation, but also of miracles. Abba Bessarion, for example, is said to have crossed a river on foot and kept the sun from setting until he reached his destination. Other fathers performed healing and saw visions of angels.

The desert fathers are perhaps most well known for their extreme ascetic practices—fasting, saying very little, going without sleep, wearing the simplest and roughest of clothing, and forsaking possessions. Many of their sayings offer specific advice for these matters. They believed that punishing or denying the needs of the body allowed them to focus more on the soul, and so their ascetic practices were regarded as a means to relinquish the hold sin had on their bodies in order to achieve a more intimate life with God. No father practiced asceticism simply to practice it or to be better at it than his fellow monk. Their discipline was moderated with common sense, as in the case of Abba Arsenius who told a monk who refused to eat until he had followed Arsenius's instructions to cut all his palm leaves, "Break your fast at once so as to celebrate the *synaxis* untroubled, and drink some water, otherwise your body will soon suffer."[2] We also see this commonsense approach in Abba Zeno, who noticed that some of his visitors were upset when he did not accept their gifts and others were hurt when they received no token from him, so he began accepting all gifts and giving them to those who asked for something.

More important than any bodily practice was the guarding of the heart. The interior was where the most intense warfare took place, and its state was not always apparent from the outside. For example, "Abba Gerontius of Petra said that many, tempted by the pleasures of the body, commit fornication, not in their body but in their spirit, and while preserving their bodily virginity, commit prostitution in their soul. 'Thus it is good, my well-beloved, to do that which is written, and for each one to guard his own heart with all possible care.' (Prov 4:23)."[3]

Humility was also paramount. The desert fathers never displayed pride in their ascetic achievements, and any visitor displaying such pride was likely to be subtly but effectively corrected. In contrast, the fathers practiced their ascetic acts in secret and spoke often of their own sinfulness. They also demonstrated a remarkable lack of judgment of others. When a bishop brought a young pregnant girl (presumably unmarried) to Abba Ammonas so he could give her a penance, Abba Ammonas instead made the sign of the cross over her and commanded that she be given six pairs of fine linen sheets in case she or the baby should die in childbirth and not have anything for the burial. "But her accusers resumed, 'Why did you do that? Give her a punishment.' But he said to them, 'Look, brothers, she is near to death; what am I to do?' Then he sent her away and no old man dared accuse anyone any more."[4] And as is told of Abba Bessarion: "A brother who had sinned was turned out of the church by the priest; Abba Bessarion got up and went with him, saying, 'I, too, am a sinner.' "[5]

Another virtue the monks refer to often is charity. Since most of the desert fathers lived together as monks, it was of the utmost importance that they cultivate charity, a sense of loving and caring for one another, of putting others' needs before their own. As Abba Anthony said, "Our life and death is with our neighbour. If we gain our brothers, we have gained God, but if we scandalise our brother, we have sinned against Christ."[6]

Abba Achilles, for example, did not make fishing nets for the first two men who asked him but consented to make one for the third, since he was of bad reputation and would have considered a refusal as a reflection on his own sin. With characteristic humility, Abba Matoes described the difficulty of achieving perfect charity: "A brother went to Abba Matoes and said to him, 'How is it that the monks of Scetis did more than the Scriptures required in loving their enemies more than themselves?' Abba Matoes said to him, 'As for me I have not yet managed to love those who love me as I love myself.' "[7]

Christians might wonder what the words of Jesus, "Deny yourself, take up your cross, and follow me," might mean; these *Sayings of the Desert Fathers* are the writings of some who took those words very seriously and stopped at nothing in striving to discipline or re-direct every aspect of their physical, intellectual and psychological lives toward God.

—Frederica Mathewes-Green

Why *The Sayings of the Desert Fathers* Is Essential

The wisdom contained in these sayings and stories has been invaluable to Christians east and west for fifteen hundred years. Truly the wisdom contained here has stood the test of time. It would be easy to write off *The Sayings of the Desert Fathers* as only meant for the monastic life, but as demonstrated by the people from all walks of life who consulted the desert fathers and mothers on all manner of things, their wholehearted commitment to Christ makes them sources of wisdom for all Christians.

Perhaps no other book on our list strikes such a contrast to modern life. As Chris Webb, Renovaré president and editorial board member, says, "The wisdom the desert fathers have is hard to get anyplace else nowadays. It's a lived experience of the gospel that is so profound, and if you're willing to sit with them and listen and reflect on what they have to say through these stories there's so much to learn. And particularly, in a church that is so keen to learn about grace the desert fathers have a lot to teach us about how you can be utterly radically committed to Jesus Christ, throwing yourself behind his cause yet becoming more committed to people, more gracious, more loving."

The desert fathers, in their radical commitment to simplicity and asceticism, present a direct challenge to comfortable Christianity. It is this very challenge that makes *The Sayings of the Desert Fathers* such important reading for spiritual formation. Their radical commitment to Christ led them to practice ascetic disciplines, something very foreign to most of us. Are we called to incorporate in our lives more of the bodily denial of the desert fathers and mothers? And despite their great commitment and discipline, we find in them deep humility. There is no competition here, no race to be more committed to Christ than the desert father down the street. We can learn from their striking reluctance to judge others. If the desert fathers, who have grown so close to Christ, can be free of judgment, what right do the rest of us have to judge each other? It is so much easier to think and talk about someone else's sins rather than our own, but if we focus on our own sinfulness we can be freed of this unhealthy judgmentalism. As Abba Moses said, "When someone is occupied with his own faults, he does not see those of his neighbour."[8] Further, we can rejoice in someone else's holiness and intimacy with God.

The desert fathers and mothers provide great examples and insight for the practice of the disciplines of simplicity, secrecy, and solitude. We can learn the most by paying close attention to those very ideas that strike us as the most countercultural. How can we recover their sense of the great value of words and thus the importance of using them sparingly and with great thought? How can we broadcast our sinfulness and hide our righteousness and obedience? What in our lives represents our cell, and how can we better meet God there?

How to Read *The Sayings of the Desert Fathers*

The Sayings of the Desert Fathers is arranged in Greek alphabetical order by the name of the father or mother to which each anecdote refers, but a reader can read them in any order. Each saying stands alone. In fact, some of them seem to directly contradict each other. For example, some of the fathers speak of the usefulness of Christian books, but others regard such books with caution or say that it is best to have no possessions. It is important to remember that each one was spoken in a particular situation to a particular person or group and was not necessarily meant to be universally true. Not every saying will speak to every reader. The desert fathers understood that each individual who comes to Christ is on a unique journey. It is also important to remember that it is a book of wisdom sayings, like the book of Proverbs, and thus not a book to sit down and read cover to cover. *The Sayings of the Desert Fathers* is a particularly important book with which to practice reflection. Try reading just a small amount at a time, allowing some time to ruminate over the particular sayings that strike you.

The world of the desert fathers may feel very different from our own, but the fathers have much to teach us. As is written in Anthony of Sourozh's preface to *The Sayings of the Desert Fathers,* "If we wish to understand the sayings of the Fathers, let us approach them with veneration, silencing our judgments and our own thoughts in order to meet them on their own ground and perhaps to partake ultimately—if we prove able to emulate their earnestness in the search, their ruthless determination, their infinite compassion—in their own silent communion with God."[9]

EXCERPTS FROM

The Sayings of the Desert Fathers

AGATHON

8. Someone asked Abba Agathon, 'Which is better, bodily asceticism or interior vigilance?' The old man replied, 'Man is like a tree, bodily asceticism is the foliage, interior vigilance the fruit. According to that which is written, "Every tree that bringeth not forth good fruit shall be cut down and cast into the fire" (Matt 3:10) it is clear that all our care should be directed towards the fruit, that is to say, guard of the spirit; but it needs the protection and the embellishment of the foliage, which is bodily asceticism.'

26. Abba Agathon said, 'If I could meet a leper, give him my body and take his, I should be very happy.' That indeed is perfect charity.

BESSARION

12. Abba Bessarion's disciples related that his life had been like that of a bird of the air, or a fish, or an animal living on earth, passing all of the time of his life without trouble or disquiet. The care of a dwelling did not trouble him, and the desire for a particular place never seemed to dominate his soul, no more

than the abundance of delights, or the possession of houses or the reading of books. But he seemed entirely free from all the passions of the body, sustaining himself on the hope of good things to come, firm in the strength of his faith; he lived in patience, like a prisoner who is led everywhere, always suffering cold and nakedness, scorched by the sun. He always lived in the open air, afflicting himself on the edge of the desert like a vagabond. Often he found it good to be carried over the sea to distant and uninhabited regions. When he happened to come into pleasanter places where the brethren lived a life in common, he would sit outside at the gate, weeping and lamenting like one shipwrecked and flung back on to the earth. Then if one of the brethren coming out found him there, sitting like one of the poor beggars living in the world, and filled with compassion approached him, asking, 'Man, why are you weeping? If you are in need of something, as far as we can we will see you receive it, only come in, share your table and rest yourself.' He would reply, 'I cannot live under a roof so long as I have not found again the riches of my house,' adding that he had lost great riches in various ways. 'I have fallen amongst pirates, I have suffered shipwreck, I have dishonoured my rank, becoming unknown, famous as I was.' The brother, moved by these words, returned, bringing a morsel of bread and giving it to him, saying, 'Take this, Father; all the rest, as you say, God will restore to you; home, honour, and riches of which you speak.' But he, bewailing himself yet more, sighed deeply, adding, 'I cannot say if I shall find again those lost good things I seek, but I am still more afflicted, every day suffering the danger of death, having no respite because of my great calamities. For always I must wander, in order to finish my course.'

JOHN THE DWARF

8. One day when he was sitting in front of the church, the brethren were consulting him about their thoughts. One of the old men who saw it became a prey to jealousy and said to him,

'John, your vessel is full of poison.' Abba John said to him, 'That is very true, abba; and you have said that when you only see the outside, but if you were able to see the inside, too, what would you say then?'

13. Abba Poemen said of Abba John the Dwarf that he had prayed God to take his passions away from him so that he might become free from care. He went and told an old man this: 'I find myself in peace, without an enemy,' he said. The old man said to him, 'Go, beseech God to stir up warfare so that you may regain the affliction and humility that you used to have, for it is by warfare that the soul makes progress.' So he besought God and when warfare came, he no longer prayed that it might be taken away, but said, 'Lord, give me strength for the fight.'

31. A camel-driver came one day to pick up some goods and take them elsewhere. Going inside to bring him what he had woven, Abba John forgot about it because his spirit was fixed in God. So once more the camel-driver disturbed him by knocking on the door and once more Abba John went in and forgot. The camel-driver knocked a third time and Abba John went in saying, 'Weaving—camel; weaving—camel.' He said this so that he would not forget again.

35. It was said of the same Abba John that when he returned from the harvest or when he had been with some of the old men, he gave himself to prayer, meditation and psalmody until his thoughts were re-established in their previous order.

ISIDORE OF PELUSIA

1. Abba Isidore of Pelusia said, 'To live without speaking is better than to speak without living. For the former who lives rightly does good even by his silence but the latter does no good even when he speaks. When words and life correspond to one another they are together the whole of philosophy.'

RICHARD J. FOSTER

Some books of genuine importance that are not in the list of twenty-five.

1 ***Hudson Taylor's Spiritual Secret***. Early in my Christian journey I was deeply nurtured by mission biography and autobiography. Hudson Taylor was the first and I would encourage serious readers of Taylor to secure the seven-volume set by A. J. Broomhall. Soon I added many other names to my study: William Cary, Adoniram Judson, George Müller, C. T. Studd, Mary Slessor, Rees Howells, Watchman Nee, Sadhu Sundar Singh, Jim Elliot, and more. Each personality helped to increase my understanding of what life with Christ can be like.

2 ***The Journal of John Woolman***. In an odd twist Woolman brought new insight into my understanding of contemporary social issues. This simple Quaker tailor from New Jersey in the eighteenth century penned a journal that remains quite contemporary, pinpointing issues we wrestle with today: racism, consumerism, militarism. He dealt with these issues with a striking combination of compassion and courage, tenderness and firmness.

3 ***Letters by a Modern Mystic***, Frank Laubach. Laubach wrote perhaps a dozen books on prayer but this is his best known. A twentieth-century international statesman for Christ, he developed a method of literacy training around the world that gave him the title "The Apostle to the Silent Billion." This book lays forth a simple and effectual way by which we can fill our minds with the reality of God, of Christ, and of his kingdom.

4 ***Repentance: The Joy-filled Life***, Basilea Schlink. Schlink founded the Evangelical Sisterhood of Mary, a Lutheran contemplative movement that grew out of the ashes of WWII and has spread around the world. My personal visit to the Evangelical Sisterhood in Darmstadt, Germany, was powerful beyond the telling. This movement and the many writings that continue to be produced by these evangelical sisters are a genuine witness to the reality of life with Christ in God.

5 ***The Divine Conspiracy***, Dallas Willard. Willard has with this book produced a masterpiece. It provides a conceptual philosophy for understanding the meaning and purpose of human existence. It presents God as real and present and ever reaching out to all of humanity. All of this is done in a way that is warm and practical and completely understandable. It is one of a small handful of books from the twentieth century that shall endure.

RICHARD J. FOSTER is the founder of Renovaré. He has authored or coauthored seven books, including *Celebration of Discipline, Prayer: Finding the Heart's True Home, Freedom of Simplicity, The Challenge of the Disciplined Life,* and *Streams of Living Water.*

JOSEPH OF PANEPHYSIS

7. Abba Lot went to see Abba Joseph and said to him, 'Abba, as far as I can say my little office, I fast a little, I pray and meditate, I live in peace and as far as I can, I purify my thoughts. What else can I do?' Then the old man stood up and stretched his hands toward heaven. His fingers became like ten lamps of fire and he said to him, 'If you will, you can become all flame.'

MOSES

2. A brother at Scetis committed a fault. A council was called to which Abba Moses was invited, but he refused to go to it. Then the priest sent someone to say to him, 'Come, for everyone is waiting for you.' So he got up and went. He took a leaking jug, filled it with water and carried it with him. The others came out to meet him and said to him, 'What is this, Father?' The old man said to them, 'My sins run out behind me, and I do not see them, and today I am coming to judge the errors of another.' When they heard that they said no more to the brother but forgave him.

POEMEN (CALLED THE SHEPHERD)

4. Before Abba Poemen's group came there, there was an old man in Egypt who enjoyed considerable fame and repute. But when Abba Poemen's group came up to Scetis, men left the old man to go see Abba Poemen. Abba Poemen was grieved at this and said to his disciples, 'What is to be done about this great old man, for men grieve him by leaving him and coming to us who are nothing? What shall we do, then to comfort this old man?' He said to them, 'Make ready a little food, and take a skin of wine and let us go to see him and eat with him. And so we shall be able to comfort him.' So they put together some food, and went. When they knocked at the door the old man's disciple answered, saying, 'Who are you?' They responded, 'Tell the abba it is Poemen who desires to be blessed by him.' The

disciple reported this and the old man sent him to say, 'Go away, I have no time.' But in spite of the heat they persevered, saying, 'We shall not go away till we have been allowed to meet the old man.' Seeing their humility and patience, the old man was filled with compunction and opened the door to them. Then they went in and ate with him. During the meal he said, 'Truly, not only what I have heard about you is true, but I see that your works are a hundred-fold greater,' and from that day, he became their friend.

12. A brother questioned Abba Poemen saying, 'I have committed a great sin and I want to do penance for three years.' The old man said to him, 'That is a lot.' The brother said, 'For one year?' The old man said again, 'That is a lot.' Those who were present said, 'For forty days?' He said again, 'That is a lot.' He added, 'I myself say that if a man repents with his whole heart and does not intend to commit the sin any more, God will accept him after only three days.'

17. It was said of Abba Poemen that if he was invited to eat against his will, he wept but he went, so as not to refuse to obey his brother and cause him pain.

20. Abba Isaiah questioned Abba Poemen on the subject of impure thoughts. Abba Poemen said to him, 'It is like having a chest full of clothes, if one leaves them in disorder they are spoiled in the course of time. It is the same with thoughts. If we do not do anything about them, in time they are spoiled, that is to say, they disintegrate.'

23. Abba Poemen said, 'If a man has sinned and denies it, saying: "I have not sinned," do not reprimand him; for that will discourage him. But say to him, "Do not lose heart, brother, but be on guard in future," and you will stir his soul to repentance.'

28. A brother came to see Abba Poemen and said to him, 'Abba, I have many thoughts and they put me in danger.' The old man led him outside and said to him, 'Expand your chest and do not breathe in.' He said, 'I cannot do that.' Then the old man said to him, 'If you cannot do that, no more can you prevent thoughts from arising, but you can resist them.'

31. Abba Joseph asked Abba Poemen, 'How should one fast?' Abba Poemen said to him, 'For my part, I think it better that one should eat every day, but only a little, so as not to be satisfied.' Abba Joseph said to him, 'When you were younger, did you not fast two days at a time, abba?' The old man said: 'Yes, even for three days and four and the whole week. The Fathers tried all this out as they were able and they found it preferable to eat every day, but just a small amount. They have left us this royal way, which is light.'

33. A brother asked Abba Poemen, 'An inheritance has been left me, what ought I to do?' The old man said to him, 'Go, come back in three days and I will tell you.' So he returned as it had been decided. Then the old man said, 'What shall I say to you, brother? If I tell you to give it to the church, they will make banquets with it; if I tell you to give it to your relations, you will not receive any profit from it; if I tell you to give it to the poor, you will not do it. Do as you like, it is none of my business.'

64. A brother questioned Abba Poemen saying, 'If I see my brother committing a sin, is it right to conceal it?' The old man said to him, 'At they very moment when we hide our brother's fault, God hides our own and at the moment when we reveal our brother's fault, God reveals ours too.'

80. He also said, 'Do not give your heart to that which does not satisfy your heart.'

92. Some old men came to see Abba Poemen and said to him, 'When we see brothers who are dozing at the *synaxis,* shall we rouse them so that they will be watchful?' He said to them, 'For my part when I see a brother who is dozing, I put his head on my knees and let him rest.'

125. Abba Poemen said that the blessed Abba Anthony used to say, 'The greatest thing a man can do is to throw his faults before the Lord and to expect temptation to his last breath.'

164. Abba Poemen said, 'Teach your mouth to say what is in your heart.'

177. He also said, 'Wickedness does not do away with wickedness, but if someone does you wrong, do good to him, so that by your action you destroy his wickedness.'

SIMON

1. A magistrate came to see Abba Simon one day. When he heard of it, he put on his apron and went out to attend to a palm-tree. When the visitors arrived they called out to him, 'Old man, where is the anchorite?' He replied, 'There is no anchorite here.' Hearing these words, they went away again.

SYNCLETICA

1. Amma Syncletica said, 'In the beginning there are a great many battles and a good deal of suffering for those who are advancing towards God and afterwards, ineffable joy. It is like those who wish to light a fire; at first they are choked by the smoke and cry, and by this means obtain what they seek (as it is said: "Our God is a consuming fire" (Heb 12:24): so we also must kindle the divine fire in ourselves through tears and hard work.'

4. She also said, 'Do not let yourself be seduced by the delights of the riches of the world, as though they contained something

useful on account of vain pleasure. Worldly people esteem the culinary art, but you, through fasting and thanks to cheap food, go beyond their abundance of food. It is written: "He who is sated loathes honey" (Prov 27:7). Do not fill yourself with bread and you will not desire wine."[10]

A Study Guide for *The Sayings of the Desert Fathers*

1. What is the difference between a desert father (abba) and a preacher/priest/spiritual director? Is there a modern parallel to the desert fathers in your church or community? Who in your life encourages and teaches you and holds you accountable?

2. The monks went into the desert not to avoid temptation, but to invite it, believing that it would strengthen their souls. Many of the fathers advise not praying for such temptations to be removed, but for the strength to resist them. In what place or time in your life have you met with the most temptation? How did your battles there strengthen your soul?

3. Much of what the fathers advise may strike us as excessive. For example, Abba Anthony says, "Hate the world and all that is in it. Hate all peace that comes from the flesh. . . . Suffer hunger, thirst, nakedness, be watchful and sorrowful; weep, and groan in your heart; test yourselves, to see if you are worthy of God; despise the flesh, so that you may preserve your souls."[11] How are we to take such advice?

4. Despite all those who wanted to consult with the fathers, they were often extremely reluctant to meet with visitors. From what did this reluctance stem? Do you know anyone who is equally reluctant to share his or her wisdom or teachings? What kind of feeling would such a reaction evoke in you?

5. One rationale for the extreme asceticism practiced by many of the desert fathers can be found in the words of Abba Daniel: "The body prospers in the measure in which the soul is weakened, and the soul prospers in the measure in which the body is weakened."[12] How have you found this to be true or not in your spiritual practice? Is it important to achieve a balance between the body and the soul? Why or why not?

6. Giving up food, in particular, is said to make our inner vision more keen. How have you experienced this? If you have not tried fasting before, why not?

7. Many of the fathers practiced their asceticism in secrecy so as not to invite praise. Why is that important? When have you sought to perform such an act in secrecy? What was the result?

8. Not only do the fathers and mothers hide their good works and acts of obedience to God, they profess openly the depths of their sinfulness. Are you able to present yourself this way to others? If not, what prevents you from doing so?

9. Isidore the Priest advises, "It is better for a man to eat meat than to be inflated with pride and to glorify himself."[13] How can we avoid feeling pride at practicing spiritual disciplines such as fasting?

10. A practice mentioned often by the fathers is that of saying few words, of not engaging in idle conversation. Why is such economy of words necessary? Why do you think this practice has fallen out of fashion? What would it mean for you to try to better incorporate such a practice into your life?

The Rule of St. Benedict

ST. BENEDICT

~ Are you hastening toward your heavenly home? Then with Christ's help, keep this little rule that we have written for beginners.

Written by St. Benedict of Nursia as a guide for monasteries, the *Rule* is a handbook to living the Christian life.

BENEDICT OF NURSIA lived in Italy in the late fifth and early to mid-sixth centuries. It was a turbulent time, characterized by the disintegration of the Roman Empire. Disgusted with the paganism he saw in Rome as a student, Benedict went to live alone in a cave in Subiaco, thirty miles east of Rome. He was asked by other monks who lived nearby to be their abbot. He reluctantly agreed, but after a time these monks chafed under his authority and tried to poison him. He later became the abbot of another group of monks, establishing twelve monasteries of twelve monks each, but he left this community because of the jealousy of the local clergy. Eventually, St. Benedict founded another monastery on the mountain above Cassino, where he lived out the rest of his life, becoming known as a holy man and a miracle worker.

The *Rule* is his greatest legacy, a set of guidelines for monks based on centuries of monastic wisdom. It deals with the whole of life, both physical and spiritual, detailing precise instructions for everything from the monks' sleeping arrangements to the proper attitude of prayer. Into a chaotic world where nothing seemed reliable (if Rome could fall, what could be depended upon?), Benedict's *Rule* offered order, routine, and peace.

Benedict sets the tone for the *Rule* in his first few words, describing the *Rule* as advice from a loving father. To him the *Rule* is the way to subvert our own wills so that we can better follow Christ's will. For a monk, every action matters. "The Lord waits for us daily to translate into action, as we should, his holy teachings."[1] In fact, the abbot of the monastery is to oversee every aspect of the monks' lives, from their diet and clothing to deciding what letters or gifts from their families they are allowed to keep.

With frequent references to the Bible, the *Rule* is an instruction book for loving God and others, honoring others, and living an ascetic, hopeful, and devout lifestyle. At the root of monastic life, however, is obedience. When we commit to Jesus, we agree not to live by our own judgment. For monks this obedience takes the form of living in a monastery and submitting to the direction of the abbot. The obedience they give to their superiors is given also to God. But obedience is "acceptable to God and agreeable to man" only if it is done willingly and is not halfhearted or grudging.

The *Rule* also calls us to guard our speech and practice humility. Practicing humility, like obedience, requires subverting our wills, obeying our superiors, and embracing suffering, but also recognizing with our mouths and our hearts that we are inferior to all. "In the monastery no one is to follow his own heart's desire."[2]

The *Rule* also describes the divine office, or daily schedule of worship, in great detail, from the time of each office to the number of psalms read and the responses. Throughout, it is clear that the practice of each office, from Vespers to Lauds to Compline, is to be the centerpiece of the day, and all that happens there carries over into the rest of life. For example, "Assuredly, the celebration of Lauds and Vespers must never pass by without the superior's reciting the entire Lord's Prayer at the end for all to hear, because thorns of contention are likely to spring up. Thus warned by the pledge they make to one another in the very words of this prayer: *Forgive us as we forgive* (Matt 6:12), they may cleanse themselves of this kind of vice."[3] All 150 psalms are to be read each week, "For monks who in a week's time say less than the full psalter with the customary canticles betray extreme indolence and lack of devotion in their service. We read, after all, that our holy Fathers, energetic as they were, did all this in a single day. Let us hope that we, lukewarm as we are, can achieve it in a whole week."[4] The mealtimes of the monks are also specified, as are times for manual labor and spiritual reading, all with an eye toward avoiding idleness.

In the *Rule* we find spiritual gems such as how to pray before God without many words, mixed right in with practical advice about how the younger monks should sleep with their beds interspersed with those of the seniors, and how all should quietly encourage one another upon rising, "for the sleepy like to make excuses."[5]

Punishments for being stubborn or prideful or resisting the authority of superiors include excommunication and exclusion from table, oratory, and fellowship. But an abbot is urged to support and console any wayward brother to the greatest extent possible, following Jesus' example in the parable of the shepherd who left the ninety-nine sheep to care for the one that was lost. The abbot is likened to a physician, who is to apply the ointment of encouragement, the medicine of Scripture, and the remedy of prayer before taking such a drastic measure as removing the diseased limb. Even brothers who have been excommunicated, however, can be received back into the fellowship, if they make full amends, up to three times.

Benedict's *Rule* displays a telling knowledge of human nature. Kitchen duties are to rotate among all, and kitchen workers are instructed to ask for a special prayer before and after their week of service. The sick are to be given the utmost care, but they are also asked not to be too demanding of their brothers. Brothers are to read and sing not according to rank but according to "their ability to benefit their hearers."[6]

Monks are to "diligently cultivate silence at all times, but especially at night."[7] Further, they are to proceed with speed but dignity to the divine office when they first hear the call. If one does arrive late, he is to stand last or in a special place so that all will know, a practice Benedict calls doing "penance by public satisfaction."[8] But it is important for them to enter and not remain outside the oratory lest they go back to sleep or engage in idle talk.

Guests, particularly the poor and pilgrims, are to be welcomed, but interactions are to be kept to a minimum. If any newcomer wants to join the monastery, he is not to be granted an easy entry, is

A lamb can bathe in it without drowning, while an elephant can swim in it.

—Unknown writer's ancient saying about the *Rule*

not allowed to enter for four or five days, and then should be given several long periods to reflect on the *Rule* before deciding whether he wants to join. Community rank is to be determined not by age, but by the date of entry to the monastery, the virtue of the monk's life, and the decision of the abbot. The abbot, who holds the place of Christ, is to be carefully chosen and always to remember that he is accountable for all the souls of the monastery. He is cautioned to use prudence and avoid extremes in punishment and strive to be loved rather than feared.

Benedict ends by telling us that while the way to perfection is found in the Old and New Testaments, "this little Rule for beginners" is a good place to start.

Why *The Rule of St. Benedict* Is Essential

This *Rule* written more than a thousand years ago is still used in almost every Western monastery, earning St. Benedict the title Father of Western Monasticism. Obviously it is hugely important for those who choose to live cloistered lifestyles, but it holds great significance for all Christians. Phyllis Tickle, editorial board member and compiler of *The Divine Hours* series, calls the *Rule* "the quintessential Western statement on how to be a Christian." Not only is it an essential and characteristic document of Western Christianity, with its emphasis on morality, but it also brims with wisdom for anyone seeking a life of yielded submission to Christ.

The *Rule*'s message is that our actions matter; they matter to God. And as anyone who has ever resolved to do one thing and ended up doing just the opposite knows, it's all very well to think and to plan—following through is another matter. The truth is, we cannot just think ourselves into a new way of being; we must *live* ourselves into a new way of being. The way we order our days affects our spiritual lives, and vice versa. The *Rule* has much to teach us about avoiding idleness, cultivating humility and obedience, and most of all, putting aside our own wills.

Although many spiritual disciplines are touched on in its pages, submission is the key discipline highlighted in the *Rule*. "In the monastery no one is to follow his own heart's desire."[9] We are to set aside our own wills for that of Christ's. Those who choose to live life in the monastery have the abbot to take the place of Christ. For the rest of us, we must appeal directly to God to replace our own wills with Christ's. From Benedict perhaps more than from any other source we can learn not only the importance of obedience but also how we can set aside our own wills and learn submission.

How to Read *The Rule of St. Benedict*

It is certainly possible to read *The Rule of St. Benedict* straight through in one sitting, and the text recommends that those considering joining a Benedictine monastery should hear it read through in its entirety several times before finalizing their decision. But we recommend not reading the *Rule* so much as savoring it, reading each passage in the slow, prayerful style of *lectio divina,* also a Benedictine tradition.

Considering the age of the *Rule,* it is perhaps rather astonishing how little of it feels irrelevant. One could certainly live a life as Benedict prescribes today, and many continue to do so. But for those of us who are not considering joining a community that lives this way, our advice would be not to read the *Rule* as a set of rules or laws exactly, but to read it symbolically, looking for the wisdom and the thought behind each guideline and regulation. Just as the monks for whom Benedict originally intended the *Rule,* we, too, seek to submit our wills to Christ, to cultivate humility and obedience, and to live in peace with our brothers and sisters in Christ. Even in the most specific of instructions for particular jobs in the monastery, we can find much to consider and apply to our own lives. How can we cultivate humility? How can we greet others with hospitality? How can we value and serve those we live with? Some may want to read through it with a journal, in order to ponder further what each part of the *Rule* might mean for them. Others of us may want to create our own Rule, by ourselves or with others. Benedict's *Rule* can serve as a good example and guide.

EXCERPTS FROM

The Rule of St. Benedict

CHAPTER 4: THE TOOLS FOR GOOD WORKS

Your way of acting should be different from the world's way; the love of Christ must come before all else. You are not to act in anger or nurse a grudge. Rid your heart of all deceit. Never give a hollow greeting of peace or turn away when someone needs your love. Bind yourself to no oath lest it prove false, but speak the truth with heart and tongue.

Do not repay one bad turn with another (1 Thess 5:15; 1 Pet 3:9). Do not injure anyone, but bear injuries patiently. *Love your enemies* (Matt 5:44; Luke 6:27). If people curse you, do not curse them back but bless them instead. *Endure persecution for the sake of justice* (Matt 5:10).

You must *not* be *proud, nor be given to wine* (Titus 1:7; 1 Tim 3:3). Refrain from too much eating or sleeping, and *from laziness* (Rom 12:11). Do not grumble or speak ill of others.

Place your hope in God alone. If you notice something good in yourself, give credit to God, not to yourself, but be certain that the evil you commit is always your own and yours to acknowledge.

Live in fear of judgment day and have a great horror of hell. Yearn for everlasting life with holy desire. Day by day remind yourself that you are going to die. Hour by hour keep careful watch over all you do, aware that God's gaze is upon you, wherever you may be. As soon as wrongful thoughts come into your heart, dash them against Christ and disclose them to your spiritual father. Guard your lips from harmful or deceptive speech. Prefer moderation in speech and speak no foolish chatter, nothing just to provoke laughter; do not love immoderate or boisterous laughter.

Listen readily to holy reading, and devote yourself often to prayer. Every day with tears and sights confess your past sins to God in prayer and change from these evil ways in the future.

Do not gratify the promptings of the flesh (Gal 5:16); hate the urgings of self-will. Obey the orders of the abbot unreservedly, even if his own conduct—which God forbid—be at odds with what he says. Remember the teaching of the Lord: *Do what they say, not what they do* (Matt 23:3).

Do not aspire to be called holy before you really are, but first be holy that you may more truly be called so. Live by God's commandments every day; treasure chastity, harbor neither hatred nor jealousy of anyone, and do nothing out of envy. Do not love quarreling; shun arrogance. Respect the elders and love the young. Pray for your enemies out of love for Christ. If you have a dispute with someone, make peace with him before the sun goes down.

And finally, never lose hope in God's mercy.

These then are the tools of the spiritual craft. When we have used them without ceasing day and night and have returned them on judgment day, our wages will be the reward the Lord has promised: *What the eye has not seen nor the ear heard, God has prepared for those who love him* (1 Cor 2:9).

The workshop where we are to toil faithfully at all these tasks is the enclosure of the monastery and stability in the community.

CHAPTER 5: OBEDIENCE

The first step of humility is unhesitating obedience, which comes naturally to those who cherish Christ above all. Because of the holy service they have professed, or because of dread of hell and for the glory of everlasting life, they carry out the superior's order as promptly as if the command came from God himself. The Lord says of men like this: *No sooner did he hear than he obeyed me* (Ps 17[18]:45); again he tells teachers: *Whoever listens to you, listens to me* (Luke 10:16). Such people as these immediately put aside their own concerns, abandon their own will, and lay down whatever they have in hand, leaving it unfinished. With the ready step of obedience, they follow the voice of authority in their actions. Almost at the same moment, then, as the master gives the instruction the disciple quickly puts it into practice in the fear of God; and both actions together are swiftly completed as one.

It is love that impels them to pursue everlasting life; therefore, they are eager to take the narrow road of which the Lord says: *Narrow is the road that leads to life* (Matt 7:14). They no longer live by their own judgment, giving in to their whims and appetites; rather they walk according to another's decisions and directions, choosing to live in monasteries and to have an abbot over them. Men of this resolve unquestionably conform to the saying of the Lord: *I have come not to do my own will, but the will of him who sent me* (John 6:38).

This very obedience, however, will be acceptable to God and agreeable to men only if compliance with what is commanded is not cringing or sluggish or half-hearted, but free from any grumbling or any reaction of unwillingness. For the obedience shown to superiors is given to God, as he himself said: *Whoever listens to you, listens to me* (Luke 10:16). Furthermore, the disciples' obedience must be given gladly, for *God loves a cheerful giver* (2 Cor 9:7). If a disciple obeys grudgingly and grumbles, not only aloud but also in his heart, then, even though he carries out the order, his action will not be accepted with favor by God, who sees that he is grumbling in his heart. He will have no reward for service of this kind; on the contrary, he will incur punishment for grumbling, unless he changes for the better and makes amends.

My Personal Top 5

EMILIE GRIFFIN

1 *Surprised by Joy*, C. S. Lewis. This book was a turning point for me in acceptance of Christ. I identified with Lewis every step of the journey, especially because my childhood reading had become a way that the Lord spoke to me through the things I loved. Lewis's influence was profound in shaping my life choices as writer and reader.

2 **The Poetry and Plays of T. S. Eliot**. In my twenties I read Eliot and was baffled by him at first, until at last (through reading Lewis, especially *The Four Loves*) I came to see what Eliot was driving at, and driven by—a deep yearning for God and a desire to know him more. The most important poems for me are "The Four Quartets," "The Love Song of J. Alfred Prufrock," and "Gerontion."

3 *The Cloud of Unknowing* and **The Confessions of St. Augustine** were both influential in my early journey. Now, amazingly, I can teach both texts with some authority, simply because of a lifetime of reading them. *The Cloud,* of course, is a primary text for prayer, after the Bible, which always stands at the head of all devotional writing. And *Augustine* manages to capture in one deeply personal story the wisdom and truth of all the ancient writers and thinkers from Aristotle to Abraham. He is the quintessential teacher who leads us into the heart of Christ.

4 *The Divine Comedy*, Dante Alighieri. I came late to loving Dante, influenced by the late-in-life experience of Dorothy L. Sayers. She loved Milton, Shakespeare, all the classical authors I had cared about, and finally, the one I found hardest to understand. She opened me up to Dante. Also, I had the blessing of reading Dante with a fine Dante scholar and historian, a process of several years that taught me to feel a confidence even in the competitive world of Dante scholarship. Dante is for me one of the greatest teachers of the spiritual life, one who has mastered the ancient teachings on virtue and love and gives them all to us, generously.

5 **Donne and the Devotional Poets of the Seventeenth Century**. Over a lifetime I have come to see how deep was the influence of my early life encounter with mystical poets: Emily Dickinson, the Latin poets, Wordsworth, Coleridge, Herbert, and Donne. Of course, both C. S. Lewis and J. R. R. Tolkien played into this, showing me how poetry and friendship conspire to lead us into the heart of God and, at last, into the heart of Christ. All the virtues and values—truth, goodness, meaning, beauty—I can discover again daily. Gerard Manley Hopkins, of course, is the latest in this great succession of mystical poets, celebrating the wonder, the words, and the Word.

EMILIE GRIFFIN is the author of *Souls in Full Sail: Christian Spirituality for the Later Years* and *Wonderful and Dark Is This Road,* a brief introduction to Christian mystics.

CHAPTER 28: THOSE WHO REFUSE TO AMEND AFTER FREQUENT REPROOFS

If a brother has been reproved frequently for any fault, or if he has been excommunicated, yet does not amend, let him receive a sharper punishment: that is, let him feel the strokes of the rod. But if even then he does not reform, or perhaps become proud and would actually defend his conduct, which God forbid, the abbot should follow the procedure of a wise physician. After he has applied compresses, the ointment of encouragement, the medicine of divine Scripture, and finally the cauterizing iron of excommunication and strokes of the rod, and if he then perceives that his earnest efforts are unavailing, let him apply an even better remedy: he and all the brothers should pray for him so that the Lord, who can do all things, may bring about the health of the sick brother. Yet even if this procedure does not heal him, then finally, the abbot must use the knife and amputate. For the Apostle says: *Banish the evil one from your midst* (1 Cor 5:13); and again, *If the unbeliever departs, let him depart* (1 Cor 7:15), lest one diseased sheep infect the whole flock.

CHAPTER 31: QUALIFICATIONS OF THE MONASTERY CELLARER

As cellarer of the monastery, there should be chosen from the community someone who is wise, mature in conduct, temperate, not an excessive eater, not proud, excitable, offensive, dilatory or wasteful, but God-fearing, and like a father to the whole community. He will take care of everything, but will do nothing without an order from the abbot. Let him keep to his orders.

He should not annoy the brothers. If any brother happens to make an unreasonable demand of him, he should not reject him with disdain and cause him distress, but reasonably and humbly deny the improper request. Let him keep watch over his own soul, ever mindful of that saying of the Apostle: *He who serves well secures a good standing for himself* (1 Tim 3:13). He must show every care and concern for the sick, children, guests and the poor, knowing for certain that he will be held accountable for all of them on the day of judgment. He will regard all utensils and goods of the monastery as sacred vessels of the altar, aware that nothing is to be neglected. He should not be prone to greed, nor be wasteful and extravagant with the goods of the monastery, but should do everything with moderation and according to the abbot's orders.

Above all, let him be humble. If goods are not available to meet a request, he will offer a kind word in reply, for it is written: A kind *word is better than the best gift* (Sir 18:17). He should take care of all that the abbot entrusts to him, and not presume to do what the abbot has forbidden. He will provide the brothers with their allotted amount of food without any pride or delay, lest they be led astray. For he must remember what that Scripture says that person deserves *who leads one of the little ones astray* (Matt 18:6).

If the community is rather large, he should be given helpers, that with their assistance he may calmly perform the duties of his office. Necessary items are to be requested and given at the proper times, so that no one may be disquieted or distressed in the house of God.

CHAPTER 68: ASSIGNMENT OF IMPOSSIBLE TASKS TO A BROTHER

A brother may be assigned a burdensome task or something he cannot do. If so, he should, with complete gentleness and obedience, accept the order given him. Should he see, however, that the weight of the burden is altogether too much for his strength, then he should choose the appropriate moment and explain patiently to his superior the reasons why he cannot perform his task. This he ought to do without pride, obstinacy, or refusal. If after the explanation the superior is still determined to hold to his original order, then the junior must recognize that this is best for him. Trusting in God's help, he must in love obey.

The reason we have written this rule is that, by observing it in monasteries, we can show that we have some degree of virtue and the beginnings of monastic life. But for anyone hastening on to the perfection of monastic life, there are the teachings of the holy Fathers, the observance of which will lead him to the very heights of perfection. What page, what passage of the inspired books of the Old and New Testaments is not the truest of guides for human life? What book of the holy catholic Fathers does not resoundingly summon us along the true way to reach the Creator? Then, besides the *Conferences* of the Fathers, their *Institutes* and their *Lives,* there is also the rule of our holy father Basil. For observant and obedient monks, all these are nothing less than tools for the cultivation of virtues; but as for us, they make us blush for shame at being so slothful, so unobservant, so negligent. Are you hastening toward your heavenly home? Then, with Christ's help, keep this little rule that we have written for beginners. After that, you can set out for the loftier summits of the teachings and virtues we mentioned above, and under God's protection you will reach them. Amen.[10]

A Study Guide for *The Rule of St. Benedict*

1. Those who choose to live in a monastery agree to submit to the will of the abbot. How can those of us who have not taken orders practice this sort of submission?

2. Why is it so important for our obedience to be cheerful and not grudging or halfhearted in order to be "acceptable to God and agreeable to men"?[11]

3. The sixth step of humility is to regard oneself as a poor and worthless worker, insignificant and ignorant, but the seventh step is to admit not only with our tongues but also

to be convinced in our hearts that we are inferior to all. When have you professed something with your tongue that you did not believe in your heart? How can we cultivate in ourselves a true sense of our own inferiority, and why should we want to?

4. What has been your experience, if any, with the rhythm of the divine office? Why is it important for the offices to be laid out here in such great detail, from the start time to the psalms read?

5. A brother can potentially be excommunicated for being stubborn, disobedient, proud, grumbling, despising the holy rule, or defying the orders of his superiors. Why would these particular characteristics lead to such a harsh punishment? Other punishments include not being allowed to share the common table or participate in the oratory or even associate or converse with the other brothers. What do these punishments indicate about life in the monastery?

6. Why are humility and obedience so prized and pride to be so carefully guarded against in the monastery? Are these the key virtues and most dangerous sin in the noncloistered life? Why or why not?

7. The *Rule* refers to private ownership as "this most evil practice."[12] What problems might arise from private ownership? What has your experience been with communal ownership? What has it taught you?

8. One of the reasons for the very detailed schedule of the monks' day is to protect against idleness. Why is idleness so feared? What has been the effect of idleness in your life?

The Divine Comedy

DANTE ALIGHIERI

> When I had journeyed half of our life's way, / I found myself within a shadowed forest, / for I had lost the path that does not stray.

In this Italian poetic masterpiece, Dante's journey through hell, purgatory, and, finally, heaven mimics the soul's journey toward God.

DANTE ALIGHIERI was born in Florence, Italy, in 1265. He served Florence in public office as a magistrate and as an envoy to the pope, but when a rival political faction seized power, he was exiled from his beloved city, sentenced to death should he return. He wrote several books in the years of his exile, but *The Divine Comedy* is considered his masterpiece. In this three-part work, Dante describes a journey in which he visits hell, purgatory, and heaven, with the poet Virgil and Beatrice, a Florentine woman for whom Dante had a courtly love, as his guides. Dante wrote the three parts over a period of about ten years, hoping that *The Divine Comedy* would be the conduit of his return to Florence, even expressing this desire within the text, but he died in 1321 without the exile having been lifted.

The Inferno begins with Dante the pilgrim as a young man of thirty-five who finds himself in a dark forest, having lost his way. He tries to climb a barren slope to reach a mountaintop bathed in sunlight, but wild animals block his path. Eventually he comes across Virgil, the famous Roman poet who lived in the first century BC, who offers to guide him out through hell and purgatory. Then if Dante still wants to climb to the blessed mountaintop, another, more worthy guide will have to lead him, since Virgil, who lived before the time of Christ, is not allowed to enter heaven. Dante expresses his own unworthiness for such a journey, and Virgil tells him that Beatrice in heaven has called Virgil to rescue Dante, at the behest of no less than the Virgin Mary.

The two continue their journey into hell itself, finding outside its gates those who had never done good or evil acts, doomed to forever exist outside of heaven or hell. Next they find in Limbo those who lived before the time of Christ, including righteous pagans such as Cicero and Homer. They proceed through the various outer circles of hell, encountering those guilty of lust, gluttony, greed, wrath, and sloth; they see that all are punished in relation to their sins, the lustful tossed about by a strong wind just as their passions ruled them in life; the gluttonous torn at by a hungry dog while enduring excessive discomfort from rain, hail, and snow; the wrathful ripping each other to shreds.

As they proceed, Dante recognizes some of the shades (those condemned to hell look less substantial than those who are alive but have enough of a body to suffer) as historical figures. Many are from Greek mythology, and others are various figures in the Church, many of whom are being punished for their greed. Other shades approach Dante and tell him their stories or ask him questions about the world. The story of two lovers condemned to the circle of lust causes Dante to faint, but he seems to relish the punishment of some of the souls he knew on earth. It is clear, however, that Dante relates to and even sees himself in the place of many of the sinners. He exclaims, "Justice of God! Who has amassed as many / strange tortures and travails as I have seen? / Why do we let our guilt consume us so?"[1]

Aided by an angel, Dante and Virgil enter the City of Dis where they encounter the heretics and then those whose sins were characterized by malice, as opposed to the sins of the outer circles, which were sins of incontinence and thus are, explains Virgil, less offensive to God. The punishments continue to be fitted to each sin, as Dante sees usurers crouching in the flames with their purses around their necks; panderers, pimps, and seducers walking naked while being lashed by the whips of devils; and flatterers smeared with excrement. Sorcerers who claimed to see the future now have their heads turned backward on their bodies, and those who have sown scandal and schism are themselves ripped in half. Finally, the pair reaches the ninth and final circle, where they find the traitors, frozen in ice; the three worst—Judas, Brutus, and Cassius—forever gnawed upon by the three heads of the gigantic Lucifer. Then Dante and his guide climb down and out on Lucifer's very body.

In the second part of *The Divine Comedy, Purgatorio,* Dante follows Virgil into the island mountain of purgatory, where souls are purified in order to enter heaven. Virgil tells Cato, the sentry, that they have been sent at the behest of a lady from heaven, in order to save Dante's soul before he dies. The two are allowed to proceed into the lovely, calm, and cool land (a sharp contrast to hell) with the caution that Dante's face must be cleansed of the filth of hell. Dante is given a tattoo of seven *P*s on his forehead and proceeds to view seven stages of purification, as each soul is rebalanced and freed from its earthly disorder. In the first stage, for example, those who were proud are literally weighed down to the ground until that pride can be transformed to humility. Dante urges the reader to understand that these punishments are not the goal or end but the process, and not to cease to repent because of them. Dante views these souls as purifying themselves in order to meet God, as he expresses to someone who is being purged of wrath: "O creature who—that you return / fair unto Him who made you—cleanse yourself."[2] Dante experiences a measure of this purification as well, feeling his own pride reduced after talking to one of the shades. As Dante and Virgil pass through each level, an angel wipes away a *P* from Dante's forehead, leaving him feeling lighter and better able to ascend. The mountain of purgatory is most difficult to climb at the beginning but gets easier and finally effortless at the top. Virgil explains that each of the sins in purgatory is a perversion of love, love that has been directed at the wrong thing (leading to pride, envy, or wrath) or even pursued as a good thing but in excess (avarice, gluttony, lust) or without enough energy (sloth).

The penance undergone in purgatory restores this love to its proper focus—God. For example, those who suffered from worldly envy have their eyes sewn shut, presumably to aid them in focusing on God and not on what is around them to covet. Through processes

The Divine Comedy is precisely the drama of the soul's choice. It is not a fairy-story, but a great Christian allegory, deriving its power from the terror and splendour of the Christian revelation.

—Dorothy L. Sayers

like these, purgatory transforms pride into humility, envy into generosity, wrath into peace, greed into a proper estimation of worldly goods, gluttony into temperance, and lust into chastity. Its inhabitants willingly submit to the process. As Dante's friend Forese, who is in the terrace of gluttony, speaks of the "pain" he feels upon constantly smelling the fruit that he cannot taste, he quickly corrects himself: "I speak of pain but I should speak of solace, / for we are guided to those trees by that // same longing that had guided Christ when He / had come to free us through the blood He shed / and, in His joyousness, called out: 'Eli.' "[3] After proceeding through all the terraces, Dante finds himself in the Garden of Eden, where humankind would still be if we had never sinned. There Virgil turns him over to Beatrice, a woman Dante loved and idealized from afar on earth, who is now capable of guiding him through heaven.

Once purified from his ascension through purgatory, Dante, in *Paradiso,* is allowed to visit Paradise, or heaven, which is celestially located among the moon, stars, and planets. Heaven is so far above his comprehension that he cannot even be sure he is really there. It is characterized by light, the light of God. Those souls Dante meets in heaven appear to him as mere reflections, since, as a living human, he is not able to see heaven as it really is. Each soul takes in the Divine light as much as he or she is able, so each is perfectly happy. As King Solomon explains to Dante, "[Our love's] brightness takes its measure from our ardor, / our ardor from our vision, which is measured / by what grace each receives beyond his merit."[4] In other words, all has begun from grace. Even those who reside in the lower parts of heaven express perfect happiness and contentment since to express otherwise would make them not in accord with God's will. Emperor Justinian tells him, "Thus does the Living Justice make so sweet / the sentiments in us, that we are free / of any turning toward iniquity. // Differing voices join to sound sweet music; / so do the different orders in our life / render sweet harmony among these spheres."[5]

As Beatrice, his guide, takes Dante through the nine lower heavens, she explains God's truths to him, growing ever more beautiful in the process. In Canto VII, for example, she explains that humankind, once separated from God by sin, could never be reconciled by any human effort. So when God took on humankind's sins through the lofty and magnificent gesture of Jesus' death and resurrection, then God's deed "shows / the goodness of the heart from which it springs," giving so much more than if God had simply annulled the debt.[6] As Dante journeys through heaven, he becomes more and more attuned to God's divine light, even forgetting about Beatrice in the realm of the sun, to her approval. Imagery abounds, particularly that of light and circles. First in Beatrice's eyes and then in all of Paradise he finds the divine love, which frees his heart of any other longing. Dante catches a glimpse of Jesus ascending in triumph in the upper reaches of heaven, and he also sees Mary. Until this point Dante has been the one asking questions, but in heaven he is questioned by Peter, James, and John about faith, hope, and charity. Eventually Dante reaches the apex of heaven, and there *his* eyes are able to reflect and receive God's light. He sees the elect gathered there, and Beatrice is now with them. The elect are divided into those who lived before Christ but put their hope in him to come, and those who lived after Christ. An old man is now his guide, and he urges Dante to fix his gaze instead upward on the Virgin Mary, on whom he must now depend. Then, finally, the man, who we find is Bernard, instructs Dante to look upon God, but Dante has already done so. Lacking words to express exactly what he saw, he describes a Great Light shining in three circles, characterized by surpassing goodness. And in God, his will and his desire are perfected like a balanced wheel.

Why *The Divine Comedy* Is Essential

The Divine Comedy has long been heralded as a masterpiece of literature, theology, and poetry. Dante's journey down through the depths of hell and then up through purgatory to the celestial heights of heaven is as beautiful and evocative as it is essential for our spiritual formation. The sheer scope of Dante's work is dazzling. It would be difficult to think of a theological question that is not dealt with in the pages of *The Divine Comedy*. Indeed, Chris Webb, editorial board member and Renovaré president, describes *The Divine Comedy* as "one of the most insightful and comprehensive books on spiritual formation I've ever read." Yet despite the breadth of Dante's theology, which is heavily influenced by Thomas Aquinas, Dante presents his ideas in a gentle, accessible way with example after example, illustration after illustration. And in case his evocative imagery doesn't adequately convey his point, we are given extensive question-and-answer sessions with Dante and Virgil, Dante and Beatrice, and even Dante and the shades and souls he meets on every level. Dante the pilgrim asks all the questions that we ourselves might long to ask, even those that could be criticized as stupid or obvious. Dante very purposely paints himself as Everyperson so that we can share in his journey. Like Dante, we are lost in the woods of our own sin. Just as he travels to the depths of hell and then to the heights of heaven, so, too, can we understand the nature of sin by visiting hell and recognizing our own sins there, open ourselves to the reordering of our desires and purifying of our wills by God's grace illustrated so powerfully on the mount of purgatory, and understand the truths about God that he learns in heaven. Like us, Dante is no casual observer but both participates in the sins for which he witnesses punishment in hell and is purified as he watches others go through this process in purgatory. For example, in Canto XI of *Purgatorio* as he watches those who are repenting from pride do penance by being bowed to the ground, Dante, too, stands with his head low and body bent, and as he leaves that terrace, he also feels a lifting of his own pride.

Dante's journey is, of course, not just about the afterlife; it is about this life—the choices and temptations we face and the repercussions our actions will have. Those in the *Inferno* suffer terribly because they have sinned so grievously. Their suffering is without end. But as we learn in *Purgatorio,* a great repository of spiritual-formation instruction, we do not need to go through what they do. Those in purgatory suffer, too, but they suffer with purpose; they wouldn't have it any other way. Dante's purgatory is a great reordering of our appetites. Avarice is turned to generosity, gluttony to temperance, pride to humility, and so forth; with each reordering and resulting purification, we feel a tremendous lightening of our burdens. Purgatory can be viewed as a land of spiritual disciplines. Those who sinned by being gluttonous repent by fasting; those who sinned by being slothful must rouse themselves to activity. Although many readers may not align themselves with Dante's belief in purgatory after death, we can all relate to the way it illustrates grace purifying the soul in this life. Dante invites us to think about how we can cooperate with God, right now in this life, to reorder that which has become corrupted, out of control, disordered. Because the aim of purgatory is a rebalancing of our desires, we see that sins on the opposite ends of the spectrum are punished together—Statius who spent his money too foolishly lies prostrate with his head in the dust along with those who erred on the side of greed. Both have erred in their valuing of earthly resources and must find balance.

As Dante teaches us, that balance can only be found by focusing on God. When Virgil speaks to Dante about envy, for example, he explains how the things of this world are not worth longing for because they are diminished by each person who shares in them, but in heaven the more love there is, the more goodness and love abound for every soul, reflected by each soul as though by a mirror. Our sins come when our love is corrupted by focusing it on something other than God or by focusing it with too little or too much zeal. Seeking God first, loving God first and above all other things, is the solution. Just as Dante finds his wills and desires in perfect balance in heaven, so, too, can we seek that same balance by focusing our love on God first and letting that focus reorder all the rest of our lives.

How to Read *The Divine Comedy*

While *Inferno* has taken up permanent residence on many class reading lists, *Purgatorio* and *Paradiso* are less frequently read, despite the fact that these two titles contain most of the spiritual-formation application in *The Divine Comedy*. As Dorothy L. Sayers wrote, stopping with *Inferno* is like judging "a great city after a few days spent underground among the cellars and sewers." *The Divine Comedy* is an epic poem, a story. It is meant to be read straight through to its happy ending (the origin of the poem's name), although do not expect to do so in one sitting!

The sheer number of names and historical references can be wearying to a modern reader for whom many of the references are unfamiliar. Dante's contemporaries would have been familiar with the names of those he assigned to various places in the afterlife; for them, reading *The Divine Comedy* must have been somewhat akin to reading a political tell-all. Most versions of *The Divine Comedy* have extensive footnotes that explain each person and his or her role, but when reading *The Divine Comedy* for spiritual formation, we need not be so concerned about understanding each person's role in history and in the historical Dante's life. More important for us is simply understanding how each person represents a lesson about a certain disordering or mistake of free will.

EXCERPTS FROM

The Divine Comedy

INFERNO, CANTO I

When I had journeyed half of our life's way,
I found myself within a shadowed forest,
for I had lost the path that does not stray.

Ah, it is hard to speak of what it was,
that savage forest, dense and difficult,
which even in recall renews my fear:

so bitter—death is hardly more severe!
But to retell the good discovered there,
I'll also tell the other things I saw.

I cannot clearly say how I had entered
the wood; I was so full of sleep just at
the point where I abandoned the true path.

But when I'd reached the bottom of a hill—
it rose along the boundary of the valley
that had harassed my heart with so much fear—

I looked on high and saw its shoulders clothed
already by the rays of that same planet
which serves to lead men straight along all roads.

At this my fear was somewhat quieted;
for through the night of sorrow I had spent,
the lake within my heart felt terror present.

And just as he who, with exhausted breath,
having escaped from sea to shore, turns back
to watch the dangerous waters he has quit,

so did my spirit, still a fugitive,
turn back to look intently at the pass
that never has let any man survive.

I let my tired body rest awhile.
Moving again, I tried the lonely slope—
my firm foot always was the one below.

And almost where the hillside starts to rise—
look there!—a leopard, very quick and lithe,
a leopard covered with a spotted hide.

He did not disappear from sight, but stayed;
indeed, he so impeded my ascent
that I had often to turn back again.

The time was the beginning of the morning;
the sun was rising now in fellowship
with the same stars that had escorted it

when Divine Love first moved those things of beauty;
so that the hour and the gentle season
gave me good cause for hopefulness on seeing

that beast before me with his speckled skin;
but hope was hardly able to prevent
the fear I felt when I beheld a lion.

His head held high and ravenous with hunger—
even the air around him seemed to shudder—
this lion seemed to make his way against me.

And then a she-wolf showed herself; she seemed
to carry every craving in her leanness;
she had already brought despair to many.

The very sight of her so weighted me
with fearfulness that I abandoned hope
of ever climbing up that mountain slope.

Even as he who glories while he gains
will, when the time has come to tally loss,
lament with every thought and turn despondent,

so was I when I faced that restless beast
which, even as she stalked me, step by step
had thrust me back to where the sun is speechless.

While I retreated down to lower ground,
before my eyes there suddenly appeared
one who seemed faint because of the long silence.

When I saw him in that vast wilderness,
"Have pity on me," were the words I cried
"whatever you may be a shade, a man."

He answered me: "Not man; I once was man.
Both of my parents came from Lombardy,
and both claimed Mantua as native city.

And I was born, though late, sub Julio, and
lived in Rome under the good Augustus the
season of the false and lying gods.

I was a poet, and I sang the righteous
son of Anchises who had come from
Troy when flames destroyed the pride of Ilium.

But why do you return to wretchedness?
Why not climb up the mountain of delight,
the origin and cause of every joy?"

My Personal Top 5

FREDERICA MATHEWES-GREEN

1 *Philokalia*

2 *The Way of a Pilgrim*

3 *The Sayings of the Desert Fathers*

4 *On the Incarnation*, St. Athanasius

5 *The Ladder of Divine Ascent*, St. John Climacos

FREDERICA MATHEWES-GREEN is the author of many books about ancient Eastern Christianity, including *Facing East* and *The Illumined Heart*.

"And are you then that Virgil, you the fountain
that freely pours so rich a stream of speech?" I
answered him with shame upon my brow.

"O light and honor of all other poets, may my
long study and the intense love that made me
search your volume serve me now.

You are my master and my author, you—
the only one from whom my writing drew the
noble style for which I have been honored.

You see the beast that made me turn aside;
help me, o famous sage, to stand against her, for
she has made my blood and pulses shudder."

"It is another path that you must take,"
he answered when he saw my tearfulness,
"if you would leave this savage wilderness;

the beast that is the cause of your outcry
allows no man to pass along her track, but
blocks him even to the point of death;

her nature is so squalid, so malicious
that she can never sate her greedy will;
when she has fed, she's hungrier than ever.

She mates with many living souls and shall
yet mate with many more, until the Greyhound
arrives, inflicting painful death on her.

That Hound will never feed on land or pewter,
but find his fare in wisdom, love, and virtue; his
place of birth shall be between two felts.

He will restore low-lying Italy for which
the maid Camilla died of wounds, and
Nisus, Turnus, and Euryalus.

And he will hunt that beast through every city
until he thrusts her back again to Hell from
which she was first sent above by envy.

Therefore, I think and judge it best for you
to follow me, and I shall guide you, taking
you from this place through an eternal place,

where you shall hear the howls of desperation
and see the ancient spirits in their pain, as each
of them laments his second death;

and you shall see those souls who are content
within the fire, for they hope to reach—
whenever that may be—the blessed people.

If you would then ascend as high as these,
a soul more worthy than I am will guide
you; I'll leave you in her care when I depart,

because that Emperor who reigns above,
since I have been rebellious to His law,
will not allow me entry to His city.

He governs everywhere, but rules from there;
there is His city, His high capital: o happy
those He chooses to be there!"

And I replied: "O poet by that God whom
you had never come to know I beg you, that I
may flee this evil and worse evils,

to lead me to the place of which you spoke,
that I may see the gateway of Saint Peter and
those whom you describe as sorrowful."

Then he set out, and I moved on behind him.

When the first heaven's Seven-Stars had halted
(those stars that never rise or set, that are
not veiled except when sin beclouds our vision;

those stars that, there, made everyone aware
of what his duty was, just as the Bear
below brings helmsmen home to harbor), then

the truthful band that had come first between
the griffin and the Seven-Stars turned toward
that chariot as toward their peace, and one

of them, as if sent down from Heaven, hymned
aloud, "Veni, sponsa, de Libano,"
three times, and all the others echoed him.

Just as the blessed, at the Final Summons,
will rise up—ready—each out of his grave,
singing, with new-clothed voices, Alleluia,

so, from the godly chariot, eternal
life's messengers and ministers arose:
one hundred stood ad vocem tanti senis.

All of them cried: "Benedictus qui venis,"
and, scattering flowers upward and around,
"Manibus, oh, date lilia plenis."

I have at times seen all the eastern sky
becoming rose as day began and seen,
adorned in lovely blue, the rest of heaven;

and seen the sun's face rise so veiled that it
was tempered by the mist and could permit
the eye to look at length upon it; so,

within a cloud of flowers that were cast
by the angelic hands and then rose up
and then fell back, outside and in the chariot,

a woman showed herself to me; above
a white veil, she was crowned with olive boughs;
her cape was green; her dress beneath, flame-red.

Within her presence, I had once been used
to feeling—trembling—wonder, dissolution;
but that was long ago. Still, though my soul,

now she was veiled, could not see her directly,
by way of hidden force that she could move,
I felt the mighty power of old love.

As soon as that deep force had struck my vision
(the power that, when I had not yet left
my boyhood, had already transfixed me),

I turned around and to my left—just as
a little child, afraid or in distress,
will hurry to his mother—anxiously,

to say to Virgil: "I am left with less
than one drop of my blood that does not tremble:
I recognize the signs of the old flame."

But Virgil had deprived us of himself,
Virgil, the gentlest father, Virgil, he
to whom I gave my self for my salvation;

and even all our ancient mother lost
was not enough to keep my cheeks, though washed
with dew, from darkening again with tears.

"Dante, though Virgil's leaving you, do not
yet weep, do not weep yet; you'll need your tears
for what another sword must yet inflict."

Just like an admiral who goes to stern
and prow to see the officers who guide
the other ships, encouraging their tasks;

so, on the left side of the chariot
(I'd turned around when I had heard my name—
which, of necessity, I transcribe here),

I saw the lady who had first appeared
to me beneath the veils of the angelic
flowers look at me across the stream.

Although the veil she wore—down from her head,
which was encircled by Minerva's leaves—
did not allow her to be seen distinctly,

her stance still regal and disdainful, she
continued, just as one who speaks but keeps
until the end the fiercest parts of speech:

"Look here! For I am Beatrice, I am!
How were you able to ascend the mountain?
Did you not know that man is happy here?"

My lowered eyes caught sight of the clear stream,
but when I saw myself reflected there,
such shame weighed on my brow, my eyes drew back

and toward the grass; just as a mother seems
harsh to her child, so did she seem to me—
how bitter is the savor of stern pity!

Her words were done. The angels—suddenly—
sang, "In te, Domine, speravi"; but
their singing did not go past "pedes meos."

Even as snow among the sap-filled trees
along the spine of Italy will freeze
when gripped by gusts of the Slavonian winds,

then, as it melts, will trickle through itself
—that is, if winds breathe north from shade-less lands—
just as, beneath the flame, the candle melts;

so I, before I'd heard the song of those
whose notes always accompany the notes
of the eternal spheres, was without tears

and sighs; but when I heard the sympathy
for me within their gentle harmonies,
as if they'd said: "Lady, why shame him so?"—

then did the ice that had restrained my heart
become water and breath; and from my breast
and through my lips and eyes they issued—anguished.

Still standing motionless upon the left
side of the chariot, she then addressed
the angels who had been compassionate:

"You are awake in never-ending day,
and neither night nor sleep can steal from you
one step the world would take along its way;

therefore, I'm more concerned that my reply
be understood by him who weeps beyond,
so that his sorrow's measure match his sin.

Not only through the work of the great spheres—
which guide each seed to a determined end,
depending on what stars are its companions—

but through the bounty of the godly graces,
which shower down from clouds so high that we
cannot approach them with our vision, he,

when young, was such—potentially—that any
propensity innate in him would have
prodigiously succeeded, had he acted.

But where the soil has finer vigor, there
precisely—when untilled or badly seeded—
will that terrain grow wilder and more noxious.

My countenance sustained him for a while;
showing my youthful eyes to him, I led
him with me toward the way of righteousness.

As soon as I, upon the threshold of
my second age, had changed my life, he took
himself away from me and followed after

another; when, from flesh to spirit, I
had risen, and my goodness and my beauty
had grown, I was less dear to him, less welcome:

he turned his footsteps toward an untrue path;
he followed counterfeits of goodness, which
will never pay in full what they have promised.

Nor did the inspirations I received—
with which, in dream and otherwise, I called
him back—help me; he paid so little heed!

He fell so far there were no other means
to lead him to salvation, except this:
to let him see the people who were lost.

For this I visited the gateway of
the dead; to him who guided him above
my prayers were offered even as I wept.

The deep design of God would have been broken
if Lethe had been crossed and he had drunk
such waters but had not discharged the debt

of penitence that's paid when tears are shed."[7]

A Study Guide for *The Divine Comedy*

1. Hell is divided into two main parts, according to Aristotle's scheme. The sins of incontinence incur a lesser punishment than the sins of the will because the latter are caused by a desire to do evil rather than just weakness. Do you agree with this categorization? Why or why not? Which sins do you fall most prey to—those of incontinence or those of the will?

2. If you were condemned to hell, what circle of hell would Minos send you to? Which punishment would be most difficult for you to bear? What do you think Dante most wished to convey with his depiction of those in hell?

3. Ciacco, whom Dante meets in the third circle of hell with the other gluttons, and many of the other shades ask Dante to remember them to the world. And at one point, Virgil urges Dante to rise and keep moving for he will never gain fame if he rests too long. Then in the ninth circle, one of the shades refuses to give Dante his name, saying that fame is the last thing he wants in that place. Finally, in heaven, Cacciaguida tells Dante that the reason Dante has met such famous men in heaven is so that those on earth would trust his words. What do you think is Dante's overall message about fame?

4. What are the major differences between those souls in hell, purgatory, and heaven? How are the differences demonstrated in how they respond to Dante, the requests they make of him? How do Dante's reactions to the shades change as he proceeds through hell and then purgatory?

5. The mountain of purgatory is most difficult to climb at the beginning but gets easier and finally effortless at the top. How does this correspond to your experience of repentance?

6. In purgatory Statius tells Dante and Virgil that souls who erred at the opposite ends of a spectrum of sin are punished together, so he who sinned by his profligacy suffered with those who were guilty of avarice, greed. What does this teach us about the goal of purgatory? What are some ways we can experience the corrections of purgatory here on earth?

7. Throughout *The Divine Comedy* we see many condemnations of the society and Church of Dante's day. Which of these are still applicable today? If Dante were writing today, what might he condemn?

8. Only in the far reaches of heaven can Dante actually see the features of the souls to which he speaks. As he proceeds, all he can see of the souls is light. Why do you think Dante chose light as a symbol of God and love? Who have you known who radiated God's love more so than their own features?

9. In paradise, Thomas Aquinas warns Dante about rash opinions, both because they might lead one to heresy and because they might cause one to second-guess God. Similarly, as he and Dante enter purgatory, Virgil says, "Foolish is he who hopes our intellect / can reach the end of that unending road / only one Substance in three Persons follows."[8] Among all this theology, Dante seems to be reminding us that some things must remain mystery. How does this perspective affect your reading of *The Divine Comedy*? How can we avoid rushing to judgment?

10. Looking down on the earth from heaven, Dante sees it as "the little threshing floor / that so incites our savagery."[9] How might viewing earth this way reorder your own desires and priorities?

The Cloud of Unknowing

ANONYMOUS

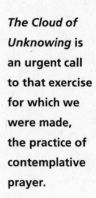

> ⟶ *Beat on that thick cloud of unknowing with the sharp arrow of longing and never stop loving, no matter what comes your way.*

The Cloud of Unknowing is an urgent call to that exercise for which we were made, the practice of contemplative prayer.

THE CLOUD WAS WRITTEN by an English monk in the fourteenth century—the time of the plague, the Hundred Years' War between England and France, and the Peasants' Revolt. The chaos of this era sparked some of the all-time best-known devotional classics, including *The Imitation of Christ* and *Revelations of Divine Love* as well as *The Cloud of Unknowing.* Like Julian of Norwich in her *Revelations of Divine Love,* the author of *The Cloud* chose to write in Middle English rather than the more customary Latin, presumably to make his book more accessible. The author also chose to remain anonymous, despite the immediate popularity of his book. He writes in the form of a dialogue, his words directed to a young person of twenty-four, perhaps a monastery novice, or simply a student of the author's.

The author's aim is to recommend and teach the exercise that is "worth more than all other exercises," namely lifting up our hearts to God and having God alone as our aim. "You were made for contemplation, and everything in the universe conspires to help you with it," he writes.[1] He describes this contemplation as "a sudden impulse coming out of nowhere and flying up to God like a spark from a burning coal."[2] Yet at this point we will also find between us and God the cloud from which the book's title is taken. He writes, "The first time you practice contemplation, you'll only experience a darkness, like a cloud of unknowing. You won't know what this is. You'll only know that in your will you feel a simple reaching out to God. You must also know that this darkness and this cloud will always be between you and your God, whatever you do. They will always keep you from seeing him clearly by the light of understanding in your intellect and will block you from feeling him fully in the sweetness of love in your emotions. So, be sure you make your home in this darkness. Stay there as long as you can, crying out to him over and over again, because you love him. It's the closest you can get to God here on earth, by waiting in this darkness and in this cloud."[3] This cloud in which we are to make our home is not a literal one or one we might draw with our imaginations. Such thinking is unhelpful. Indeed, we cannot approach God with our intellect or with our imagination. We can reach God only through love, with our hearts.

To aid ourselves in our practice, we must put everything else, all of creation, under "a cloud of forgetting." Nor should we think of God's qualities or of our love for God. All we need is "a naked intent for God."[4] To help us, we can gather this focus into one word, one syllable, such as *God* or *love,* which we can fasten on our hearts and use as a sword or a spear with which we beat upon the cloud of unknowing. For our task is to rid ourselves of all extraneous thoughts, even those that seem holy and helpful, so that we can come out of ourselves and approach God. We cannot love and praise God fully while we are about the business of life. God asks of us complete dedication. In this exercise that we practice, of seeking to beat upon the cloud of unknowing between us and God, the author advises no moderation. Far from it, we are to indulge ourselves in contemplation. Excess in contemplation leads to balance in the rest of our lives. He writes, "I hope you'll never stop doing this loving work as long as you live."[5]

In this single-minded pursuit of God, he advises simplicity (short prayers—the shorter the better) and also a kind of ruthlessness and reductionism. "Loathe everything not God that crosses your mind or influences your will. Grow weary of it, because—whatever it is—it stands between you and God. Little wonder that you hate thinking about yourself, because you have a constant sense of your own sinfulness—that revolting, stinking, incomprehensible lump between you and God. And you know that lump is none other than you, inseparable from who you are, glued to your very essence."[6] Contemplative prayer reduces things down to just two—we, lumps of sin, and God. Eventually we hope to lose even this feeling of our naked selves so that we can focus on God alone.

And finally, despite his enthusiastic advocacy, the author assures us that it is okay if we find ourselves ill-suited to this type of praying; we can try another if it does not work well for us. He offers us a test we can use to see if we are called to this exercise: "Let them see if the desire for contemplation presses on their minds at all times, attracting their attention more than any other spiritual discipline. Also, if their conscience can find no peace in any physical or spiritual good they do, unless they make this secret little love-longing the primary spiritual reason for everything they do, then it's proof that they are called by God to do this work. Otherwise, the answer is no."[7]

Why *The Cloud of Unknowing* Is Essential

The Cloud of Unknowing is an essential work of the contemplative tradition. During the fourteenth century it was passed from monastery to monastery. Over the centuries it has also become a valued devotional text for laypeople for its thoughtful lessons on how to pray. It is easy to see why. It would be hard to find a more practical or thorough guide to contemplative prayer. *The Cloud of Unknowing* boils contemplative prayer down to its essential parts. As Chris Webb, president of Renovaré and editorial board member, explains, "*The Cloud* would teach you how to pray. It goes past liturgy or quiet times or techniques. It takes away all that stuff, and it says, 'I want to teach you how to sit with God. Even though God is hidden away, that's okay. Let me teach you how to just be with God.' And that's the heart of prayer. Then everything else can follow on."

The Cloud presents, in its purest form, the case for pursuing God alone. And it does so in a way unrivalled anywhere in the panoply of Christian literature. Some books can be eaten whole. Like fast food they fill a gap in a busy day focussed on other things. Not so *The Cloud of Unknowing*. It is to be savoured with a small spoon, one tiny piece at a time.

—James Catford

First, the author ably demonstrates for us the urgency and importance of pursuing the practice of contemplative prayer, explaining that this would be the central focus of our lives had we not been sidetracked by the Fall. He cautions us about the precious quality of time and the accounting of it we will one day owe to God, while at the same time assuring us that if we but just begin with the practice of contemplative prayer, our ability and desire to continue it will be provided. This focus on the contemplative rather than the active life is another reason this book is essential reading. Today we often tend to value the active parts of life over the contemplative, perhaps because the active life is more public and yields tangible results. *The Cloud* can help us reclaim a countercultural focus on our interior lives, accompanied by the further countercultural disciplines of solitude and silence.

Few books have captured the experience of contemplative prayer so evocatively as *The Cloud,* from the beautiful image of prayer as sparks flying up to God to the title phrase "the cloud of unknowing." Yet the author takes pains to point out that we must not get caught up in these images or think that there is literally a cloud between us and God. As humans, we often rely on our imaginations and seek to understand things by comparing them to other things we have experienced. Many of us, even if only at a subconscious level, cling to a physical image of God, and any such image falsely limits God. Thus this insistence on the essentially spiritual nature of contemplative prayer is an important corrective to us, for no matter how good and helpful an image we may have of God, we always need to remember that God is beyond the physical. Our bodies do not physically go up to God; nor do we see God with our eyes. We must forget time, place, and body in our spiritual exercises. As our teacher instructs, "I . . . don't want you outside, above, behind, or on one side or the other of yourself. / 'Where then,' you ask, 'will I be? If I take your advice, I'll end up "nowhere"!' You're right. Well said. That's exactly where I want you, because nowhere physically is everywhere spiritually."[8]

In the end, we cannot reach God with our minds or our imaginations. Only the heart is equal to the task of meeting God in all

God's mystery. While we are on this earth, we can never know God fully, and the author is entirely comfortable with such mystery. When he anticipates that his student will ask, "How do I think on God as God, and who is God?" he responds, "I can only answer, 'I don't know.'"[9] If we allow him, the author will teach us that such mystery is nothing to fear; instead we can join him, seek the cloud of unknowing, and "make our home in this darkness."

How to Read *The Cloud of Unknowing*

The Cloud of Unknowing is a relatively short book comprised of seventy-five brief chapters. From the very outset, the author offers us instruction for reading. We are to look at the book as a whole, straight through, and not just at one part, for, as the writer warns, looking at one part and not another may lead us into error. And the author also advises multiple readings: "Read it through two or three times, the more the better. Each time it will make more sense. Some section that was too hard for you to understand on a first or second reading will eventually seem easy."[10] Once we have read through the book in its entirety, we can go back to some of the chapters that particularly spoke to us and read them again, using the ancient Benedictine technique of *lectio divina,* or "holy reading." To practice *lectio divina* is simply to read slowly and thoughtfully, savoring each word, giving plenty of time and space for God to speak to us through them. *The Cloud*'s short chapters offer a perfect opportunity to practice this style of reading.

One final note: the author mentions several times that he has written this book only for those who have resolved to be perfect followers of Christ and have been working at this goal in both the active and the contemplative life. The author also makes clear his strong preference for those who have chosen a contemplative life. Those who of necessity have active lives but find themselves drawn to the contemplative life, the life of the interior, are granted permission to read the book, but only somewhat grudgingly, it may seem. The author only wishes to say that he has written the book for someone who has a serious interest in contemplative prayer. He has no interest in teaching the casual or curious reader but only the earnest Christian who truly wants to know God. We honor his intention by reading the book with this purpose.

EXCERPTS FROM

The Cloud of Unknowing

3. HOW TO DO THE WORK OF CONTEMPLATION, AND WHY IT IS THE BEST WORK

Lift up your heart to God with a gentle stirring of love. Focus on him alone. Want him, and not anything he's made. Think on nothing but him. Don't let anything else run through your mind and will. Here's how. Forget what you know. Forget everything God made and everybody who exists and everything that's going on in the world, until your thoughts and emotions aren't focused on or reaching toward anything, not in a general way and not in any particular way. Let them be. For the moment, don't care about anything.

This is the work of the soul that most pleases God. All saints and angels rejoice in it, and they're always willing to help you when you're spending time in contemplation. They rush to your side, their powers ready. But contemplation infuriates the devil and his company. That's why they try to stop you in any way they can. Everyone on earth has been helped by contemplation in wonderful ways. You can't know how much. This spiritual exercise even lessens the pain for souls in purgatory. And no other discipline can purify your soul as deeply or make you as virtuous. But it's the easiest work of all, when a soul is helped by grace to feel a pure desire—contemplation follows. Otherwise, it's hard, nearly impossible to do.

So stop hesitating. Do this work until you feel the delight in it. In the trying is the desire. The first time you practice contemplation, you'll only experience a darkness, like a cloud of unknowing. You won't know what this is. You'll only know that in your will you feel a simple reaching out to God. You must also know that this darkness and this cloud will always be between you and your God, whatever you do. They will always keep you from seeing him clearly by the light of understanding in your intellect and will block you from feeling him fully in the sweetness of love in your emotions. So, be sure you make your home in this darkness. Stay there as long as you can, crying out to him over and over again, because you love him. It's the closest you can get to God here on earth, by waiting in this darkness and in this cloud. Work at this diligently, as I've asked you to, and I know God's mercy will lead you there.

4. CONTEMPLATION'S BREVITY, AND WHY KNOWLEDGE AND IMAGINATION CAN'T ACQUIRE IT

So you won't go down the wrong path in this work, thinking contemplation is something it's not, I'll tell you more about it. Some people believe contemplation is time-consuming, but it's not. In fact, it takes less time than anything else you'll ever do. It's as brief as an atom, which excellent philosophers in the science of astronomy define as the smallest particle of time. An atom's littleness makes it indivisible, nearly inconceivable, and also invaluable. On this subject, it has been written, "Every moment of time is a gift to you, and one day you'll be asked how you spent each one." And you should be held responsible for it, because this briefest moment of time is exactly how long it takes your will, that strong architect of your soul, to desire something and to act on that desire. In an hour, you experience the same number of aspirations and cravings as there are atoms in that space of time, and if you were restored by grace to the original purity of your soul, you'd be the master of every impulse. You'd never feel out of control, because your every desire would be directed toward the most desirable and highest good, who is God.

He measures us and makes his divinity fit our souls, and our souls are able to take the measure of him because he created us in his image and made us worthy. He alone is complete and can fulfill our every longing. God's grace restores our souls and teaches us how to comprehend him through love. He is incomprehensible to the intellect. Even angels know him by loving him. Nobody's mind is powerful enough to grasp who God is. We can only know him by experiencing his love.

Look. Every rational creature, every person, and every angel has two main strengths: the power to know and the power to love. God made both of these, but he's not knowable through the first one. To the power of love, however, he is entirely known, because a loving soul is open to receive God's abundance. Each person loves uniquely, and God's limitlessness can fill all angels and all souls that will ever exist. His very nature makes love endless and miraculous. God will never stop loving us. Consider this truth, and, if by grace you can make love your own, do. For the experience is eternal joy; its absence is unending suffering.

If you were changed enough by God's grace, you could continue controlling the unceasing and inherent impulses of your will, and by succeeding in this exercise here on earth, you'd never be without a taste of the eternal sweetness, and later, in the joy of heaven, you'd never be without every food. So don't be surprised if I direct you to the work of contemplation. If humanity had never sinned, this work would not have stopped. You were made for contemplation, and everything in the universe conspires to help you with it. And contemplation will heal you. I'll tell you more about this subject later. The person who shirks this exercise falls deeper and deeper into sin, moving further and further from God, but the one who practices this discipline rises higher and higher above sin, drawing nearer and nearer to God.

So take good care of your time. Watch how you spend it, for nothing is more precious. In the twinkling of an eye, heaven can be won or lost. Here's how we know time is precious. God, the giver of time, never gives us two moments simultaneously; instead, he gives them to us one after another. We never get the future. We only get the present moment. He does this to establish order in his creation and to keep cause and effect in place. Time is made for us; we're not made for time. God is the ruler

My Personal Top 5

MICHAEL G. MAUDLIN

1 *Surprised by Joy*, C. S. Lewis. As an atheist, I became open to the supernatural after reading Narnia in college. I became a Christian the night I finished *Surprised by Joy,* Lewis's own testimony to his conversion. Then I was tutored by *Mere Christianity* and deepened by *Screwtape Letters* and *The Great Divorce.* No other author has influenced me more.

2 *Basic Christianity*, John Stott, and *The Fight*, John White. I read them at the same time—shortly after becoming a Christian—and to the same effect. Later I underestimated how formative these wise Christian sages were only to reread them and find that they had formed in me what I considered the "common sense" view of the faith.

3 *Run with the Horses*, Eugene Peterson. Before this, I stayed away from the Old Testament. Peterson's account of Jeremiah opened up the full story of God. In fact, I read Peterson regularly for his expansive view of the living God.

4 *The Book of Bebb*, Frederick Buechner. These four novels and his autobiographical works humanized and grounded me spiritually and opened up a richer and deeper way of seeing God.

5 *The Lord of the Rings*, J. R. R. Tolkien. Ten years ago I would not have listed Tolkien on this kind of list, but I keep being confronted with how deeply these characters have shaped my understanding of truth, goodness, character, purpose, and the meaning of one's life.

MICHAEL G. MAUDLIN is a senior vice president, executive editor, and director of Bible Publishing for HarperOne, the religion and spirituality imprint of HarperCollins.

of nature, but his gift of time has no strings attached—it never determines our own nature and natural impulses. Instead, each of these exactly corresponds to one atom of time. That way, none of us has an excuse on Judgment Day when we go before God to give an account of how we spend our time. We won't be able to say, "You gave me two moments at once to my every single impulse."

I can hear you complaining: "What am I supposed to do then? I know you're right, but how can I give an itemized account of each moment? I'm twenty-four already. I never noticed time before. Your argument has already convinced me there's no way I can go back in time and change things. Time doesn't work that way, nor does ordinary grace. I can't go back in time and make amends. I'm also well aware that because I'm weak and slow about some things spiritually, I can no more control the time to come than I did the time past. At best, I'll manage maybe one in a hundred impulses well. So tell me what to do. Help me now, for the love of Jesus."

It is good that you said, "for the love of Jesus." For in the love of Jesus you'll find your help. Love is so powerful that it shares everything. So love Jesus, and everything he has will be yours. Through his divinity, he is the maker and giver of time, and through his humanity, he is the true keeper of time. His divinity and his humanity combined make him the best judge, the one most qualified to question how we've spent our time. Cling to him in love and in faith, and through that powerful bonding, you'll become his companion. His friends will be your friends. By "friends," I mean our Lady, St. Mary, who was full of grace and made the most of her time; the heavenly angels, who never waste time; and the saints in heaven and on earth, who by the grace of Jesus and through the power of love make best use of their time.

See? This truth will comfort you and give you strength. Think clearly about what I've said, and your soul will grow. I do want to warn you about one thing in particular. I don't believe anyone can have a fellowship with Jesus, his holy Mother, the angels on high, and his saints, if that person doesn't make the effort to understand and appreciate time, with the help of grace. No matter how small the contribution, every person must work to strengthen the fellowship, as it does them.

Start practicing contemplation and watch how this spiritual exercise makes a difference in your life. When contemplation is genuine, it's nothing but a sudden impulse coming out of nowhere and flying up to God like a spark from a burning coal. It's awesome to count how many times your soul stirs like that in an hour, but, of these, you may only have one instant where you suddenly realize you've completely forgotten every attachment you have on earth. You'll also notice that, because of our human frailty, each impulse rising to God immediately falls to earth in the form of a thought about something you've done or something that is still on your list to do. But so what? Right after that, it rises up again as fast as it did before.

See how it works? Contemplation is quite different from daydreaming or a delusion or a strange superstition. These don't come from a sincere and humble blind stirring of love, but from an arrogant, curious, and over-imaginative mind. The self-important, hyper-analytical intellect must always and in every way be squashed. Stomp it under foot, if you want to do the work of contemplation with integrity.

A person hearing this book read or quoted may misunderstand my point. I'm not saying that if a person thinks hard enough, he or she will succeed in the work of contemplation. I do not want people sitting around analyzing, racking their brains, their curiosity forcing their imagination to go entirely the wrong way. It's not natural. It's not wise for the mind, and it's not healthy for the body. These people are dangerously deluded, and it would take a miracle to save them. God in his infinite goodness and mercy would have to intervene, making these people stop such a wrong-minded approach and seek the counsel of experienced contemplatives; otherwise, such erring souls could succumb to madness, frenzied fits, or the devil's lies, which lead to the profound misery of sin and eventually to the loss of body and soul, for all eternity.

So, for the love of God, be careful in this work. Don't in any way approach contemplation with your intellect or your imagination. I'm telling you the truth—these won't help you. Leave them be and don't try to do the work of contemplation with them.

Also, don't get the wrong idea about my use of *darkness* and *cloud*. When I refer to this exercise as a darkness or a cloud, I don't want you to imagine the darkness that you get inside your house at night when you blow out a candle; nor do I want you to imagine a cloud crystallized from the moisture in the air. It's easy for your mind to picture either of these at any time. For example, even on the brightest, clearest summer day, you can imagine darkness or a cloud. Conversely, on the darkest night of winter, you can form a mental picture of a clear and shining light. They're not what I mean at all. Leave them alone. This way of thinking is nonsense.

When I say "darkness," I mean the absence of knowing. Whatever you don't know and whatever you've forgotten are "dark" to you, because you don't see them with your spiritual eyes. For the same reason, by "cloud" I don't mean a cloud in the sky, but a cloud of unknowing between you and God.

6. A SHORT LOOK AT CONTEMPLATION, THROUGH DIALOGUE

I know you'll ask me, "How do I think on God as God, and who is God?" and I can only answer, "I don't know."

Your question takes me into the very darkness and cloud of unknowing that I want you to enter. We can know so many things. Through God's grace, our minds can explore, understand, and reflect on creation and even on God's own works, but we can't think our way to God. That's why I'm willing to abandon everything I know, to love the one thing I cannot think. He can be loved, but not thought. By love, God can be embraced and held, but not by thinking. It is good sometimes to meditate on God's amazing love as part of illumination and contemplation, but true contemplative work is something entirely different. Even meditating on God's love must be put down and covered with a cloud of forgetting. Show your determination next. Let that joyful stirring of love make you resolute, and in its enthusiasm bravely step over meditation and reach up to penetrate the darkness above you. Then beat on that thick cloud of unknowing with the sharp arrow of longing and never stop loving, no matter what comes your way.[11]

A Study Guide for *The Cloud of Unknowing*

1. Why do you think the author advises readers not even to attempt the book if they are not determined and resolved to be perfect followers of Christ? How do you react to such a warning?

2. The author warns that we cannot reach God through study or intellect, or even through our imaginations, but only through "loving power." Why can love do what the mind and the imagination cannot?

3. The author warns us to take good care of our time. How do you feel about the idea of giving God an accounting of your time, as the author suggests we will be asked to do? Does such an idea motivate you to do things differently? If so, how?

4. How have you experienced the cloud or darkness that the author describes between God and humanity? What do you think the author means by instructing us to make our home in this darkness?

5. Why do you think we must put all creatures and their works under a "cloud of forgetting" while we are coming to the cloud of unknowing? How might this task be made

more complicated by the connections you have made to people in your life?

6. What must you work to keep under your "cloud of forgetting"—people, past or present sins? One device the author suggests for beating on the cloud is to admit defeat by all those thoughts you cannot overcome, to "fall down before them and cower like a captive or a coward overcome in battle. Give up."[12] What is it about admitting defeat that can allow God to break through to us?

7. Why do you think the author recommends short prayers—the fewer words the better? How does this speak to your prayer experience?

8. The author advises playing a sort of game with God, namely trying to hide from God our very desire to see and experience God. What is the purpose of such game-playing? What does the answer tell you about our relationship with God?

Revelations of Divine Love (Showings)

JULIAN OF NORWICH

Fourteenth-century anchoress Julian of Norwich describes her powerful visions of God, offering us insights into God's goodness and the shelter we have in God.

For God loves and enjoys us—and the Divine Will wants us to love and enjoy God in return, and rest in this strength. And all shall be well.

JULIAN OF NORWICH was born in England in 1342 and died around 1412. She lived as an anchoress, voluntarily confining herself to a cell next to a church. It was a way of withdrawing from the world, but also remaining "anchored" in it. As an anchoress, Julian would not have experienced complete solitude but would have been consulted through an opening in her cell by churchgoers asking for wisdom and advice. As a young woman, Julian became so ill she almost died. During that illness, she experienced a series of visions and revelations she called "showings." She wrote her experiences down and later, as she reflected on them, added additional thoughts, analyzing and explaining what she was shown. The resulting book, *Revelations of Divine Love,* is believed to be the first ever written by a woman in the English language.

Julian wrote in the plain vernacular of the common people, underscoring her desire for her revelations to be available to all. The inclusive nature of God's community is one of her major themes. In spite of the visions she received, she emphasizes that she was not extraordinary but just one in the unity of God's people. Although she seems to skirt close to advocating universal salvation at times, she is careful to stay within Church doctrine by saying that God did not show her the fate of the damned, only that of the redeemed. Her caution is understandable. At the time of her writing, John Wycliffe and his supporters were being killed by the Church for heresy.

From the beginning of the book, we learn that she longs for a life-threatening illness to help her understand more of Christ's endurance and death. She hopes that such a sickness will leave her "scrubbed clean."[1] When she does fall seriously ill at age thirty (just when she had wished to become sick, to coincide with Jesus' age when he started his ministry), her curate brings her a crucifix on the fourth day of her illness. Since her lower body is paralyzed, she fixes her eyes on the crucifix and wishes again to experience the mental and physical pains of Christ's endurance. Then she sees blood trickling down from the crucifix. Knowing that Jesus is the one showing this to her, she is filled with joy. God goes on to show her other sights, both those she can see with her physical eyes and images in her mind, such as a vision of the Virgin Mary. God also reveals spiritual insights; for example, she is shown an object the size of a hazelnut, and she sees that God made it, God loved it, and God kept it.

Despite the spiritual nature of many of the revelations, Julian's showings also include a graphic physical description of Jesus' face and body as he dies. She is surprised at how he looks. God shows her that "Jesus' bright loveliness was hidden inside our dying flesh."[2] Jesus' death, the pain he suffered, is at the center of the showings. She refers to Christ as a "glad giver," who thought more of the pleasure to the recipient than of the pain and cost of the gift.[3]

Yet our flesh is also good; even bodily functions are lovely in their efficiency, because they were created and designed by God. Just as we are clothed in flesh, we are also clothed in God. But the flesh does not endure, only God endures; and the moment of our passing into death is a moment of joy because we are no longer separated from God.

Julian describes God's overwhelming goodness and how God is in everything good. She even goes on, in the third revelation, to say that God is at work in all things, as the "Midpoint" of all things. For Julian, all actions are God's doing. Even Satan is so completely overcome as to be not even worthy of our thoughts. Thus our only response can be to turn to God. "Seeking is as good as seeing," she writes.[4] "Our only job is to cling to God with total trust."[5]

In the thirteenth revelation, while reflecting on sin, Julian is told by Christ, "All shall be well, and all shall be well, and absolutely everything shall be well."[6] Even though we cannot yet know why sin was allowed into the world, Julian is shown that sin has no being or substance and can only be known by the pain it causes us—pain that purifies us, teaches us, and prompts us to rely on God. In this discussion, Julian demonstrates her comfort with paradox and ambiguity, asking Christ how all can be well if the Bible tells us some will be condemned to hell? Jesus' answer to her is, "That which is impossible for you is not impossible for Me. I will keep My word in all things, and I will make everything absolutely well."[7] To which Julian responds, "And so I learned to believe these two seemingly contradictory truths, holding them both in my mind at the same time. . . . This is the Great Deed our Protector shall do; in this deed, He will keep the Divine Word revealed in Scripture, but at the same time, He will make absolutely everything well. How Christ can do this no one knows, and no one will ever know until it has been accomplished."[8]

Again she emphasizes unity: the unity of God, unity with God and with other people, and even the unity of material things. We are to enjoy God's worth in all things, in a big-picture sense in order to avoid unnecessary attachment to particular things. We can experience unity with God through prayer. In the fourteenth revelation, one of the longest, Julian describes prayer as our natural state, "stretched out straight and true toward God."[9] Our prayers come from the deepest part within us, the "Ground" at our core, which is God within. We are to unite our prayers (requests) with our awareness of what God is doing in the world. "For prayer is like an arrow shot straight toward joy's completion in Heaven—and prayer is also like a shelter that covers us with the knowledge that we can trust God to grant all for which we yearn."[10]

God is unchangeable, and God's nature is love, not anger. Anger is human, which is covered by God's mercy and grace. Most of all, Julian finds peace in her vision of God, even in the violence and

Revelations of Divine Love may well be the most important work of Christian reflection in the English language.

—Rowan Williams, Archbishop of Canterbury

chaos of her world. As she writes, "God wants to be in an intimate relationship with us; and if we know God, love God, and are filled with reverence and awe for God, we shall have peace. Our minds will be at rest. Everything God does will create in our minds an enclosed garden of joy and delight, a place where we can be safe and happy."[11] And fifteen years after the showings, she writes that she was shown their clear meaning. "And so I finally understood: Love was the meaning in everything God had shown me. I saw completely and certainly that before we were ever made, we were loved. God's love for us has never diminished, and it never will."[12]

Why *Revelations of Divine Love* Is Essential

Julian's book is a true devotional classic; its wisdom has been recognized and appreciated for centuries. No one writes more eloquently than Julian about God's goodness—that God is in charge and that we are safe with God. As Thomas Merton wrote, "The theology of Julian of Norwich is a theology of mercy, of joy, and of praise. Nowhere in all Christian literature are the dimensions of her Christian optimism excelled." God has made everything, and it is all good, from the hazelnut to even our bodily functions. The fact that Julian came to this conclusion in the chaotic and turbulent time in which she lived makes her insight about the good in all things all the more remarkable.

She also brings out an important sense of the female aspects of God, of Christ as Mother. Julian develops the image of Christ as Mother who gave birth to us, shares our lives, and keeps us safe. This image for her evokes Christ's tenderness and intimacy, the idea of suffering for us, but also the sense of letting us experience life, even when doing so means we fail, so that we may learn and grow. These nurturing, feminine aspects of God are often downplayed, even now.

Julian's writing is notable for her focus on the physical—the suffering Jesus felt when he died, what his face and body looked like as he was on the cross. Julian spends more time writing about Jesus' death than his resurrection, the opposite of what we might read or hear today. If so much attention on bodily suffering makes us uncomfortable, it might be good to reflect on the reasons why. Too often we view our faith as something that concerns only our spiritual sides. Julian made no such distinction between spiritual and corporeal matters. She truly understands that we are not immune to pain in this world, but that we are free from eternal harm. Ultimately we find our rest in God.

Finally, Julian is one of the few examples we have in Christian devotional writing of the wise, older woman. Julian is at the end point of her journey, resting in God, hidden with God. Truly she is an example of the discipline of submission, and we can all learn from the joy she found in her practice of clinging to God with total trust. She is no longer thrown by the emotional and physical upheavals of her life. Julian has truly achieved the peace toward which all the rest of us strive.

How to Read *Revelations of Divine Love*

Julian's writings are available in many good modern translations. Since her aim was to write for everyone, *Revelations* is not difficult reading. The book is divided into many short chapters, making it easy to read slowly and reflectively chapter by chapter.

One of the most surprising things about her book may be her description of longing for illness. For someone who had lived during the ravages of the plague, or Black Death, such a longing was perhaps not as strange as it might seem to us today. It is estimated that at least half of the population of Norwich died from the plague. In addition, other sicknesses struck livestock and crops at the same time, leading the desperate people to revolt and loot churches and monasteries. As Julian scholar Ellyn Sanna writes, "By identifying with Christ's death and making it the focus of her thoughts, Julian was struggling to find meaning in her reality. . . . She no doubt wondered why she survived when so many died, and 'survivor guilt,' as well as the longing to be closer to her lost loved ones, may have been what drove her to ask God for a serious illness, one that would help her better understand others' suffering."[13]

It may also feel strange to read about her intense visions since few of us are accustomed to such phenomena. Julian takes pains to point out that the visions do not make her extraordinary and to say that even for her the intense feelings she had during the showings themselves would not last, that she would have to rely on faith to keep them alive.

Revelations of Divine Love

V. THE HAZELNUT

During this first showing, our Protector showed me a spiritual view of the Divine One's intimate love for us. I saw that the Divine Spirit is everything that is good, everything that comforts us and gives us pleasure. This Spirit is our clothing. In love, the Divine One wraps us up, holds us tight, and encloses us with tenderness. The Spirit lives in everything good that we encounter, the entire universe, and we shall never be abandoned.

At the same time, the Spirit showed me a tiny thing the size of a hazelnut, as round as a ball and so small I could hold it in the palm of my hand. I looked at it in my mind's eye and wondered, "What is this?" The answer came to me: "This is everything that has been made. This is all Creation." It was so small that I marveled it could endure; such a tiny thing seemed likely to simply fall into nothingness. Again the answer came to my thoughts: "It lasts, and it will always last, because God loves it." Everything—all that exists—draws its being from God's love.

I saw that the Little Thing has three properties: First, God made it. Second, God loves it. And third, God keeps it; its ongoing existence depends on God. But to go further than that—to understand the actual relation of the Maker, the Keeper, and the Lover to my own being—I cannot understand. Until my very essence is united with the Divine, I will never be completely at rest, nor will I be totally happy until I am so firmly joined with God that there is nothing—no intervening or mediating aspect of Creation—between God and me.

We need to understand how small and inconsequential Creation is compared to God (who was never created but simply IS). When we perceive the nothingness in reality, we find God there. This is why our minds and souls are often restless and uncomfortable, because we rely on things that are so small, which can offer us no real rest or security, while we fail to realize that God is Almighty, All-Wise, All-Good. The Divine One is the essence of rest and security, the only true comfort. God wants to be known; the Divine One is pleased when we rest in the Spirit's presence, since all that was created will never be enough in and of itself to give us what we need. This is the reason why no soul finds peace until it achieves nothingness even in the midst of the created world. When we willingly, lovingly detach our minds from the world around us, we have the One who is all—and we find rest for our spirits.

Our Protector God also showed me the Divine joy when a soul comes, helpless, without any strength of its own, simply, intimately, with ordinary familiarity, into God's presence. This is the soul's natural tendency when the Spirit touches it. This showing helped me understand this, and I said, "God, in Your goodness, give me Yourself, for You are enough for me. If I ask for less than You, then my life no longer worships You, and I am lacking. Only in You do I have everything."

These words express the soul's loveliness, and they come close to expressing the will of God, the will of goodness, for Creation. All Creation, all the Divine works, are contained within the Divine Unity, even as that Unity transcends all Creation. God is That-Which-Has-No-End, the source of Eternity, and we are made so that we are only complete when we are joined with the

Divine. Although we have separated ourselves, with His Endurance Jesus restored our intimacy, and He keeps us safe in His love. And He does all this out of His goodness.

XLI. ALL YOU ASK IS GROUNDED IN ME

After this, our Protector showed me insights into prayer. In this showing, I saw two perspectives on our Protector's meaning: one is the sense of rightfulness, that prayer makes us as we should be, stretched out straight and true toward God; the other has to do with our assurance that through prayer we are totally safe.

And yet oftentimes, our trust is incomplete, for we are not sure God hears us, or we think we are unworthy, or our emotions are empty (for many times we feel as barren and dry after we pray as we did before). Our foolish feelings make us weak. I know this from experience.

All these thoughts our Protector brought suddenly to my mind, showing me these words: "I am the Ground of each thing for which you ask. It is My will first that you have whatever it is, and then I make you yearn for it, and then you ask Me for it—so why would I not give you that for which I have made you yearn?"

Our Protector gives us great comfort with these words. When the Divine Voice spoke this message, it revealed the endless reward we shall have for all our seeking. It is impossible that we should seek mercy and grace and not receive them. Each thing that we ask, God has already laid out for us from before the beginning of time.

This shows that we do not make God act with our prayers, as though we could move the Divine Essence to be what we want, but rather that the Divine lives in our true desires. This is what our Protector meant with the words, "I am the Ground." God wants all lovers of the Divine to understand this, for the more we grasp this truth, the more we will pray, pouring out our hearts' desires to God.

Seeking and asking is a true, joyful, and enduring soul-quality, a part of who we are as human beings, a quality that unites us and fastens us tight to the Divine Will at work in Creation by the sweet, internal workings of the Holy Spirit. First, Christ receives each prayer from us, and then I imagine He sets it in the Treasure House, where it will never fade away or perish. Our prayers rest there before God and all the Holy Ones, where they are continually received and endlessly answered, so that our needs become sources of prosperity that send us speeding forward toward God. When we reach Heaven, these prayers will be given back to us, delighting us as we thank God with endless worship.

My Personal Top 5

RICHARD ROHR

These are my top five in the sense that they most foundationally formed me at the right time.

1 *The Perfect Joy of St. Francis*, Felix Timmermans

2 *The Story of a Soul*, St. Thérèse of Lisieux

3 *Confessions*, St. Augustine

4 *New Seeds of Contemplation*, Thomas Merton

5 *Showings*, Julian of Norwich

FR. RICHARD ROHR is the founder of the Center for Action and Contemplation in Albuquerque and the author of many books, including *Everything Belongs, The Naked Now,* and *Falling Upward.*

Our Protector laughs with gladness at our prayers. He takes care of them and works through them to change our lives, for Divine grace makes us like God, not only because we are connected to Christ with the bonds of family love and relationship, but because we are becoming like Him. That is why God directs us, "Pray inside your minds, even if you feel no emotional satisfaction from doing so, for it is good for you, even if you can't feel the benefits, even if you can't see them, even if you think you are incapable of prayer. In the midst of dryness and barrenness, in your sickness and weakness, your prayers always make Me happy, even if you feel your prayer is flavorless and dry. I treasure all your prayers."

Because of the reward and the endless thanks God gives us, the Divine Will urges us to pray continually. God accepts our good intentions and our hard work, no matter how we feel emotionally. That is why we please God when we exert all our strength to pray and live united with the Divine; with God's help and grace, then, we keep all our abilities, our mental focus, our body's perceptions turned toward God, until we have what we seek, until our joy is complete, until we have Jesus. (Christ showed this to me in the fifteenth revelation, a little further on, when He said, "I am your reward.")

In addition, giving thanks is a part of prayer, a true heart-knowledge. When, with great reverence and loving awe, we use all our strength to turn ourselves to the work our good Protector inspires in us, our hearts fill up with pleasure and gratitude. Sometimes, this thankfulness becomes so great that it spills out of our minds into speech, and we cry, "Thank You, Protector! Blessed are You!" And sometimes when our hearts are dry and numb, or when the Enemy tempts us, we cry out loud so that we can hear in our own words the echo of Christ's Endurance and His great unity with God. Then the strength of our Protector's words spoken through our own mouths turns inward into our souls, bringing out hearts to life, leading them into Divine grace where they are restored to healthy function so that our prayers become straight and true, exactly what they are meant to be.

Simply enjoying our Protector is the best thanks we can give.

LIX. CHRIST IS THE TRUE MOTHER

The Divine Nature does good in the face of evil, and it is in this way that Jesus Christ is our truest Mother, for from Christ springs our life (as it did with our human mothers), and Christ's sheltering love follows us throughout our entire life. Yes, God is our Father—and yes, God is also our Mother. The Divine demonstrates this in all that exists, saying, "I am the strength and goodness of Fatherhood; I am the wisdom of Motherhood; I am the light and grace that comes from all true love; I am the Trinity; I am Unity; I am the authority of goodness living in all things. I am the One who makes you love; I am the One who makes you yearn for more; and I am the endless fulfillment of all true desires."

When the soul is at its lowest, humblest, and gentlest, there it is also at its highest, noblest, and worthiest. From this reality grows all our sense-soul's strengths; they spring up from this soil naturally, and mercy and grace water them, or we would never grow. Our High Father, God All-Strong who is Being, knew and loved us before time existed. This Divine knowledge, alongside a deep and amazing love, chose with the foreknowledge of the Trinity the Second Person to become our Mother. This was our Father's intention; our Mother brought it about; and our Protector the Holy Spirit made it firm and real. For this reason we love our God in whom we have our being. We thank and praise our Father for our creation; we pray with our entire intellects to our Mother for mercy and understanding; and we ask our Protector the Holy Spirit for help and grace.

In these three—nature, mercy, grace—are contained our entire life. From these we have gentleness and humility; patience and kindness; and we turn away from sin and human arrogance. Our truest strength relies on this turning away. And in this way Jesus is our True Mother, the Mother of our human nature, that which we were created to be—and Jesus is also our True Mother by grace, because He chose to take on our human nature. All the qualities of motherhood come from the Second Person of the Trinity, where we are kept whole and safe, both in our human nature and by spiritual grace, fed by Christ's particular goodness.

I understand that we can consider God's Motherhood from three perspectives: the first is that the Divine Mother gave birth to us and gave us life; the second is that She shared our lives; and the third is that She works always to keep us safe. Through the Divine Mother, grace is spread out wide and long, deep and high, like a blanket that has no edges or binding.

And all is one love.[14]

A Study Guide for *Revelations of Divine Love*

1. Can you relate to Julian's desire for a serious illness? How in your life has illness brought you closer to or further from God?

2. Julian saw some parts of her revelations with her eyes, and others with her mind, yet she seems to find both types of visions equally valid. Would your feelings differ? Why or why not?

3. Julian notes that catching a mere glimpse of God made her long to see him even more clearly. How has experiencing God in your life made you long for more?

4. Julian writes that God is at work in all things, as the "Midpoint" of all creation. In fact, to her, sin is nothing—the absence of action, the absence of reality. How does this match up with your ideas about sin?

5. Julian writes, "It is easy to understand that good needs—what we consider to be high and moral actions—are well done, but from God's perspective, the highest level of action and the lowest are equally well done. . . . All this God showed me with utter joy, as if to say: 'See! I am God. See! I am in all things. See! I never lift My hands from Creation, nor shall I ever, world without end. See! I complete all things, leading them to the goal I have ordained for them without any beginning, by the same strength, wisdom, and love through which I created them. How can anything be wrong with the world, when all this is the case?'"[15] How can you reconcile such a thought with what you know of the world? With what Julian knew of hers?

6. In the sixth revelation, Julian sees God as a homeowner providing welcome and hospitality, thanking each of us for our earthly efforts. How does such an image fit or not fit with your ideas of God? Does this idea of thanks from God make you more eager to serve God? Why or why not?

7. In the twelfth revelation, Julian sees Christ, who tells her, "It is I, I am the One: I am the One who is highest, I am the One you love."[16] She writes that the joy this showing gave her was beyond anything she could describe. Why do you think these words mean so much to Julian? What would hearing these words from Christ mean to you?

8. In the fourteenth revelation, Julian writes that when we pray, we pray for the action that is already being accomplished by God. For her, praying is uniting ourselves with God's work, so it is important that we both pray and recognize this work that God is already doing in the world. Which one are you better at doing—asking or recognizing what God has done? What is the danger of doing one without the other?

9. One of Julian's central messages is that we are kept safe in God. What does Julian mean by this? Is this part of your belief in God? Why or why not?

10. Julian was not the first to speak of Christ as Mother, but she does carry this image further than her predecessors. How do you react to this image?

The Imitation of Christ

THOMAS À KEMPIS

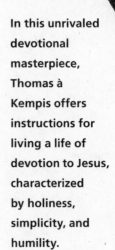

If you want to learn something that will really help you, learn to see yourself as God sees you and not as you see yourself in the distorted mirror of your own self-importance. This is the greatest and most useful lesson we can learn: to know ourselves for what we are, to admit freely our weaknesses and failings, and to hold a humble opinion of ourselves because of them.

In this unrivaled devotional masterpiece, Thomas à Kempis offers instructions for living a life of devotion to Jesus, characterized by holiness, simplicity, and humility.

THOMAS À KEMPIS was born in Kempen, Germany, c. 1379. He entered the Mount St. Agnes monastery at the age of nineteen and remained there until his death at ninety-two. An ordained priest, writer, and copyist, Kempis served for a time as subprior of the monastery, a job that also included service as novice master, instructing the newest members of the community. *The Imitation of Christ* is addressed to these young novitiates and others like them. Since Kempis never claimed authorship for anything, scholars have debated whether he is the true author or simply the scribe of *The Imitation of Christ*. Regardless, Kempis's name is forever entwined with this devotional classic.

Kempis's monastery was part of the New Devotion movement. Followers of Gerard Groote, they called themselves the Brothers and Sisters of the Common Life. Their method of dealing with the uncertainties of life in the time of the plague, Church schisms, and class revolts was to retreat behind the monastery walls and live lives of simplicity and devotion, concerned less with doctrine and theological correctness than with fostering an intimate relationship with

God. Kempis and his brothers and sisters spent their lives creating an inner room within their souls, one in which they could meet Christ.

We see these emphases on every page of *The Imitation of Christ*. In Book 1: Useful Reminders for the Spiritual Life, Kempis stresses the essentialness of imitating Christ in our lives. In all things we can find guidance through Jesus: "A religious person who trains himself intently and devoutly in the holy life and Passion of the Lord will find everything he needs, and he will find it in abundance."[1] Most important is to cultivate humility, to see ourselves as God sees us. For pride makes us weak and easily toppled, focused on things that lead to more restlessness rather than peace. As he writes, "A humble understanding of yourself is a surer way to God than a profound searching after knowledge."[2] Echoing Ecclesiastes, he points out that both intellectual and material vanity can interfere with our relationship with God.

For the author, a certain amount of withdrawing from the world is essential to the spiritual life. Thomas à Kempis himself only ventured outside the monastery walls twice after he took his vows. What can we find outside the monastery that is not within its doors? he asks. Even the biological necessities of life "can be a great bother to a devout person who wishes to concentrate on the spiritual life," he writes.[3] Yet he also urges us to take care of ourselves so that we can do good work for God, since we can do more good things when we are healthy.

In Book 2: Suggestions Drawing One Toward the Inner Life, Kempis instructs us to focus inward on the care of our own souls; as a result, we will pay less attention to other people's business. For indeed if we love Jesus above all things, if we place God where God should be, we do not need other people. We are called to take up our own crosses and follow Jesus. And we will always find the cross to be some form of suffering. If we bear it willingly, our burden will be less. "Know for certain that you must lead a life that focuses less and less on yourself. The less self-centered you become, the more you become centered in God."[4]

Book 3: Of Inner Comfort is a series of dialogues between Jesus and a disciple. Jesus takes up the themes of the earlier two books, speaking of love and a focus on him alone. He offers strong words for overcoming our self-centeredness. "Why is it so remarkable if you, who are dust and nothingness, submit yourself to another person for God's sake, when I, the Almighty and Most High, who created all things out of nothing, humbly subjected myself to others for you? I became the most humble and abject of all, so that you might conquer your pride through my humility."[5] He also mentions intense spiritual feelings and advises that we enjoy and be thankful for them, but that we not seek them out. Instead, we are to maintain spiritual calm. This focus on cultivating an even-keeled calm and peace continues throughout. Jesus says, "Strive, my friend, to do another's will rather than your own; always prefer to have less than more; always seek the lower place and be submissive in all things; always wish and pray that God's will may be entirely fulfilled in you, for you see, the person who does all this enters a place of peace and rest."[6]

Book 4 continues this conversation between Jesus and the disciple, but now focused on Communion. The disciple expresses his unworthiness for the awesome gift of receiving Christ's body in Holy Communion. He expresses regret for not truly appreciating Communion and shares with us stirring words about its power: "Through it, you comfort your beloved people in every trial, and you lift them from the depths of dejection to the hope of your protection. You continually refresh and enlighten them with some new grace. Though they may at first have felt uneasy and unloving before Holy Communion, afterward they always find themselves changed for the better, having restored themselves with this heavenly food and drink."[7] We must prepare ourselves for Communion with confession of sins, and with "deep awe, profound reverence, and unutterable love."[8]

No Book, I believe, except the Bible, has been so universally read and loved by Christians of all tongues and sects.

—Thomas Carlyle

Why *The Imitation of Christ* Is Essential

For more than five hundred years, *The Imitation of Christ* was *the* classic devotional work, enjoying almost continual success and praise. It has been published in literally thousands of editions and read by millions. Many consider it second only to the Bible in readership and impact. St. Thomas More chose it as one of three books every Christian should read. Other fans included George Eliot, John Wesley, and Matthew Arnold. Our editorial board member Dallas Willard refers to it as "absolutely indispensable."

It is only in relatively recent times that *The Imitation of Christ* has diminished in popularity. Its message of unworldliness, withdrawal, and humility seems almost shockingly countercultural today. And, of course, the challenge that the book poses to our modern worldview is in large part what makes it essential. Kempis was reacting to the doctrinal schisms of his own time with a passionate declaration that theological learning matters not at all if we do not have an intimate relationship with Jesus. His book tells us how to cultivate that relationship, by creating an inner room where we can meet Jesus in prayer. At its heart *The Imitation of Christ* is a work of encouragement, designed to build up our desire for prayer, to clear our minds and schedules of everything that would distract us from this most central of purposes.

In his practical advice Kempis demonstrates great clarity and insight into the human spirit. Kempis knows what distracts us and prevents us from meeting Jesus in prayer, and he wants to help us get past all that. Christ is there waiting for us, he tells us, and if we allow him, he will change our lives. As Richard J. Foster writes, "Why, you might ask, has this tradition had such an extensive and profound effect? Well, first of all, because it understands Jesus is a living Teacher showing us daily how to live our lives as he would live our lives if he were us. Then second, because it focuses not on any particular set of external actions but upon how we become a particular kind of person, namely, a person who will do naturally the kinds of things Jesus would do. And third, because it ushers us into living interaction with the living Christ who comes alongside us empowering us to be the right kind of people doing the right kind of things in the midst of everyday life."[9]

How to Read *The Imitation of Christ*

Kempis's book is made up of many short, bite-size chapters. He wrote it as a daily reflection book, with the intention that upon reading, people would find motivation to come closer to God. We can certainly read it this way, a chapter a day before a time of reflection or prayer, as Christians have done for hundreds of years. Others may wish to read in larger chunks, taking on each of the four books in turn or working through the whole book to see the entire scope of Kempis's thoughts.

First, a word about tone. As mentioned before, *The Imitation of Christ* has become less popular in modern times. This is in large part because its tone can feel dour and pessimistic. "Prepare yourself for enduring hardships rather than for comforts," writes Kempis.[10] His focus on withdrawal from the world can also feel off-putting. But whether we live in a monastery or an apartment building, we are still called to engage in the creation of our inner rooms with Jesus. We still must figure out how to meet Jesus amid the distractions of our daily lives and needs. And for someone living in a world devastated by the plague, or Black Death, reminding his readers of the sufferings and hardships they must endure was not pessimistic but practical. We, too, need to know that the spiritual life is no safeguard against suffering. When we remove the blinders of our self-interest and see ourselves as God really sees us, when we allow Christ to cultivate within us his love for the world and all its people, we see these hardships as God does and our faith is not rocked by them. *The Imitation of Christ* is meant primarily to *encourage* us—to lead us to deep spiritual lives, to show us how all of us are called to this wonderful experience of prayer, to meeting Jesus, who waits for us in our inner rooms. Keep this focus on encouragement in mind as you read.

The Imitation of Christ

BOOK I, CHAPTER I: OF THE IMITATION OF CHRIST

"Anyone who follows me shall not walk in darkness," says the Lord. These are the words of Christ, and by them we are reminded that we must imitate his life and his ways if we are to be truly enlightened and set free from the darkness of our own hearts. Let it be the most important thing we do, then, to reflect on the life of Jesus Christ.

Christ's teaching surpasses all the teachings of the saints, and the person who has his spirit will find hidden nourishment in his words. Yet, many people, even after hearing scripture read so often, lack a deep longing for it, for they do not have the spirit of Christ. Anyone who wishes to understand Christ's words and to savor them fully should strive to become like him in every way.

What good does it do, then, to debate about the Trinity, if by a lack of humility you are displeasing to the Trinity? In truth, lofty words do not make a person holy and just, but a virtuous life makes one dear to God. I would much rather feel profound sorrow for my sins than be able to define the theological term for it. If you knew the whole Bible by heart and the sayings of all the philosophers, what good would it all be without God's love and grace? Vanity of vanities and all is vanity, except to love God and to serve only him. This is the highest wisdom: to see the world as it truly is, fallen and fleeting; to love the world not for its own sake, but for God's; and to direct all your effort toward achieving the kingdom of heaven.

So, it is vanity to seek material wealth that cannot last and to place your trust in it. It is also vanity to seek recognition and status. It is vanity to chase after what the world says you should want and to long for things you should not have, things that you will pay a high price for later on if you get them. It is vanity to wish for a long life and to care little about a good life. It is vanity to focus only on your present life and not to look ahead to your future life. It is vanity to live for the joys of the moment and not to seek eagerly the lasting joys that await you.

Often remember that saying: "The eye is not satisfied with seeing, nor is the ear filled with hearing." Make every effort, then, to shift your affections from the things that you can see to the things you cannot see, for people who live in the world on its terms instead of on God's stain their conscience and lose God's grace.

BOOK 2, CHAPTER 1: OF GOD SPEAKING WITHIN YOU

"The kingdom of God is within you," says the Lord.[11] Turn to the Lord with your whole heart, let him be the most important part of your life, and your soul will find rest. If you put God first, you will see his kingdom blossom within you, for the kingdom of God is living in peace and joy with the Holy Spirit, a thing not given to those who do not yearn for him with all their hearts. Christ will come to you and comfort you if you prepare a worthy place for him in your heart. All his glory and beauty lies within you, and he finds great delight in living there. He often visits the person who has a rich inner life, holding sweet conversation with him, granting delightful comfort, much peace and intimate friendship.

So get up, faithful soul, and prepare your heart for this Bridegroom so that he will want to come to you and live in your heart, for he says: "If anyone loves me he will keep my word, and we shall come to him, and we shall make our home with him." Make room for Christ, then, and place him at the center of your life. When he alone rests there, you will have great wealth, and he will be all you need. He will care for you, and he will provide for you faithfully in everything; you will not have to depend on anyone else, for people soon change and they fall short of your expectations before you know it. Only Christ remains constant forever, and he will stand by you to the very end.

Do not rely too heavily on other people, for, like all of us, they have their flaws and foibles. Even if you love someone very much, and that person has been a great blessing to you, do not be disappointed if sometimes the two of you disagree. Those who are your greatest help today may not be tomorrow; their needs change, and so do yours. Place all your trust in God; worship and love him. He will defend you and do what is best for you. This world is not your permanent home; wherever you may be you are a stranger, a pilgrim passing through. You will never find peace unless you are united with Christ in the very depths of your heart.

Why do you look around here to find peace when you do not really belong here? Your place is in heaven, and you should see everything else in terms of heaven. All things pass away, and you pass away with them, too. See that you do not cling to passing things, lest you become caught up in them and perish along with them.

Let your highest thoughts be with the Most High and your prayer be directed to Christ without ceasing. If you cannot contemplate high and heavenly things, rest your thoughts on Christ's Passion, and dwell freely on his Sacred Wounds. If you go for refuge to Jesus's Wounds and to the precious marks of his Passion with humility and love, you will feel great comfort in troubled times, you will not be too concerned about what other people think of you, and it will not be hard to put up with the humiliating things that they may say about you. Christ was also scorned by many people, and in his greatest need he was abandoned by his friends as others heaped insults on his head. Christ was willing to suffer and to be despised, and do you presume to complain of anything? Christ had those who did not like him and those who disagreed with him, and would you have everyone be your friends and supporters? How will your patience be rewarded if you meet with no hardships? If you never encounter opposition, how will you be Christ's friend?

Prop yourself up with Christ and for Christ if you wish to live with Christ. If just once you could perfectly enter the inner life of Jesus and experience a little of his passionate love, then you would not care at all about what you might gain or lose in life. You would even bear insults gladly, for the love of Jesus makes a person think of himself in a very humble way. A lover of Jesus and of truth, a genuinely spiritual person who is free from a troubled heart, can turn himself to God at any time, rise above himself, and rest joyfully in the Lord.

The person who understands all things as they are and not as they are said to be, is truly wise and is taught more by God than by others. The person who knows how to walk by an inner

My Personal Top 5

LYLE SMITHGRAYBEAL

1 *The Grapes of Wrath*, John Steinbeck. The vivid and heartfelt portrayal of the trials of the family Joad moving west along Route 66 from Oklahoma to California during the Great Depression is epic and empathy-producing.

2 *With Justice for All*, John Perkins. While written for a social justice application, Perkins's "3 R's" for Christian Community Development—Relocation, Reconciliation, and Redistribution—have usefulness in any situation where renewal is needed.

3 *Life Together*, Dietrich Bonhoeffer. My pick as Bonhoeffer's most important work, *Life Together* is the primary antidote for the individualism and consumerism of contemporary society.

4 *The Technological Society* and *The Meaning of the City*, Jacques Ellul. Looking at the same human predicament of over-reliance on self rather than God from a sociological (*Society*) and a theological (*City*) perspective, Ellul's writing has trained me to question the value of efficiency and look for the variety of metanarratives present in Scripture.

5 *Freedom of Simplicity*, Richard J. Foster. Richard, echoing Jesus in his life and writing, has helped me to see that while the outward manifestation is of importance, it is the inner disposition that is determinative, in our practice of simplicity and all else.

LYLE SMITHGRAYBEAL is the Renovaré USA Coordinator, where he works on print and electronic publishing, event planning, international projects, and other fun stuff.

light is not overly influenced by his surroundings, and he needs neither special places nor special times for prayer. A person who can quickly focus inwardly is at one with himself, because he never completely loses himself in his outside affairs. He is not distracted by such things, nor does occasional necessary business sidetrack him, but he adjusts himself to such things as they come. The person whose inner life is well-ordered and set in place is not troubled by the strange and twisted things that people do. A person is hindered and distracted in life in proportion to the cares he clutters about himself.

If everything were right with you and if you were pure throughout, everything would work to your advantage. As it is, many things often make you unhappy and upset you because you have not successfully shifted your attention from yourself to God, nor have you let go of the things that the world has set in your path. Nothing so stains and entangles a person's heart as a love of material things that is tarnished by self-interest. If you could put aside all those distracting things that the world has to offer, you could then contemplate heavenly things and you would often experience a deep inner joy.[12]

A Study Guide for *The Imitation of Christ*

1. Why is reflecting on the life of Jesus Christ the most important thing we can do?

2. In what ways does the author suggest that we cultivate humility? Why is humility such a key element of the spiritual life?

3. How does the writing reflect Kempis's life within the monastery walls? Do you experience any difficulty translating this focus to your life? Why or why not?

4. Why is it good for us to face troubles and temptations? How have troubles and temptations shaped you?

5. We read, "What can you see elsewhere that you cannot see here? . . . Go into your room, shut your door, and call upon Jesus, your Beloved. Stay with him in the privacy of your own room, for you will not find such peace anywhere else."[13] Why does Kempis recommend staying home or withdrawing from the noise of the world? How have you been able to experience withdrawing as he suggests?

6. How have you prepared an inward dwelling place for Christ? What distractions in the past and now have prevented you from meeting him there?

7. Kempis urges us to love Jesus better than all others, stating, "When we feel at one with God, it is easy not to need others."[14] What does it mean to you not to need others? Is this practical advice for your life? Why or why not? What does it mean to you to focus all of your love on God? Would this advice differ for those who aren't monks or nuns? Why or why not?

8. Throughout, Kempis seems to prize an even-keeled peace and calm and even advises that although we should be thankful for intense spiritual feelings, we should not seek them. When have you experienced this kind of spiritual high? In hindsight, what was this experience's effect on your faith journey?

The Philokalia

VARIOUS

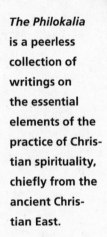

> _Spiritual knowledge comes through prayer, deep stillness, and complete detachment, while wisdom comes through humble meditation on Holy Scripture, and above all, through grace given by God._

T HIS FIVE-VOLUME COLLECTION (only four have been translated into English) is an anthology of writings from the fourth to the fourteenth century by monks and abbots who applied Jesus' teachings to their own lives. It was assembled on Mount Athos, a peninsula in northern Greece, which is the historic center of Eastern Orthodox spirituality, by St. Nicodemus of the Holy Mountain and St. Makarios of Corinth and first published in 1782. The title is the Greek word for "love of the beautiful, holy, exalted." According to the subtitle of the original edition, it is through such love that "the intellect is purified, illumined and made perfect."[1] The English translators refer to _The Philokalia_ as "an itinerary through the labyrinth of time, a silent way of love and gnosis through the deserts and emptinesses of life."[2]

The Philokalia provides numerous examples of how the Eastern Orthodox Church interprets the Bible. As the eponymous pilgrim was told in the Russian nineteenth-century classic _The Way of a Pilgrim, The Philokalia_ is a magnifying glass that allows us to see the Bible properly. One element of this interpretation is the belief that _theosis,_ or deification, is the true aim of salvation. Christ's Incarnation and his victory over death enable us to grow into our true nature as "children of God" (John 1:12), and to realize "the measure of the full stature of Christ" (Eph 4:13). Although we were orig-

The Philokalia is a peerless collection of writings on the essential elements of the practice of Christian spirituality, chiefly from the ancient Christian East.

inally made in "the image and likeness of God" (Gen 1:26), this inheritance was damaged in the fall of Adam and Eve. Through Christ the divine image can be restored, as we are gradually healed in body and soul and increasingly united with him. St. Maximos the Confessor writes, "To reconcile us with the Father, at his Father's wish the Son deliberately gave himself to death on our behalf so that, just as he consented to be dishonored for our sake by assuming our passions, to an equal degree he might glorify us with the beauty of his own divinity."[3] The term *deification* has connotations in English that are misleading; the doctrine does not imply that humans become independent gods. In the fourteenth century Gregory Palamas clarified that God's essence remains inaccessible, beyond human contact or knowledge, but we are invited to share in God's "energies," God's activity in the life of all creation (*energies* and *energize* being Greek words St. Paul frequently used, but for which no Latin equivalent could be found when the Western Bible was being prepared in the fifth century). *Theosis* is a gift by grace, as St. Maximos makes clear: "God made us so that we might become 'partakers of the divine nature' (2 Pet 1:4) and sharers in His eternity, and so that we might come to be like Him (1 John 3:2) through deification [*theosis*] by grace. It is through deification [*theosis*] that all things are reconstituted and achieve their permanence; and it is for its [deification's] sake that what is not is brought into being and given existence."[4] Yet although the initiative for our deification and salvation rests with God, we must respond and accept God's grace. As St. Maximos writes, "Created man cannot become a son of God and god by grace through deification [*theosis*], unless he is first through his own free choice begotten in the Spirit by means of his self-loving and independent power dwelling naturally within him. The first man neglected this divinizing, divine, and immaterial birth by choosing what is manifest and delectable to the senses in preference to the spiritual blessings that were as yet unrevealed. In this way he fittingly condemned himself to a bodily generation that is without choice, that is material, and that is subject to death."[5]

The Philokalia is also a guide to contemplative, inward prayer, which results in increased sensitivity to the presence and voice of God. St. Evagrios the Solitary writes extensively about prayer, describing it as "the ascent of the intellect to God." Many of *The Philokalia* writers emphasize that prayer has little to do with our physical posture or positions, but is greatly affected by our behavior and lifestyle. Like St. Evagrios, many of these authors lived ascetic lifestyles. He writes, "When the soul has been purified through the keeping of all the commandments, it makes the intellect steadfast and able to receive the state needed for prayer."[6] Many other monks wrote of the discipline and vigilance necessary for a fruitful prayer life. St. Makarios of Egypt writes, "He who cultivates prayer has to fight with all diligence and watchfulness, all endurance, all struggle of soul and toil of body, so that he does not become sluggish and surrender himself to distraction of thought, to excessive sleep, to listlessness, debility, and confusion, or defile himself with turbulent and indecent suggestions, yielding his mind to things of this kind, satisfied merely with standing or kneeling for a long time, while his intellect wanders far away."[7] These writings remind us of similar themes in *The Sayings of the Desert Fathers,* and indeed many of the authors of *The Philokalia* were desert fathers.

Another frequent theme of *The Philokalia* is that of continuous prayer, most often the Jesus Prayer—"Lord Jesus Christ, Son of God, have mercy on me." The authors of *The Philokalia* found that constant recitation of this prayer would banish evil. St. Hesychios the Priest writes, "We will travel the road of repentance correctly if, as we begin to give attention to the intellect, we combine humility with watchfulness, and prayer with the power to rebut evil thoughts. In this way we will adorn the chamber of our heart with the holy and venerable name of Jesus Christ as with a lighted lamp, and we will sweep our heart clean of wickedness, purifying and embellishing it."[8] The Jesus Prayer is also described as a way of focusing the mind, banishing the passions, and as a help on the path to theosis.

Finally, *The Philokalia* illuminates the concept of *hesychia*, translated as stillness or tranquility. *Hesychia* is the desired outcome of the Jesus Prayer. St. Peter of Damaskos defines stillness as "living a life without distraction, far from all worldly care."[9] St. Thalassios the Libyan advises "enclos[ing] your senses in the citadel of stillness

The content of this book is of such depth and usefulness that it is considered to be the primary teacher of contemplative life. . . . It contains clear exposition of the ideas that are mysteriously presented in the Bible and are not easy for our finite mind to understand. I will give you an illustration. The sun—a great, shining, and magnificent light—cannot be contemplated and looked at directly with the naked eye. An artificial glass, a million times smaller and dimmer than the sun, is needed to look at the great king of lights to be enraptured by its fiery rays. In a similar way the Holy Bible is a shining light and *The Philokalia* is the necessary glass.

—*The Way of a Pilgrim*

so that they do not involve the intellect in their desires."[10] Stillness is something everyone, not just clergy and monastics, is called to seek. As Abba Philimon writes, "The only path leading to heaven is that of complete stillness, the avoidance of all evil, the acquisition of blessings, perfect love toward God and communion with him in holiness and righteousness. If a man has attained these things, he will soon ascend to the heavenly realm."[11]

Why *The Philokalia* Is Essential

Apart from the Bible, *The Philokalia* is the principal spiritual text in the Eastern Christian tradition. The sayings within it have been treasured in one form or another by Eastern Christians for centuries. Editorial board member Frederica Mathewes-Green, author of *The Illumined Heart,* describes it as "an invaluable foundational description of Orthodox spirituality." Like many writings from the Eastern Christian tradition, *The Philokalia* focuses less on external rules of behavior and action and more on the inner life, which is always seeking to increase its ability to commune with God. While moderation and holiness in outward behavior is important, it would be meaningless without the accompanying inner growth. This attitude is a valuable corrective to the focus on external behavior that frequently characterizes Western Christianity. As Jesus told the Pharisees, it is the inner life that is of the greatest importance: "Woe to you, scribes and Pharisees, hypocrites! For you clean the outside of the cup and of the plate, but inside they are full of greed and self-indulgence. You blind Pharisee! First clean the inside of the cup, so that the outside also may become clean" (Matt 23:25–26).

We can also learn from *The Philokalia*'s emphasis on organic integration of all aspects of life. There are no lines here between theology and spirituality, knowledge and belief, the actions of our bodies and the actions of our hearts; it is all one. We bow and prostrate ourselves when we pray with our hearts because what we do with our bodies is intrinsically connected to what we think about God. The Jesus Prayer, as a form of continuous prayer, is another good example of this holism. Life cannot be separated from prayer; prayer is our life.

The Philokalia also emphasizes the concept of *hesychia,* or stillness. Stillness is almost a completely alien notion to the Western Church, at least as a goal of the spiritual life. Stillness in *The Philokalia* is also viewed holistically: the stillness of the body is a prerequisite for the stillness of the mind. Through this stillness, or tranquility, we can conquer our desires and reach out for God. A time-tested way to reach stillness is through the practice of the Jesus Prayer.

Finally, in its very breadth and diversity *The Philokalia* shows us the way in which a devout follower of God gains knowledge of God through a variety of spiritual practices.

How to Read *The Philokalia*

Four of the five volumes of *The Philokalia* are widely available in English. But *The Philokalia* is a challenging work, and in the Orthodox tradition it is not recommended that a reader take it on without the direction of a knowledgeable spiritual mother or father (having such a guide is an important component of the Eastern tradition). A couple of places to begin with *The Philokalia* might be "On Prayer" by Evagrios in volume 1 and the section of Maximos the Confessor in volume 2. At least one abridged and annotated edition is available in English as well, with commentary to help guide the reader.

EXCERPTS FROM

The Philokalia

VOLUME I: EVAGRIOS THE SOLITARY: ON PRAYER

Do not despise the humble appearance of these texts, for you know how to be content with much or little (Phil 4:12). You will recall how Christ did not reject the widow's mites (Mark 12:44), but accepted them as greater than the rich gifts of many others. Showing in this way charity and love towards your true brethren, pray for one who is sick that he may 'take up his bed' and walk (Mark 2:11) by the grace of Christ. Amen.

1. Should one wish to make incense, one will mingle, according to the Law, fragrant gum, cassia, aromatic shell and myrrh in equal amounts (Exod 30:34). These are the four virtues. With their full and balanced development, the intellect will be safe from betrayal.

2. When the soul has been purified through the keeping of all the commandments, it makes the intellect steadfast and able to receive the state needed for prayer.

3. Prayer is communion of the intellect with God. What state, then, does the intellect need so that it can reach out to its Lord without deflection and commune with Him without intermediary?

4. When Moses tried to draw near to the burning bush he was forbidden to approach until he had loosed his sandals from his feet (Exod 3:5). If, then, you wish to behold and commune with Him who is beyond sense-perception and beyond concept, you must free yourself from every impassioned thought.

5. First pray for the gift of tears, so that through sorrowing you may tame what is savage in your soul. And having confessed your transgressions to the Lord, you will obtain forgiveness from Him.

6. Pray with tears and all you ask will be heard. For the Lord rejoices greatly when you pray with tears.

7. If you do shed tears during your prayer, do not exalt yourself, thinking you are better than others. For your prayer has received help so that you can confess your sins readily and make your peace with the Lord through your tears. Therefore do not turn the remedy for passions into a passion, and so again provoke to anger Him who has given you this grace.

8. Many people, shedding tears for their sins, forget what tears are for, and so in their folly go astray.

9. Persevere with patience in your prayer, and repulse the cares and doubts that arise within you. They disturb and trouble you, and so slacken the intensity of your prayer.

10. When the demons see you truly eager to pray, they suggest an imaginary need for various things, and then stir up your remembrance of these things, inciting the intellect to go after them; and when it fails to find them, it becomes very depressed and miserable. And when the intellect is at prayer, the demons keep filling it with the thought of these things, so that it tries to discover more about them and thus loses the fruitfulness of its prayer.

11. Try to make your intellect deaf and dumb during prayer; you will then be able to pray.

12. Whenever a temptation or a feeling of contentiousness comes over you, immediately arousing you to anger or to some senseless word, remember your prayer and how you will be judged about it, and at once the disorderly movement within you will subside.

13. Whatever you do to avenge yourself against a brother who has done you a wrong will prove a stumbling-block to you during prayer.

14. Prayer is the flower of gentleness and of freedom from anger.

15. Prayer is the fruit of joy and thankfulness.

16. Prayer is the remedy for gloom and despondency.

17. 'Go and sell all you have and give to the poor' (Matt 19:21); and 'deny yourself, taking up your cross' (Matt 16:24). You will then be free from distraction when you pray.

18. If you wish to pray as you should, deny yourself all the time, and when any kind of affliction troubles you, meditate on prayer.

19. If you endure something painful out of love for wisdom, you will find the fruit of this during prayer.

20. If you desire to pray as you ought, do not grieve anyone; otherwise you 'run in vain' (Phil 2:16).

21. 'Leave your gift before the altar; first go away and be reconciled with your brother' (Matt 5:24), and when you return you will pray without disturbance. For rancor darkens the intellect of one who prays, and extinguishes the light of his prayers.

22. Those who store up grievances and rancor in themselves are like people who draw water and pour it into a cask full of holes.

23. If you patiently accept what comes, you will always pray with joy.

24. When you pray as you should, thoughts will come to you which make you feel that you have a real right to be angry. But anger with your neighbor is never right. If you search you will find that things can always be arranged without anger. So do all you can not to break out into anger.

My Personal Top 5

PHYLLIS TICKLE

These, in retrospect, seem not only to have formed me, but also to have remained dear to my heart.

1 Above them all, **Benedictine Daily Prayer—A Short Breviary** from Liturgical Press. Over the years, I have worn out two previous copies/editions and am now on my third. It is the companion of my soul, a portable sanctuary, an anchor to my wandering mind and spirit.

2 **The Soul's Sincere Desire** by Glenn Clark was first published by Little, Brown in 1948; and I must have received the first copy off the press as a gift from a family friend. I devoured it—several times—over the last six years of my adolescence. I have visited it many times since [it is still in print] and always discover there the girl who was the woman I have become. It's like a diary someone else wrote for me.

3 **In This House of Brede** by Rumer Godden was the book that showed me, as a young matron and college teacher, what mature vocation was about. I have held it to me all the years since. It is probably not a great book, but it is and was for me a compelling one. In 2005, Loyola Press re-issued it as part of their *Christian Classics* series; and one of the proudest, happiest moments of my writing life was to be asked to furnish the foreword for that edition. It was a chance to say "thank you" publicly for a book I treasure.

4 **The Book of Common Prayer**, essentially in all its editions, but especially the 1979. It is my companion in worship week in and week out, shaping me to the praxis of my communion within the faith and connecting me constantly to the history of what has been, as well as to the present of what is.

5 Because, if I am to be honest, I must mention it: **Bible Stories and What They Teach Us** by Charles Foster and first published in 1886 by Holman and then, over and over again through all the years of my childhood. It was my bible, my schoolteacher and instructor, my joy beyond all others as a child. From it I learned to love the narrative and from it I learned, to the extent that I have done so at all, to tell the stories of God and his ways among us.

PHYLLIS TICKLE is the compiler of *The Divine Hours* series of manuals for observing fixed-hour prayer and the author of some two dozen books in the field of religion, including the bestselling *The Great Emergence—How Christianity Is Changing and Why*.

1. First the intellect marvels when it reflects on the absolute infinity of God, that boundless sea for which it longs so much. Then it is amazed at how God has brought things into existence out of nothing. But just as 'His magnificence is without limit' (Ps 145:3, LXX), so 'there is no penetrating His purposes' (Isa 40:28).

2. How can the intellect not marvel when it contemplates that immense and more than astonishing sea of goodness? Or how is it not astounded when it reflects on how and from what source there have come into being both nature endowed with intelligence and intellect, and the four elements which compose physical bodies, although no matter existed before their generation? What kind of potentiality was it which, once actualized, brought these things into being? But all this is not accepted by those who follow the pagan Greek philosophers, ignorant as they are of that all-powerful goodness and its effective wisdom and knowledge, transcending the human intellect.

3. God is the Creator from all eternity, and He creates when He wills, in His infinite goodness, through His coessential Logos and Spirit. Do not raise the objection: 'Why did He create at a particular moment since He is good from all eternity?' For I reply that the unsearchable wisdom of the infinite essence does not come within the compass of human knowledge.

4. When the Creator willed, He gave being to and manifested that knowledge of created things which already existed in Him from all eternity. For in the case of almighty God it is ridiculous to doubt that He can give being to anything when He so wills.

5. Try to learn why God created; for that is true knowledge. But do not try to learn how He created or why He did so comparatively recently; for that does not come within the compass of

your intellect. Of divine realities some may be apprehended by men and others may not. Unbridled speculation, as one of the saints has said, can drive one headlong over the precipice.

6. Some say that the created order has coexisted with God from eternity; but this is impossible. For how can things which are limited in every way coexist from eternity with Him who is altogether infinite? Or how are they really creations if they are coeternal with the Creator? This notion is drawn from the pagan Greek philosophers, who claim that God is in no way the creator of being but only of qualities. We, however, who know almighty God, say that He is the creator not only of qualities but also of the being of created things. If this is so, created things have not coexisted with God from eternity.

7. Divinity and divine realities are in some respects knowable and in some respects unknowable. They are knowable in the contemplation of what appertains to God's essence and unknowable as regards that essence itself.

8. Do not look for conditions and properties in the simple and infinite essence of the Holy Trinity; otherwise you will make It composite like created beings—a ridiculous and blasphemous thing to do in the case of God.

9. Only the infinite Being, all-powerful and creative of all things, is simple, unique, unqualified, peaceful and stable. Every creature, consisting as it does of being and accident, is composite and always in need of divine providence, for it is not free from change.

10. Both intelligible and sensible nature, on being brought into existence by God, received powers to apprehend created beings. Intelligible nature received powers of intellection, and sensible nature powers of sense perception.

11. God is only participated in. Creation both participates and communicates: it participates in being and in well-being, but communicates only well-being. But corporeal nature communicates this in one way and incorporeal nature in another.

12. Incorporeal nature communicates well-being by speaking, by acting, and by being contemplated; corporeal nature only by being contemplated.

13. Whether or not a nature endowed with intelligence and intellect is to exist eternally depends on the will of the Creator whose every creation is good; but whether such a nature is good or bad depends on its own will.

14. Evil is not to be imputed to the essence of created beings, but to their erroneous and mindless motivation.

15. A soul's motivation is rightly ordered when its desiring power is subordinated to self-control, when its incensive power rejects hatred and cleaves to love, and when its power of intelligence, through prayer and spiritual contemplation, advances towards God.

16. If in time of trial a man does not patiently endure his afflictions, but cuts himself off from the love of his spiritual brethren, he does not yet possess perfect love or a deep knowledge of divine providence.

17. The aim of divine providence is to unite by means of true faith and spiritual love those separated in various ways by vice. Indeed, the Savior endured His sufferings so that 'He should gather together into one the scattered children of God' (John 11:52). Thus, he who does not resolutely bear trouble, endure affliction, and patiently sustain hardship, has strayed from the path of divine love and from the purpose of providence.

18. If 'love is long-suffering and kind' (1 Cor 13:4), a man who is fainthearted in the face of his afflictions and who therefore behaves wickedly towards those who have offended him, and stops loving them, surely lapses from the purpose of divine providence.

19. Watch yourself, lest the vice which separates you from your brother lies not in him but in yourself. Be reconciled with him without delay, so that you do not lapse from the commandment of love.

20. Do not hold the commandment of love in contempt, for through it you will become a son of God. But if you transgress it, you will become a son of Gehenna.

21. What separates us from the love of friends is envying or being envied, causing or receiving harm, insulting or being insulted, and suspicious thoughts. Would that you had never done or experienced anything of this sort and in this way separated yourself from the love of a friend.

22. Has a brother been the occasion of some trial for you and has your resentment led you to hatred? Do not let yourself be overcome by this hatred, but conquer it with love. You will succeed in this by praying to God sincerely for your brother and by accepting his apology; or else by conciliating him with an apology yourself, by regarding yourself as responsible for the trial and by patiently waiting until the cloud has passed.

23. A long-suffering man is one who waits patiently for his trial to end and hopes that his perseverance will be rewarded.

24. 'The long-suffering man abounds in understanding' (Prov 14:29), because he endures everything to the end and, while awaiting that end, patiently bears his distress. The end, as St.

Paul says, is everlasting life (Rom 6:22). 'And this is life eternal, that they might know Thee the only true God, and Jesus Christ whom Thou hast sent' (John 17:3).

25. Do not lightly discard spiritual love: for men there is no other road to salvation.[12]

A Study Guide for *The Philokalia*

1. What has been your experience with a continuous prayer such as the Jesus Prayer? Do you find the image of the prayer as light in the darkness helpful?

2. Do you find your prayer to be more powerful when you combine certain actions of the body, postures, bowing, or even walking, with the words of your heart? Why or why not?

3. What does the concept of *hesychia* mean to you? How have you experienced *hesychia*?

4. What do you think is meant by *theosis*/deification? Do you agree with this concept?

5. Prayer is often described in *The Philokalia* as the communion of the intellect with God. In what ways do we prepare the intellect for such a meeting?

6. Evagrios instructs us to pray with tears, saying that the Lord delights of such sorrow in prayer. When have you been sorrowful in prayer? Why? What was the result of your coming to God in that way?

7. How does Maximos the Confessor seem to understand love?

Institutes of the Christian Religion

JOHN CALVIN

> *We must be persuaded not only that as [God] once formed the world, so he sustains it by his boundless power, governs it by his wisdom, preserves it by his goodness, in particular, rules the human race with justice and Judgment, bears with them in mercy, shields them by his protection; but also that not a particle of light, or wisdom, or justice, or power, or rectitude, or genuine truth, will anywhere be found, which does not flow from him, and of which he is not the cause; in this way we must learn to expect and ask all things from him, and thankfully ascribe to him whatever we receive. For this sense of the divine perfections is the proper master to teach us piety, out of which religion springs.*

Still the foundation of today's Protestant Church, *Institutes of the Christian Religion* is Calvin's *magnum opus*, describing God's sovereignty and the piety we are called to exhibit in response.

JOHN CALVIN was born in Noyon, France, in 1509. Raised a Roman Catholic, he experienced a kind of conversion while studying law at university and became convinced of the strong need for reform within the Church. Calvin was outspoken about these beliefs, and his association with the Protestant reform movement put him in danger in strongly Catholic France. After fleeing the country when an uprising put his life at risk, at age twenty-six Calvin wrote *Institutes* as a statement of what the reformers believed. *Institutes* was his first and most important expression of his theology, and throughout his lifetime he revised and reordered the material several times. In its final version, the work is divided into four parts: Father, Son, Holy Spirit, and Church.

Calvin believed that the two parts of wisdom are knowledge of God and knowledge of self, and that the two are inextricably linked. Since God is so much greater than we, however, we should begin by seeking knowledge of God, and knowing God requires piety. Indeed, piety is at the center of Calvin's work. He defines it as "that union of reverence and love to God which the knowledge of his benefits inspires."[1] Because we belong not to ourselves, but to God, all our actions and thoughts should serve not our own interests, but God's. We are subject to God in all things and are as nothing compared to God. Even when we seek to know God, it is God who must take the initiative. But with God's help, we can know God through three primary sources: ourselves, since we are created in God's image; the universe God created; and the Scriptures that are God's Word.

Yet our estrangement from God is so complete that we need Christ for redemption. God's law itself cannot bridge our separation from God, so Christ came to complete the law. Jesus did not throw out the law—we are still to live under the law in a moral sense. Instead, Jesus, fully human and fully divine, taught us what living under God's law truly looks like. Jesus' life, properly understood, embodies the Ten Commandments. The law also serves to show us just how much we need Jesus Christ, since we cannot possibly obey it perfectly or satisfy it on our own.

According to Calvin, the Holy Spirit enables us to trust God and our knowledge of God, by its testimony on our hearts. It is through the grace and energy of the Spirit that we are united to Christ. The Holy Spirit also enables us to understand Scripture and its reliability. The work of the Spirit is to be found in our church communities. Central to our lives as Christians, the Church is where we learn to fulfill that mandate of the Ten Commandments, loving God and loving our neighbor.

But it is his teachings on the Christian life for which Calvin is perhaps best known today. For him, there is no greater principle than the biblical directive to be holy as God is holy. Calvin offers many reasons why we must seek to be holy and undefiled: because we are God's children, because we have been purified by Christ's baptism, since we are members of Christ's body as the Church, and since our bodies are temples of the Holy Spirit. Holiness means life characterized by sobriety, righteousness, and godliness. It is only with restraint and moderation that we can truly appreciate God's earthly blessings. The Christian life is one in which we renounce our false appetites, humble ourselves, and esteem others.

Why *Institutes of the Christian Religion* Is Essential

As the founder of the Reformed or Presbyterian Church, John Calvin is one of the key figures in Church history, and *Institutes* is his *magnum opus*. The theology he develops in this book in large part laid the foundation for the Protestant Church as it is today. Building on Augustine's theology, Calvin is often remembered for his ideas about predestination and his commitment to holiness by way of asceticism. But *Institutes* contains so much more that is relevant for our spiritual formation. "No other single book from the sixteenth century does more to define the nature of our life with God than *The Institutes of the Christian Religion*," writes editorial board member Gayle Beebe in *Longing for God*.

Perhaps most notable is Calvin's working premise of God's sovereignty over all life. We owe everything that we are to God, and so everything that we do should be subject to God's will, not our own interests. Nothing that we do ultimately endures without God's help; we cannot even seek the knowledge of God unless God first reaches out to us. Calvin's teachings present a sharp contrast to our culture's emphasis on each person's independence and control of his or her individual destiny. Calvin reminds us that our ultimate happiness rests in God alone. We are called to dependence and submission, not independence and autonomy, and as uncomfortable as it may feel against the mind-set of our popular culture, it is only when we surrender to God that we can experience our humanity as God intended.

> Among all those who have been born of women, there has not risen a greater than John Calvin; no age before him ever produced his equal, and no age afterwards has seen his rival. In theology, he stands alone, shining like a bright fixed star, while other leaders and teachers can only circle round him, at a great distance—as comets go streaming through space—with nothing like his glory or his permanence.
>
> —Charles Spurgeon

Following closely on this understanding is Calvin's teaching about prayer. His section about prayer is by far the longest section on any single subject in *Institutes,* and his thoughts represent an important teaching for our age. Prayer is not a method for convincing God or trying to change God's mind. Indeed we have no basis to make any requests since we can never be righteous or perfect enough to offer anything in return. So for Calvin prayer is primarily a way for us to become conformed to God's will. Only after we have become attuned to God's righteousness and will do we make our requests. Prayer thus becomes a conversation as we learn to ask truly for God's will to be done.

Being conformed to God's will inevitably involves the denial of our own wills. Calvin calls us to a life of holiness and restraint, to sobriety and frugality. It is tempting for modern readers to dismiss Calvin's pivotal teachings about the Christian life, about self-denial and moderation, because of the many ways they have been twisted and then wielded as a puritanical, legalistic blade. Yet every time we correct an excess, we risk the pendulum's swinging too far the other way, and if Calvin's calls to restraint and moderation rankle us, it is certainly worth considering if our reaction stems from being too accustomed to immoderation and excess. For it is moderation to which Calvin calls us. He emphasizes the beauty and blessings of the earth and the fact that nature's beautiful colors and the smell and taste of our food are far more than required to meet our basic needs. Calvin can offer us insight into our practice of the discipline of celebration. Calvin wants us to enjoy all of God's blessings, and he believes that moderation is the best way to fully do that. Too much wine or food or any good thing only dulls our senses and prevents us from truly appreciating that in which we have overindulged. This excess can then lead us to ignore spiritual things. These are the reasons we are to rein in our desires, not out of masochism or a hatred of the body.

Finally, Calvin's teachings about Christ are crucial for our spiritual formation. He famously explains how Christ fulfills all our needs in his threefold office of prophet, priest, and king. In Christ we find all the major roles of the biblical narrative. Christ prophesies the truth about God, ourselves, and our need for God; he mediates our salvation; and he reigns over us. Christ is alive and continuing to work in us today, giving us knowledge, reconciling us to God, using his power to take away our sins. His work is not over but continues in us, in our hearts if we but open them to him.

How to Read *Institutes of the Christian Religion*

The figure of Calvin looms so large, and, sometimes, so dour, over Church tradition that meeting Calvin in his own words in the pages of *Institutes* is most rewarding and refreshing. Yet tackling all four volumes of Calvin's massive masterwork can feel intimidating to the most motivated theological reader. One option is to choose from among a number of abridged editions available, including one edited by Tony Lane and Hilary Osborne (Baker, 1987). Another good entry point to *Institutes* is Calvin's *Golden Booklet of the True Christian Life,* a short devotional book that is included in *Institutes* (Book 3, chapters 6–10) but also published separately. Here we find some of Calvin's key teaching on humility, self-denial, and right living. A third helpful place to begin might be Calvin's writings about prayer, which are found in chapter 20 of the third book.

EXCERPTS FROM

Institutes of the Christian Religion

BOOK I, CHAPTER I

1. Our wisdom, in so far as it ought to be deemed true and solid Wisdom, consists almost entirely of two parts: the knowledge of God and of ourselves. But as these are connected together by many ties, it is not easy to determine which of the two precedes and gives birth to the other. For, in the first place, no man can survey himself without forthwith turning his thoughts towards

the God in whom he lives and moves; because it is perfectly obvious, that the endowments which we possess cannot possibly be from ourselves; nay, that our very being is nothing else than subsistence in God alone. In the second place, those blessings which unceasingly distil to us from heaven, are like streams conducting us to the fountain. Here, again, the infinitude of good which resides in God becomes more apparent from our poverty. In particular, the miserable ruin into which the revolt of the first man has plunged us, compels us to turn our eyes upwards; not only that while hungry and famishing we may thence ask what we want, but being aroused by fear may learn humility. For as there exists in man something like a world of misery, and ever since we were stript of the divine attire our naked shame discloses an immense series of disgraceful properties every man, being stung by the consciousness of his own unhappiness, in this way necessarily obtains at least some knowledge of God. Thus, our feeling of ignorance, vanity, want, weakness, in short, depravity and corruption, reminds us, that in the Lord, and none but He, dwell the true light of wisdom, solid virtue, exuberant goodness. We are accordingly urged by our own evil things to consider the good things of God; and, indeed, we cannot aspire to Him in earnest until we have begun to be displeased with ourselves. For what man is not disposed to rest in himself? Who, in fact, does not thus rest, so long as he is unknown to himself; that is, so long as he is contented with his own endowments, and unconscious or unmindful of his misery? Every person, therefore, on coming to the knowledge of himself, is not only urged to seek God, but is also led as by the hand to find him.

2. On the other hand, it is evident that man never attains to a true self-knowledge until he has previously contemplated the face of God, and come down after such contemplation to look into himself. For (such is our innate pride) we always seem to ourselves just, and upright, and wise, and holy, until we are convinced, by clear evidence, of our injustice, vileness, folly,

and impurity. Convinced, however, we are not, if we look to ourselves only, and not to the Lord also—He being the only standard by the application of which this conviction can be produced. For, since we are all naturally prone to hypocrisy, any empty semblance of righteousness is quite enough to satisfy us instead of righteousness itself. And since nothing appears within

My Personal Top 5

CHRIS WEBB

1 **The Divine Comedy**, Dante Alighieri. This is the single greatest work on spiritual formation I've yet read. It's a tragedy that most readers never get past the darkness of the first part, the *Inferno*; it's the second and third parts of the poem that contain the delights and wonders. I've loved Dante for decades, and will re-read him as long as I live.

2 **The Republic**, Plato. Even though Plato was a pagan philosopher, *The Republic* is a foundational work for anyone who wants to understand the Christian spiritual tradition. I love him for his depth, his brilliance, his quirky ideas, and for his sneaky sense of humor. He's influenced us all profoundly, whether we've read him or not—as those who dive in will quickly discover.

3 **The Conferences**, John Cassian. If I could travel in time and meet one figure from Christian history, I might choose Cassian. A towering figure in Christian monasticism, his writing is challenging, deep, warm, pastoral, practical, and provocative all at once. Over the years I've come to see Cassian less as a great theologian and more as a companion, a soul friend from another age.

4 **The Rule**, St. Benedict of Nursia. Benedict has consistently helped me understand how communities can intentionally pursue spiritual formation. I shaped much of my pastoral ministry around my reading of the *Rule*. And I've found a depth of wisdom in this little text that outstrips pretty much all contemporary writing on leadership.

5 **The Book of Common Prayer** (1662). This treasury of Anglican liturgy has helped me understand and experience the Christian life as *prayer*. Drawing on Scripture, on the heritage of ancient and medieval Christianity, and on the profound insights of the Reformation, this beautiful text gives voice to my heart's longing for God. I would be empty without it.

CHRIS WEBB is president of Renovaré USA, a Christian ministry dedicated to helping people experience a richer life with God through spiritual formation.

us or around us that is not tainted with very great impurity, so
long as we keep our mind within the confines of human pollution, anything which is in some small degree less defiled delights us as if it were most pure just as an eye, to which nothing
but black had been previously presented, deems an object of a
whitish, or even of a brownish hue, to be perfectly white. Nay,
the bodily sense may furnish a still stronger illustration of the
extent to which we are deluded in estimating the powers of the
mind. If, at mid-day, we either look down to the ground, or on
the surrounding objects which lie open to our view, we think
ourselves endued with a very strong and piercing eyesight; but
when we look up to the sun, and gaze at it unveiled, the sight
which did excellently well for the earth is instantly so dazzled
and confounded by the refulgence, as to oblige us to confess that
our acuteness in discerning terrestrial objects is mere dimness
when applied to the sun. Thus too, it happens in estimating our
spiritual qualities. So long as we do not look beyond the earth,
we are quite pleased with our own righteousness, wisdom, and
virtue; we address ourselves in the most flattering terms, and
seem only less than demigods. But should we once begin to
raise our thoughts to God, and reflect what kind of Being he
is, and how absolute the perfection of that righteousness, and
wisdom, and virtue, to which, as a standard, we are bound to be
conformed, what formerly delighted us by its false show of righteousness will become polluted with the greatest iniquity; what
strangely imposed upon us under the name of wisdom will
disgust by its extreme folly; and what presented the appearance
of virtuous energy will be condemned as the most miserable
impotence. So far are those qualities in us, which seem most
perfect, from corresponding to the divine purity.

3. Hence that dread and amazement with which as Scripture
uniformly relates, holy men were struck and overwhelmed
whenever they beheld the presence of God. When we see those
who previously stood firm and secure so quaking with terror,
that the fear of death takes hold of them, nay, they are, in a

manner, swallowed up and annihilated, the inference to be drawn is that men are never duly touched and impressed with a conviction of their insignificance, until they have contrasted themselves with the majesty of God. Frequent examples of this consternation occur both in the Book of Judges and the Prophetical Writings (Judg 13:22; Isa 6:5; Ezek 1:28; 3:14; Job 9:4, &c.; Gen 17:27; 1 Kings 19:13); so much so, that it was a common expression among the people of God, "We shall die, for we have seen the Lord." Hence the Book of Job, also, in humbling men under a conviction of their folly, feebleness, and pollution, always derives its chief argument from descriptions of the Divine wisdom, virtue, and purity. Nor without cause: for we see Abraham the readier to acknowledge himself but dust and ashes the nearer he approaches to behold the glory of the Lord, and Elijah unable to wait with unveiled face for His approach; so dreadful is the sight. And what can man do, man who is but rottenness and a worm, when even the Cherubim themselves must veil their faces in very terror? To this, undoubtedly, the Prophet Isaiah refers, when he says (Isa 24:23), "The moon shall be confounded, and the sun ashamed, when the Lord of Hosts shall reign;" *i.e.*, when he shall exhibit his refulgence, and give a nearer view of it, the brightest objects will, in comparison, be covered with darkness.

But though the knowledge of God and the knowledge of ourselves are bound together by a mutual tie, due arrangement requires that we treat of the former in the first place, and then descend to the latter.

BOOK 3, CHAPTER 6

1. We have said that the object of regeneration is to bring the life of believers into concord and harmony with the righteousness of God, and so confirm the adoption by which they have been received as sons. But although the law comprehends within it that new life by which the image of God is restored in us, yet, as our sluggishness stands greatly in need both of helps and incentives it will be useful to collect out of Scripture a true account of this

reformations lest any who have a heartfelt desire of repentance should in their zeal go astray. . . .

2. The Scripture system of which we speak aims chiefly at two objects. The former is, that the love of righteousness, to which we are by no means naturally inclined, may be instilled and implanted into our minds. The latter is (see chap. 7), to prescribe a rule which will prevent us while in the pursuit of righteousness from going astray. It has numerous admirable methods of recommending righteousness. Many have been already pointed out in different parts of this work; but we shall here also briefly advert to some of them. With what better foundation can it begin than by reminding us that we must be holy, because "God is holy?" (Lev 19:1; 1 Pet 1:16). For when we were scattered abroad like lost sheep, wandering through the labyrinth of this world, he brought us back again to his own fold. When mention is made of our union with God, let us remember that holiness must be the bond; not that by the merit of holiness we come into communion with him (we ought rather first to cleave to him, in order that, pervaded with his holiness, we may follow whither he calls), but because it greatly concerns his glory not to have any fellowship with wickedness and impurity. Wherefore he tells us that this is the end of our calling, the end to which we ought ever to have respect, if we would answer the call of God. For to what end were we rescued from the iniquity and pollution of the world into which we were plunged, if we allow ourselves, during our whole lives, to wallow in them? Besides, we are at the same time admonished, that if we would be regarded as the Lord's people, we must inhabit the holy city Jerusalem (Isaiah rev. 8, *et alibi*); which, as he hath consecrated it to himself, it were impious for its inhabitants to profane by impurity. Hence the expressions, "Who shall abide in thy tabernacle? Who shall dwell in thy holy hill? He that walketh uprightly, and worketh righteousness," (Pss 15:1, 2; 24:3, 4); for the sanctuary in which he dwells certainly ought not to be like an unclean stall.

3. The better to arouse us, it exhibits God the Father, who, as he hath reconciled us to himself in his Anointed, has impressed his image upon us, to which he would have us to be conformed (Rom 5:4). Come, then, and let them show me a more excellent system among philosophers, who think that they only have a moral philosophy duly and orderly arranged. They, when they would give excellent exhortations to virtue, can only tell us to live agreeably to nature. Scripture derives its exhortations from the true source, when it not only enjoins us to regulate our lives with a view to God its author to whom it belongs; but after showing us that we have degenerated from our true origin—viz. the law of our Creator, adds, that Christ, through whom we have returned to favour with God, is set before us as a model, the image of which our lives should express. What do you require more effectual than this? Nay, what do you require beyond this? If the Lord adopts us for his sons on the condition that our life be a representation of Christ, the bond of our adoption,—then, unless we dedicate and devote ourselves to righteousness, we not only, with the utmost perfidy, revolt from our Creator, but also abjure the Saviour himself. Then, from an enumeration of all the blessings of God, and each part of our salvation, it finds materials for exhortation. Ever since God exhibited himself to us as a Father, we must be convicted of extreme ingratitude if we do not in turn exhibit ourselves as his sons. Ever since Christ purified us by the laver of his blood, and communicated this purification by baptism, it would ill become us to be defiled with new pollution. Ever since he ingrafted us into his body, we, who are his members, should anxiously beware of contracting any stain or taint. Ever since he who is our head ascended to heaven, it is befitting in us to withdraw our affections from the earth, and with our whole soul aspire to heaven. Ever since the Holy Spirit dedicated us as temples to the Lord, we should make it our endeavour to show forth the glory of God, and guard against being profaned by the defilement of sin. Ever since our soul and body were destined to heavenly incorruptibility and an unfading crown, we should earnestly

strive to keep them pure and uncorrupted against the day of the Lord. These, I say, are the surest foundations of a well-regulated life, and you will search in vain for any thing resembling them among philosophers, who, in their commendation of virtue, never rise higher than the natural dignity of man.[2]

A Study Guide for *Institutes of the Christian Religion*

1. Do you think of yourself as belonging to God? If so, how does it affect your thoughts and actions? If not, how might adopting this mind-set change your life?

2. Calvin describes those who do not surrender to God as restless. Why? How have you experienced this restlessness?

3. Calvin lists three main ways we can know God: ourselves, since we are made in God's image; the universe God created; and Scripture. Which has been most instrumental for you? What are some of the insights you have gleaned?

4. How does it help you to think of Christ as prophet, priest, and king? Which understanding of Christ are you most comfortable with? Why?

5. Some of the most controversial parts of *Institutes* are Calvin's teachings about predestination. What is Calvin's rationale for why some people must be saved and others must be damned? Do you agree? Why or why not?

6. Why is our conduct so important to Calvin? What do you consider his most compelling reason for seeking to be holy?

7. Why does God call us to self-denial? In what ways have you practiced self-denial?

8. Part of surrendering, or resigning ourselves to the Lord, is meditating on his goodness and justness even in terrible

circumstances. When have you been able to do this? What did it teach you?

9. Calvin writes that God afflicts us with terrible things that we are to bear as crosses in order to remain humble, obedient, and hopeful. Where do you see this idea expressed in today's world? Do you agree with Calvin? Why or why not?

10. How can we love and appreciate the blessings and beauty of this earth while still practicing moderation and restraint? How have you been successful at living in moderation? In what areas have you struggled?

11. What were your thoughts about Calvin before you read this work? How has *Institutes* affected your understanding of what it means to be a Christian?

The Interior Castle

ST. TERESA OF ÁVILA

I thought of the soul as resembling a castle, formed of a single diamond or a very transparent crystal, and containing many rooms, just as in heaven there are many mansions. If we reflect, sisters, we shall see that the soul of the just man is but a paradise, in which, God tells us, He takes His delight. What, do you imagine, must that dwelling be in which a King so mighty, so wise, and so pure, containing in Himself all good, can delight to rest? Nothing can be compared to the great beauty and capabilities of a soul; however keen our intellects may be, they are as unable to comprehend them as to comprehend God, for, as He has told us, He created us in His own image and likeness.

Carmelite nun and reformer Teresa of Ávila describes her vision from God of a crystal globe in the shape of a castle with seven mansions, each of which represents a stage in our faith journey toward union with God.

TERESA DE CEPEDA DE AHUMADA was born in Ávila, Spain, in 1515. She became a Carmelite nun at the age of twenty. After some years of struggle with prayer, she started to receive supernatural visions. Inspired by her visions, she became a reformer within the Carmelite order, founding the Discalced Carmelite Sisters with the goal of emphasizing poverty and enforcing a stricter rule. She later enlisted John of the Cross to implement similar reforms within the Carmelite monasteries. Through her reforms, Teresa's ideas about prayer spread and her spiritual director guided her to write several books, including her autobiography and *The Interior Castle,* in order to teach others about prayer.

Teresa begins *The Interior Castle* by describing the vision that inspired the book. She envisioned the soul like a beautiful castle made of a diamond or crystal with many rooms, at the center of which God resides. Through prayer and meditation and God's grace we can enter into the "castle" and proceed all the way to this center, where we can experience union with God. Teresa describes each of the castle's dwelling places in great symbolic detail. Some souls remain out in the courtyard, not knowing or caring to enter the beautiful castle, but others are bid by God to rise. These who first enter "are still very worldly, yet have some desire to do right, and at times, though rarely, commend themselves to God's care. They think about their souls every now and then; although very busy, they pray a few times a month, with minds generally filled with a thousand other matters, for where their treasure is, there is their heart also."[1] Once our infrequent prayers and meditations have gotten us into this first room, we meditate on Christ's humility and our lack thereof, since something black looks even blacker placed against something white and vice versa. While in this first stage of prayer, we encounter devils in the form of thoughts such as worry about failure, or conversely, concern about becoming too virtuous or fear that even beginning such a path would be presumptuous. At first, our eyes are too crusted over with sin and the blackness and creatures from the outside to see anything but dimly. And as those in this first room are still preoccupied with worldly things such as riches or often fall prey to criticizing the holiness of others, they may never proceed.

But if we proceed through the castle to the second dwelling place, our eyes open more and we can better see the light the castle is bathed in. We also suffer more since as our senses become more attuned to the things of God, we can better understand what we are missing and how far we still have to go. At this stage, too, we are attacked by devils and demons in the form of reminders of earthly pleasures and the esteem that we enjoy in the world. We can help ourselves by associating with those who lead spiritual lives and have advanced further. Above all, Teresa advises that we seek to conform our will to God's. If we proceed to the third castle, which is characterized by spiritual aridity, and have not yet succeeded in conforming our will to God's, the answer is humility, which she refers to as "the ointment for our wounds."[2] A spiritual director can also help us greatly in overcoming our own will.

Generally, Teresa writes, a soul must spend a great deal of time in the first three dwelling places before reaching the fourth, although there is no fixed rule. God quietly and lovingly calls us inward, or recollects us, to this fourth dwelling place. Although there are some areas in which we can make progress, such as prayer, penance, and good works, the prayer of recollection comes when God wishes to grant it. We cannot induce it. Instead, she advises that "We should rather abandon our souls into the hands of God, leaving Him to do as He chooses with us, as far as possible forgetting all self-interest and resigning ourselves entirely to His will."[3] The fourth dwelling place is where God gives us what Teresa terms "consolations." She likens these feelings of joy and delight to water flowing into a basin that increases itself in proportion to the water. To receive such consolations we must make no efforts to acquire them since that would imply a lack of humility. She advises us that "to make rapid progress and to reach the mansions we wish to enter, it is not so essential to *think* much as to *love* much: therefore you must practise whatever most excites you to this. Perhaps we do not know what love is, nor does this greatly surprise me. Love does not consist in great sweetness of devotion, but in a fervent determination to strive to please God in all things."[4]

In describing the fifth through seventh dwelling places, Teresa starts to speak of union with God, and her tone changes from one of extreme humility, even reluctance, to one of exuberance and delight. The fifth stage is almost free of poisonous thoughts. All of our work of prayer, penance, good works, etc., up to this point can be compared to a caterpillar assiduously creating his cocoon, the house he will die in before being reborn as a butterfly. Once our cocoon is complete, we, too, emerge from our cocoons reborn, returning to the world after having experienced a brief union with God. Once reborn we experience great peace but also severe sorrows since we cannot return to the world without feeling a great

Teresa is an absolute master of the spiritual life and possesses an amazing depth and richness of spiritual theology. . . . You can put what she says to the test.

—Dallas Willard

disconnect and sorrow at its state. In the sixth dwelling place, then, the soul wishes for nothing more than to experience this union again. Trials come fast and furious now, from the ridicule and accusations of self-righteousness from friends to severe illness. But also come words from the Lord, which are characterized by their power and authority and the peace and interior delight they leave in their wake. The soul also experiences rapture, which Teresa describes as God carrying off the soul and showing it little parts of the kingdom it has gained by being united with God. But torment of the soul comes, too, which Teresa compares to what souls in purgatory must feel. All of this is preparation for the seventh castle or dwelling place, spiritual marriage. Until this point the union Teresa describes has always been brief and finite, but spiritual marriage is a joining that cannot be separated. After such a marriage, the soul has an even greater fear of offending God and a stronger desire to serve. The passions have finally been conquered, and the soul may dwell here in peace, even as the body is continually subjected to war. But the end result is never to be withdrawal from the world, for Teresa tells us that the reason for prayer and the purpose of spiritual marriage is always good works. Through these works we show God our love.

Why *The Interior Castle* Is Essential

Teresa's *The Interior Castle* has been considered a masterpiece of teaching on prayer. Editorial board member Richard J. Foster refers to it as "one of the finest books on prayer in the Christian tradition." One of her most important insights is that we can make progress in the spiritual life. There is an orderly progression, a reliable sequence to the life of the spirit and as we go forward and grow more consistent in our prayer, temptations lose their grip on us. Teresa's work has great practical application. It can show us where we are on our journey and how we can hope to progress forward, and even help us to assist others in their spiritual journeys. The book contains, for example, a most helpful description of how to discern God's voice from that of the devil or our imagination. It is also reassuring to note that even, and perhaps especially, those who have progressed well into the castle suffer trials and spiritual dryness. Such difficulties can be seen as part of our spiritual progress, rather than as a sign that we have lost all hope of continuing in our journey.

But perhaps Teresa's most important legacy is that she teaches us the value of the soul. The metaphor from her vision, the diamond castle, shows us how beautiful our soul is, what care and attention it deserves, and most important, how beloved it is to God. Throughout Teresa reminds us how eager God is to communicate with us. "So desirous is He that we should seek Him and enjoy His company, that in one way or another He never ceases calling us to Him," she writes.[5] We are often so accustomed to thinking of the evil within ourselves that we can forget how beautiful we are to God. Reading her descriptions of a God who seeks with such love awakens an answering longing within us.

These evocative images are another of Teresa's great gifts for our spiritual formation. In addition to her butterfly analogy, she describes the soul in a state of grace as "like a well of limpid water, from which flow only streams of clearest crystal. Its works are pleasing both to God and man, rising from the River of Life, beside which it is rooted like a tree. Otherwise it would produce neither leaves nor fruit, for the waters of grace nourish it, keep it from withering from drought, and cause it to bring forth good fruit. But the soul by sinning withdraws from this stream of life, and growing beside a black and fetid pool, can produce nothing but disgusting and unwholesome fruit."[6] And who could fail to be moved by her image of God recollecting us to the castle: "The King, Who holds His court within it, sees their good will, and out of His great mercy desires them to return to Him. Like a good Shepherd, He plays so sweetly on His pipe, that although scarcely hearing it they recognize His call and no longer wander, but return, like lost sheep, to the mansions. So strong is this Pastor's power over His flock, that they abandon the worldly cares which misled them and re-enter the castle."[7] Such images offer us a new window of understanding into the spiritual life.

It is hard to think of a better description of union with Christ and with God than Teresa's description of what we experience in the fifth through seventh dwelling places. She inspires us to believe that such union is possible on earth and describes as much as is possible the peace of our soul resting with God while at the same time remaining active and even at war within the world. For in the end, Teresa reminds us that this contemplative focus does not give us permission to withdraw from the world. Instead, she leads us to the discipline of service. All our interior progress has the aim of kindling within us a desire to serve the Lord, preparing us for doing good works in the world as a grateful response to God's great love.

How to Read *The Interior Castle*

Despite the humility Teresa professes, her book expresses a knowledge of God and union that is humbling, even intimidating, to the reader. Yet her message is that we can indeed make progress in the spiritual life, and moreover that God is longing for us, calling us, waiting to love us and be our truest friend. Instead of feeling intimidated by her level of spiritual mastery, we can read Teresa's book as a response to this call, as a way to learn how to meet God to the best of our abilities.

Dallas Willard offers specific instructions for reading, suggesting approaching it "as if you were mining for treasure—which you are."[8] First, he suggests reading it through nonstop, pushing through to the end to perceive the overall view. Mark themes and sections as you proceed, and upon finishing, make an outline of the entire book's progression. Next, read it through slowly, marking all the sections to which you want to return for further study. Finally, return to these passages as your heart calls you for meditative reading and contemplation.

The Interior Castle

THE FIRST MANSIONS

1. While I was begging our Lord to-day to speak for me, since I knew not what to say nor how to commence this work which obedience has laid upon me, an idea occurred to me which I will explain, and which will serve as a foundation for that I am about to write.

2. I thought of the soul as resembling a castle, formed of a single diamond or a very transparent crystal, and containing many rooms, just as in heaven there are many mansions. If we reflect, sisters, we shall see that the soul of the just man is but a paradise, in which, God tells us, He takes His delight. What, do you imagine, must that dwelling be in which a King so mighty, so wise, and so pure, containing in Himself all good, can delight to rest? Nothing can be compared to the great beauty and capabilities of a soul; however keen our intellects may be, they are as unable to comprehend them as to comprehend God, for, as He has told us, He created us in His own image and likeness.

3. As this is so, we need not tire ourselves by trying to realize all the beauty of this castle, although, being His creature, there is all the difference between the soul and God that there is between the creature and the Creator; the fact that it is made in God's image teaches us how great are its dignity and loveliness. It is no small misfortune and disgrace that, through our own fault, we neither understand our nature nor our origin. Would it not be gross ignorance, my daughters, if, when a man was questioned about his name, or country, or parents, he could not answer? Stupid as this would be, it is unspeakably more foolish to care to learn nothing of our nature except that we possess

bodies, and only to realize vaguely that we have souls, because people say so and it is a doctrine of faith. Rarely do we reflect upon what gifts our souls may possess, Who dwells within them, or how extremely precious they are. Therefore we do little to preserve their beauty; all our care is concentrated on our bodies, which are but the coarse setting of the diamond, or the outer walls of the castle.

4. Let us imagine, as I said, that there are many rooms in this castle, of which some are above, some below, others at the side; in the centre, in the very midst of them all, is the principal chamber in which God and the soul hold their most secret intercourse. Think over this comparison very carefully; God grant it may enlighten you about the different kinds of graces He is pleased to bestow upon the soul. No one can know all about them, much less a person so ignorant as I am. The knowledge that such things are possible will console you greatly should our Lord ever grant you any of these favours; people themselves deprived of them can then at least praise Him for His great goodness in bestowing them on others. The thought of heaven and the happiness of the saints does us no harm, but cheers and urges us to win this joy for ourselves, nor will it injure us to know that during this exile God can communicate Himself to us loathsome worms; it will rather make us love Him for such immense goodness and infinite mercy. . . .

EFFECTS OF UNION

1. You may imagine that there is no more left to be described of the contents of this mansion, but a great deal remains to be told, for as I said, it contains favours of various degrees. I think there is nothing to add about the prayer of union, but when the soul on which God bestows this grace disposes itself for their reception, I could tell you much about the marvels our Lord works in it. I will describe some of them in my own way, also the state in which they leave the soul, and will use a suitable comparison to elucidate the matter, explaining that though

we can take no active part in this work of God within us, yet we may do much to prepare ourselves to receive this grace. You have heard how wonderfully silk is made—in a way such as God alone could plan—how it all comes from an egg resembling a tiny pepper-corn. Not having seen it myself, I only know of it by hearsay, so if the facts are inaccurate the fault will not be mine. When, in the warm weather, the mulberry trees come into leaf, the little egg which was lifeless before its food was ready, begins to live. The caterpillar nourishes itself upon the mulberry leaves until, when it has grown large, people place near it small twigs upon which, of its own accord, it spins silk from its tiny mouth until it has made a narrow little cocoon in

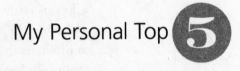

My Personal Top 5

DALLAS WILLARD

I cannot be very precise about the effect, but in general these all worked toward giving me a vivid sense of the reality of God with me and the importance of holiness and obedience to Jesus Christ as the foundation of life and ministry.

1 *Deeper Experiences of Famous Christians*, J. Gilchrist Lawson

2 *The Imitation of Christ*, Thomas à Kempis

3 *Autobiography*, Charles Finney

4 *The Writings of John Wesley*

5 *The Kingdom of God*, John Bright

DALLAS WILLARD is a professor in the School of Philosophy at the University of Southern California, an ordained minister, and the author of several books, including *The Divine Conspiracy*.

which it buries itself. Then this large and ugly worm leaves the cocoon as a lovely little white butterfly.

2. If we had not seen this but had only heard of it as an old legend, who could believe it? Could we persuade ourselves that insects so utterly without the use of reason as a silkworm or a bee would work with such industry and skill in our service that the poor little silkworm loses its life over the task? This would suffice for a short meditation, sisters, without my adding more, for you may learn from it the wonders and the wisdom of God. How if we knew the properties of all things? It is most profitable to ponder over the grandeurs of creation and to exult in being the brides of such a wise and mighty King.

3. Let us return to our subject. The silkworm symbolizes the soul which begins to live when, kindled by the Holy Spirit, it commences using the ordinary aids given by God to all, and applies the remedies left by Him in His Church, such as regular confession, religious books, and sermons; these are the cure for a soul dead in its negligence and sins and liable to fall into temptation. Then it comes to life and continues nourishing itself on this food and on devout meditation until it has attained full vigour, which is the essential point, for I attach no importance to the rest. When the silkworm is full-grown as I told you in the first part of this chapter, it begins to spin silk and to build the house wherein it must die. By this house, when speaking of the soul, I mean Christ. I think I read or heard somewhere, either that our life is hid in Christ, or in God (which means the same thing) or that Christ is our life. It makes little difference to my meaning which of these quotations is correct.

4. This shows, my daughters, how much, by God's grace, we can do, by preparing this home for ourselves, towards making Him our dwelling-place as He is in the prayer of union. You will suppose that I mean we can take away from or add something to God when I say that He is our home, and that we can make this

home and dwell in it by our own power. Indeed we can: though we can neither deprive God of anything nor add aught to Him, yet we can take away from and add to ourselves, like the silkworms. The little we can do will hardly have been accomplished when this insignificant work of ours, which amounts to nothing at all, will be united by God to His greatness and thus enhanced with such immense value that our Lord Himself will be the reward of our toil. Although He has had the greatest share in it, He will join our trifling pains to the bitter sufferings He endured for us and make them one.

5. Forward then, my daughters! hasten over your work and build the little cocoon. Let us renounce self-love and self-will, care for nothing earthly, do penance, pray, mortify ourselves, be obedient, and perform all the other good works of which you know. Act up to your light; you have been taught your duties. Die! die as the silkworm does when it has fulfilled the office of its creation, and you will see God and be immersed in His greatness, as the little silkworm is enveloped in its cocoon. Understand that when I say 'you will see God,' I mean in the manner described, in which He manifests Himself in this kind of union.

6. Now let us see what becomes of the 'silkworm,' for all I have been saying leads to this. As soon as, by means of this prayer, the soul has become entirely dead to the world, it comes forth like a lovely little white butterfly! Oh, how great God is! How beautiful is the soul after having been immersed in God's grandeur and united closely to Him for but a short time! Indeed, I do not think it is ever as long as half an hour. Truly, the spirit does not recognize itself, being as different from what it was as is the white butterfly from the repulsive caterpillar. It does not know how it can have merited so great a good, or rather, whence this grace came which it well knows it merits not. The soul desires to praise our Lord God and longs to sacrifice itself and die a thousand deaths for Him. It feels an unconquerable desire for

great crosses and would like to perform the most severe penances; it sighs for solitude and would have all men know God, while it is bitterly grieved at seeing them offend Him. These matters will be described more fully in the next mansion; there they are of the same nature, yet in a more advanced state the effects are far stronger, because, as I told you, if; after the soul has received these favours, it strives to make still farther progress, it will experience great things. Oh, to see the restlessness of this charming little butterfly, although never in its life has it been more tranquil and at peace! May God be praised! It knows not where to stay nor take its rest; everything on earth disgusts it after what it has experienced, particularly when God has often given it this wine which leaves fresh graces behind it at every draught.

7. It despises the work it did while yet a caterpillar—the slow weaving of its cocoon thread by thread—its wings have grown and it can fly; could it be content to crawl? All that it can do for God seems nothing to the soul compared with its desire. It no longer wonders at what the saints bore for Him, knowing by experience how our Lord aids and transforms the soul until it no longer seems the same in character and appearance. Formerly it feared penance, now it is strong: it wanted courage to forsake relations, friends, or possessions: neither its actions, its resolutions, nor separation from those it loved could detach the soul, but rather seemed to increase its fondness. Now it finds even their rightful claims a burden, fearing contact with them lest it should offend God. It wearies of everything, realizing that no true rest can be found in creatures.[9]

A Study Guide for *The Interior Castle*

1. Teresa writes that many of us forget the beauty of the soul and focus entirely on the beauty of the body. Does it change your outlook to see the soul as something that

requires tending and care just as your physical body does? If so, how?

2. Where do you think you are in your spiritual journey in relation to the dwelling places or castles Teresa describes?

3. In the second dwelling place, Teresa tells us that hearing God's voice can be more painful than not hearing it because, "So sweet is His voice, that the poor soul is disconsolate at being unable to follow his bidding at once, and therefore, as I said, suffers more than if it could not hear him."[10] Why would this hearing of God's voice be so hard?

4. In the second dwelling place, God speaks to us not directly but through the words of others, sermons, books, or even sickness and troubles. What are some ways God has spoken to you through these mediums?

5. Teresa advises that we associate with others who live the spiritual life, particularly those who have progressed further than we have. What value have you found in such associations?

6. Teresa directs us not to seek many of the consolations we will find in the various dwelling places, but to seek instead to abandon ourselves to God. Why is seeking after particular spiritual gifts unhelpful and even dangerous? How do you seek in your life to find the balance between the work you do in actively seeking God and the passivity of abandoning yourself to God?

7. How do you respond to the image of preparing a cocoon in which your soul can die to this world and be reborn? What have you done to prepare such a cocoon?

8. The further a soul progresses, the more terrible the idea of offending God becomes to it. Even in the seventh dwelling place, Teresa writes, the soul goes about with greater fear than before. Why?

9. Teresa tells us that trials are meant to fortify our weaknesses, so that we might be able to imitate Christ in his sufferings. How have trials in your life benefited you by bringing you closer to God?

10. In a work as focused on the interior life as this one, does it surprise you that Teresa ends by saying all this interior work is meant to result in good works in the world? Do you find yourself more inclined to Mary's worship or Martha's works? How have you sought to balance the two in your life?

Dark Night of the Soul

ST. JOHN OF THE CROSS

> *When they are going about these spiritual exercises with the greatest delight and pleasure, and when they believe that the sun of Divine favour is shining most brightly upon them, God turns all this light of theirs into darkness, and shuts against them the door and the source of the sweet spiritual water which they were tasting in God whensoever and for as long as they desired.*

J OHN OF THE CROSS was born in Fontiveros, Spain, in the sixteenth century and became a Carmelite monk as a young man. Shortly thereafter, he met Teresa of Ávila and joined her in her work reforming the Carmelite orders. She was quick to recognize the young monk's spiritual mastery, and despite being twenty-seven years her junior, John became her confessor and spiritual director. The pair's reformation work was not always popular, and at one time John was imprisoned and beaten for nine months by Carmelite superiors. He eventually escaped through a window in his tiny cell, but the suffering he experienced influenced many of his writings. John is perhaps best known for his poetry, *Spiritual Canticle,* which he wrote while imprisoned, and *Dark Night of the Soul. Dark Night of the Soul* is first and foremost a poem, but John also wrote a commentary of the same name, in which he explains his poem line by line. John's work and his concept of the dark night have become a integral part of how we understand our spiritual journeys.

John explains that the dark night happens when God moves us from a state of being spiritual beginners to a state of what he calls

Dark Night of the Soul is sixteenth-century Spanish Carmelite priest John of the Cross's poem and commentary about the journey of purification on which God takes us from times of spiritual dryness to an understanding of divine union.

progressives. He compares God to a mother who, after holding and nursing her baby for a time, puts her child down so he or she can walk. Spiritual beginners have several negative qualities that the dark night purges from us, namely pride, envy, and a lack of understanding of our sinfulness and thus a tendency to fall into despair when we fall prey to sin. Passing through the dark night allows us to progress spiritually and view others as better than ourselves, feel that we can never do enough for God, and become always willing to be taught.

John describes two dark nights that believers can go through—a dark night of the senses and a dark night of the spirit. The former night is common to many believers, but the second is much more rare. First he deals with the night of the senses, in which a person who has found constant consolation and pleasure in spiritual things such as meditation suddenly finds only dryness, despair, and bitterness, feeling that God has abandoned him or her. John explains that God has seen that this person has grown enough to progress to the next level, so God takes away these spiritual swaddling clothes so that the person can walk on his or her own. We can distinguish a God-caused dark night from any other kind of melancholy because when experiencing God's dark night, we can find no consolation in any created thing and are terribly upset because we can no longer find sweetness in the things of God. The reason for such a feeling is that what we used to experience with our senses is now transferred to our spirits. Because we are so used to the pleasures of the senses, we feel this lack greatly, even though the pleasures of the spirit are so much greater.

But eventually, as we find within us a longing to be in solitude and quiet, we can return to seeking God, albeit in a different way. John sees this night as God's way of drawing us from meditation, the acts and exercises of spiritual practice, to contemplation, a gift of God's grace that we cannot practice or seek. We are to react to this dark night by persevering, avoiding anxiety, and thinking of God with peaceful attentiveness. Perhaps most of all, we are not to make an effort or yearn for experiences of God as we had them before, but just to relax in the peace and ease of contemplation. We should view this night as a happy one, with benefits that include knowledge of oneself and one's misery and also a recognition of God's greatness, drawing us to treat God with more respect and courtesy. This knowledge of our own lowliness also cultivates a love for others, since we can no longer pretend at our own superiority, and a sense of obedience, since we realize how much we still have to learn. Most important, perhaps, we learn to seek God for God's sake alone and not for any pleasures or consolations we might receive. Once we have experienced this dark night, we can better receive wisdom from God. John also notes that God gives each a different experience of the night, as befits each one's differing level; for those who are weaker, he gives shorter periods of dryness and occasional tastes of the senses so that they will not completely lose hope. Those who are stronger can expect longer periods of dryness.

Next John turns to the second night, the dark night of the spirit, or the night of contemplation. This night often comes some time after the first night. In the meantime the soul will likely have enjoyed great satisfaction and delight in the things of God, now being able to experience the joys of contemplation "without the labour of meditation."[1] Periods of dryness may continually occur, however. Although they have undergone the first purging, these "proficients," as he refers to them, still cannot receive "very strong or very intense or very spiritual" communications. Those ready for the second night still experience the stain of some of the sins of which they were purged and can fall prey to false visions and prophecies, causing them to be less humble before God. Thus a second purging is necessary, in which both the sensual and spiritual parts of the soul must be completely purged, "since the one is never truly purged without the other, the purgation of sense becoming effective when that of the spirit has fairly begun."[2] For even these proficients are as little children before God and must undergo this second purging in order to experience true divine union, in which even our wills become divine.

This second night is really "the inflowing of God into the soul,"[3] and the reason we experience it as darkness is because God is so

> He is a man whose home is in heaven, full of God. I can assure you that since we went down there, I have found no one like him in all Castile. . . . The sisters should open their souls to him—they will see how much good it does them.
>
> —Teresa of Ávila

much greater than our souls and because the human soul is so impure in contrast. To make a human soul new, to rid it of all the habits and affections it has gained during life, is a painful process. As John writes, "The Divine assails the soul in order to renew it and thus to make it Divine; and, stripping it of the habitual affections and attachments of the old man, to which it is very closely united, knit together and conformed, destroys and consumes its spiritual substance, and absorbs it in deep and profound darkness."[4] Indeed, the soul feels abandoned by God and by friends. John mentions and quotes from the biblical examples of Job, David, Jeremiah, and Jonah as those who have been brought low by God. This process goes on for years, and God only occasionally relieves the darkness with peace and a sense of friendship with God so that the sufferer can know the process is working. One of the most difficult aspects of the second night is that the sufferer feels that his or her prayers cannot pass through to God. Even when the soul longs for the peace formerly felt, he or she must remember that peace was not really peace, so tainted as it was by the soul's imperfections.

John compares the purgation to a log of wood in a fire, which is blackened and transformed by the fire but ultimately takes on some of the same qualities of the fire itself. He is careful to point out that any afflictions or sufferings felt do not come from God and God's fire itself but from the weaknesses and imperfections in us, the wood. As the purging process continues, we will be ever more aware of the imperfections still within because of their stark contrast to what has already been purged. John compares the process to purgatory in the afterlife, in which souls are physically cleansed with fire. In this life they are cleansed with love.

Next God kindles love within the person's soul, so that the person wishes to devote all his or her energy to God alone. Throughout the dark night the person has always yearned for God, but later in the process this love is "enkindled."

The darkness is a cloud between God and us that prevents our understanding, prevents our feeling God's presence, but God is with us regardless of whether we feel it or not. To experience God's presence, divine union, we must take untraveled and unfamiliar paths to reach a place we have not been before. And the closer we get to God, the blacker is the darkness, since God's light is so great that it makes all around it look darker. This journey of ours culminates in the infusion of God's secret wisdom into our souls. The Holy Spirit does the work of infusion and not even the soul can understand it. It is beyond our ability to describe it.

This process of divine union is described as a ladder of ten steps of first, progressively seeking and yearning for God; next, touching God with increasing boldness and holding fast to God; and finally, becoming wholly assimilated by God. It is only at this last step that we will understand all, that the veil of mystery will be entirely lifted.

John's manuscript is unfinished, for reasons that are unknown.

Why *Dark Night of the Soul* Is Essential

Dark Night has been hugely influential in Christianity and still holds a unique place in devotional literature. Editorial board member James Catford of the British and Foreign Bible Society writes, "Even to receive a few pages of truth from this book and the Church will be set on fire with a renewed love of God. Ordering our passions, waiting on Christ and developing a 'white-hot burning love for God' are all essential for the Church to play its rightful role in our world. If the purpose of God in history is the formation of an all-inclusive community of loving persons with Jesus Christ at its center, then *Dark Night* will help make this a reality working from the core of our very beings."

Dark Night is most obviously helpful to anyone who is struggling with spiritual dryness. Like the beginners John writes about in Book 1, most have experienced at least for a time the joy and spiritual pleasures of connecting with God as a new believer. But this initial stage does not last forever. John's writings speak particularly to those long-term believers who have experienced ups and downs in their faith, are struggling with a feeling of God's absence, a lack of joy in all things spiritual, or even questioning their faith. Mother Teresa famously suffered a long period of darkness, in which she felt abandoned by God, after a long period in which she felt a strong union with Christ. For those walking through this kind of spiritual desert, John offers the sure knowledge that such spiritual aridity is a stage, an important part of our journeys. He also promises that it will be overcome, that it will lead to even greater union with God. Or, more precisely, it will lead to a greater understanding of our union with God, since John writes that we are all already connected with God; we just don't always realize it.

And this insight is perhaps the most powerful for our spiritual formation: God is always with us, whether we feel it or not. In fact, the dark night itself is "the inflowing of God" into our souls. Reading John's words leaves little doubt that John has experienced just this sort of inflowing. He is a man brimming with passion for his God, and this passion cannot help but inspire us to seek the same relationship, to call out for God to purge our souls of all that keeps us apart. At its heart, *Dark Night* is a call to both detachment, from all in our lives that distracts us from God, and submission, to the God who created and loves us.

How to Read *Dark Night of the Soul*

Dark Night of the Soul can be a difficult book. John almost takes it for granted that anyone reading his words will have a spiritual director. And even now, *Dark Night* is often recommended as a book to read with a spiritual director or advisor. But if you do not have such a person available, it may help to read it with a commentary or with *The Dark Night of the Soul: A Psychiatrist Explores the Connection Between Darkness and Spiritual Growth* by Gerald May, a modern take on John's ideas.

Dark Night of the Soul

PROLOGUE

In this book are first set down all the stanzas which are to
be expounded; afterwards, each of the stanzas is expounded
separately, being set down before its exposition; and then each
line is expounded separately and in turn, the line itself also
being set down before the exposition. In the first two stanzas
are expounded the effects of the two spiritual purgations: of the
sensual part of man and of the spiritual part. In the other six are
expounded various and wondrous effects of the spiritual illumination and union of love with God.

STANZAS OF THE SOUL

1. On a dark night, Kindled in love with yearnings—
     oh, happy chance!—
   I went forth without being observed, My house being now
     at rest.

2. In darkness and secure, By the secret ladder, disguised—
     oh, happy chance!—
   In darkness and in concealment, My house being now
     at rest.

3. In the happy night, In secret, when none saw me,
   Nor I beheld aught, Without light or guide, save that
     which burned in my heart.

4. This light guided me More surely than the light of noonday
   To the place where he (well I knew who!) was awaiting
     me—A place where none appeared.

5. Oh, night that guided me, Oh, night more lovely than the dawn,
   Oh, night that joined Beloved with lover, Lover transformed in the Beloved!

6. Upon my flowery breast, Kept wholly for himself alone,
   There he stayed sleeping, and I caressed him, And the fanning of the cedars made a breeze.

7. The breeze blew from the turret As I parted his locks;
   With his gentle hand he wounded my neck And caused all my senses to be suspended.

8. I remained, lost in oblivion; My face I reclined on the Beloved.
   All ceased and I abandoned myself, Leaving my cares forgotten among the lilies.

Begins the exposition of the stanzas which treat of the way and manner which the soul follows upon the road of the union of love with God.

Before we enter upon the exposition of these stanzas, it is well to understand here that the soul that utters them is now in the state of perfection, which is the union of love with God, having already passed through severe trials and straits, by means of spiritual exercise in the narrow way of eternal life whereof Our Saviour speaks in the Gospel, along which way the soul ordinarily passes in order to reach this high and happy union with God. Since this road (as the Lord Himself says likewise) is so strait, and since there are so few that enter by it (Matt 7:14), the soul considers it a great happiness and good chance to have passed along it to the said perfection of love, as it sings in this first stanza, calling this strait road with full propriety "dark night," as will be explained hereafter in the lines of the said stanza. The soul, then, rejoicing at having passed along this narrow road whence so many blessings have come to it, speaks after this manner.

BOOK I, CHAPTER 8: IN A DARK NIGHT

Wherein is expounded the first line of the first stanza, and a beginning is made of the explanation of this dark night.

1. This night, which, as we say, is contemplation, produces in spiritual persons two kinds of darkness or purgation, corresponding to the two parts of man's nature—namely, the sensual and the spiritual. And thus the one night or purgation will be sensual, wherein the soul is purged according to sense, which is subdued to the spirit; and the other is a night or purgation which is spiritual, wherein the soul is purged and stripped according to the spirit, and subdued and made ready for the

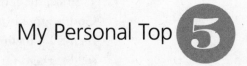

My Personal Top 5

JOHN WILSON

1 ***The Blue Flower***, Penelope Fitzgerald. Sadness and beauty intertwined with the strangeness Coleridge prized: a saying, in fiction, of what can't be spelled out (which is much of what matters most).

2 ***Hope Against Hope***, Nadezhda Mandelstam. Marriage (intimate, messy), the making of poetry, suffocating terror, Resurrection hope.

3 ***New and Collected Poems, 1931–2001***, Czeslaw Milosz. "We forget—I kept saying—that we are all children of the King."

4 ***The Lord of the Absurd***, Raymond Nogar, OP. We talk a lot about "the problem of evil," but deep down, it is the absurd that terrifies us. We need not fear. Christ is the Lord of the Absurd.

5 ***Memento Mori***, Muriel Spark. The Last Things point back to First Things and ahead to the life to come. Divine black comedy.

JOHN WILSON is the founding editor of *Books & Culture,* a bimonthly review.

union of love with God. The night of sense is common and comes to many: these are the beginners; and of this night we shall speak first. The night of the spirit is the portion of very few, and these are they that are already practised and proficient, of whom we shall treat hereafter.

2. The first purgation or night is bitter and terrible to sense, as we shall now show. The second bears no comparison with it, for it is horrible and awful to the spirit, as we shall show presently. Since the night of sense is first in order and comes first, we shall first of all say something about it briefly, since more is written of it, as of a thing that is more common; and we shall pass on to treat more fully of the spiritual night, since very little has been said of this, either in speech or in writing, and very little is known of it, even by experience.

3. Since, then, the conduct of these beginners upon the way of God is ignoble and has much to do with their love of self and their own inclinations, as has been explained above, God desires to lead them farther. He seeks to bring them out of that ignoble kind of love to a higher degree of love for Him, to free them from the ignoble exercises of sense and meditation (wherewith, as we have said, they go seeking God so unworthily and in so many ways that are unbefitting), and to lead them to a kind of spiritual exercise wherein they can commune with Him more abundantly and are freed more completely from imperfections. For they have now had practice for some time in the way of virtue and have persevered in meditation and prayer, whereby, through the sweetness and pleasure that they have found therein, they have lost their love of the things of the world and have gained some degree of spiritual strength in God; this has enabled them to some extent to refrain from creature desires, so that for God's sake they are now able to suffer a light burden and a little aridity without turning back to a time which they found more pleasant. When they are going about these spiritual exercises with the greatest delight and pleasure, and when they

believe that the sun of Divine favour is shining most brightly upon them, God turns all this light of theirs into darkness, and shuts against them the door and the source of the sweet spiritual water which they were tasting in God whensoever and for as long as they desired. (For, as they were weak and tender, there was no door closed to them, as Saint John says in the Apocalypse, 3:8). And thus He leaves them so completely in the dark that they know not whither to go with their sensible imagination and meditation; for they cannot advance a step in meditation, as they were wont to do afore time, their inward senses being submerged in this night, and left with such dryness that not only do they experience no pleasure and consolation in the spiritual things and good exercises wherein they were wont to find their delights and pleasures, but instead, on the contrary, they find insipidity and bitterness in the said things. For, as I have said, God now sees that they have grown a little, and are becoming strong enough to lay aside their swaddling clothes and be taken from the gentle breast; so He sets them down from His arms and teaches them to walk on their own feet; which they feel to be very strange, for everything seems to be going wrong with them.

BOOK 2, CHAPTER 5: ON A DARK NIGHT

Sets down the first line and begins to explain how this dark contemplation is not only night for the soul but is also grief and torment.

1. This dark night is an inflowing of God into the soul, which purges it from its ignorances and imperfections, habitual natural and spiritual, and which is called by contemplatives infused contemplation, or mystical theology. Herein God secretly teaches the soul and instructs it in perfection of love without its doing anything, or understanding of what manner is this infused contemplation. Inasmuch as it is the loving wisdom of God, God produces striking effects in the soul for, by purging and illumining it, He prepares it for the union of love with God.

Wherefore the same loving wisdom that purges the blessed spirits and enlightens them is that which here purges the soul and illumines it.

2. But the question arises: Why is the Divine light (which as we say, illumines and purges the soul from its ignorances) here called by the soul a dark night? To this the answer is that for two reasons this Divine wisdom is not only night and darkness for the soul, but is likewise affliction and torment. The first is because of the height of Divine Wisdom, which transcends the talent of the soul, and in this way is darkness to it; the second, because of its vileness and impurity, in which respect it is painful and afflictive to it, and is also dark.

3. In order to prove the first point, we must here assume a certain doctrine of the philosopher, which says that, the clearer and more manifest are Divine things in themselves the darker and more hidden are they to the soul naturally; just as, the clearer is the light, the more it blinds and darkens the pupil of the owl, and, the more directly we look at the sun, the greater is the darkness which it causes in our visual faculty, overcoming and overwhelming it through its own weakness. In the same way, when this Divine light of contemplation assails the soul which is not yet wholly enlightened, it causes spiritual darkness in it; for not only does it overcome it, but likewise it overwhelms it and darkens the act of its natural intelligence. For this reason Saint Dionysius and other mystical theologians call this infused contemplation a ray of darkness—that is to say, for the soul that is not enlightened and purged—for the natural strength of the intellect is transcended and overwhelmed by its great supernatural light. Wherefore David likewise said: That near to God and round about Him are darkness and cloud; not that this is so in fact, but that it is so to our weak understanding, which is blinded and darkened by so vast a light, to which it cannot attain. For this cause the same David then explained himself, saying: 'Through the great splendour of His presence passed

clouds'—that is, between God and our understanding. And it is for this cause that, when God sends it out from Himself to the soul that is not yet transformed, this illumining ray of His secret wisdom causes thick darkness in the understanding.

4. And it is clear that this dark contemplation is in these its beginnings painful likewise to the soul; for, as this Divine infused contemplation has many excellences that are extremely good, and the soul that receives them, not being purged, has many miseries that are likewise extremely bad, hence it follows that, as two contraries cannot coexist in one subject—the soul—it must of necessity have pain and suffering, since it is the subject wherein these two contraries war against each other, working the one against the other, by reason of the purgation of the imperfections of the soul which comes to pass through this contemplation. This we shall prove inductively in the manner following.

5. In the first place, because the light and wisdom of this contemplation is most bright and pure, and the soul which it assails is dark and impure, it follows that the soul suffers great pain when it receives it in itself, just as, when the eyes are dimmed by humours, and become impure and weak, the assault made upon them by a bright light causes them pain. And when the soul suffers the direct assault of this Divine light, its pain, which results from its impurity, is immense; because, when this pure light assails the soul, in order to expel its impurity, the soul feels itself to be so impure and miserable that it believes God to be against it, and thinks that it has set itself up against God. This causes it sore grief and pain, because it now believes that God has cast it away: this was one of the greatest trials which Job felt when God sent him this experience, and he said: 'Why hast Thou set me contrary to Thee, so that I am grievous and burdensome to myself?' For, by means of this pure light, the soul now sees its impurity clearly (although darkly), and knows clearly that it is unworthy of God or of any creature. And what

gives it most pain is that it thinks that it will never be worthy and that its good things are all over for it. This is caused by the profound immersion of its spirit in the knowledge and realization of its evils and miseries; for this Divine and dark light now reveals them all to the eye, that it may see clearly how in its own strength it can never have aught else. In this sense we may understand that passage from David, which says: 'For iniquity Thou hast corrected man and hast made his soul to be undone and consumed: he wastes away as the spider.'

6. The second way in which the soul suffers pain is by reason of its weakness, natural, moral and spiritual; for, when this Divine contemplation assails the soul with a certain force, in order to strengthen it and subdue it, it suffers such pain in its weakness that it nearly swoons away. This is especially so at certain times when it is assailed with somewhat greater force; for sense and spirit, as if beneath some immense and dark load, are in such great pain and agony that the soul would find advantage and relief in death. This had been experienced by the prophet Job, when he said: 'I desire not that He should have intercourse with me in great strength, lest He oppress me with the weight of His greatness.'

7. Beneath the power of this oppression and weight the soul feels itself so far from being favoured that it thinks, and correctly so, that even that wherein it was wont to find some help has vanished with everything else, and that there is none who has pity upon it. To this effect Job says likewise: 'Have pity upon me, have pity upon me, at least ye my friends, because the hand of the Lord has touched me.' A thing of great wonder and pity is it that the soul's weakness and impurity should now be so great that, though the hand of God is of itself so light and gentle, the soul should now feel it to be so heavy and so contrary, though it neither weighs it down nor rests upon it, but only touches it,

and that mercifully, since He does this in order to grant the soul favours and not to chastise it.[5]

A Study Guide for *Dark Night of the Soul*

1. Which characteristics of spiritual beginners do you most relate to?

2. One of the marks of a spiritual beginner is believing all experiences of God are filled with sweetness and pleasure. Was or is this the case in your life?

3. John compares those going through the first dark night of the soul, the purgation of the senses, to the Israelites in the wilderness, who longed for the tastes of the food they ate in Egypt even though God provided them with heavenly manna. In what ways do you long for the inferior tastes of this world rather than the superior heavenly offerings?

4. Throughout, John compares God to a mother who, upon seeing that her child has progressed, realized that it is time for the child to walk and to eat adult food, and so she sets the child down and stops feeding him or her breast milk. What does this image teach us about our spiritual progress and about our relationship with God?

5. One of the benefits of going through the dark night is gaining a knowledge of oneself and one's misery. Why is that of spiritual benefit? How have you experienced this?

6. Why does God's touch, which John describes as light and gentle, in the second night of the soul feel so burdensome?

7. John writes that when one is going through the second night and longs for peace, one must remember that the

peace formerly felt was no kind of peace at all, tainted as it was with life's imperfections. Does such a thought comfort you? Why or why not?

8. Why are we to perceive the dark night as such a happy occasion? If you have experienced such a period or periods in your life, were you able to see it that way at the time? Now, with the benefit of hindsight? Why or why not?

9. What exactly is the darkness John describes?

Pensées

BLAISE PASCAL

Jesus Christ is the object of all things, the centre towards which all things tend. Whoever knows him knows the reason for everything.

A collection of intensely personal meditations on wide-ranging topics—from sin to human suffering—Blaise Pascal's *Pensées* is a comprehensive, passionate defense of the Christian faith.

THE FRENCH SCIENTIST, mathematician, and thinker Blaise Pascal (1623–1662) is perhaps best known for his contributions to math and science—his theorem of geometry, the invention of the mechanical adding machine, and the theory of probability, among others—but late in his life he had a powerful experience of the presence of God that led him to a Jansenist monastery, where he lived until his death eight years later. There he resumed his mathematical work and also wrote some religious works, including *Pensées,* his defense of the Christian faith. Always sickly, Pascal wrote when and what he could, a major reason for the fragmentary nature of the book, and died before he could finish it.

The purpose of *Pensées* is to bring people to God. Pascal seeks to establish the essential reasonableness of Christianity. One of his major themes is the fallen nature of humankind and the wretchedness of people without God. We are created in God's image, which makes us glorious, but sin has corrupted us. We are driven almost entirely by concupiscence, our desire for that which brings us pleasure. He paints a picture of the human condition as boredom, inconstancy, and anxiety. Uncomfortably aware of "the natural unhappiness of our feeble mortal condition,"[1] we seek to distract ourselves with various diversions such as sport or shows or even war.

More so than any other religion or philosophy, Pascal argues, Christianity recognizes our true state and offers a remedy.

As humans, we like to believe that we are ruled by reason, but the truth is that our imagination and senses affect us much more than we realize. We are affected by the way people look and sound; we judge people's competence and worth based on their trappings rather than what they actually say or do. Our purported use of reason, tainted as it is with imagination, actually prevents us from seeing ourselves as we truly are. Having made this point, Pascal presents his theory of the three levels of reality, that of the body, the mind, and the heart. Pascal's theory is that we must apply the appropriate senses and methods to different phenomena. For physical matters, we examine them best by our bodies or senses. Those people ruled by the body focus on materialism and physical appearance but cannot appreciate reason (intellect) and wisdom. In the next level we use our minds to analyze and apply reason, but if we are ruled by this level, we can become stymied by pride and cannot appreciate the wisdom and holiness of God. For supernatural or spiritual matters, we can trust only our hearts, the final level. Therefore, both the senses and reason are inadequate to fully comprehend the nature of God's truth. Only the heart can do this. If we are ruled by this highest order of reality, that of the heart, we orient our wills to God and are thus guided as to how to properly satisfy the needs of our bodies and our minds.

Once we see ourselves as we truly are, we can accept the ultimate solution to our dual nature of gloriousness and wretchedness, Jesus Christ, who shows us both God and our own darkness. Jesus Christ, who neither demonstrated material power or authority nor expected to be respected for his brilliance, shows us a different way to be, characterized not by outward trappings or analytical reasoning, but by holiness.

Why *Pensées* Is Essential

Even unfinished, *Pensées* still remains one of the most compelling and comprehensive Christian works of apologetics ever written. It is the most well-known of Pascal's several theological works. It is comprehensive and wide-ranging, addressing a dizzying array of issues of the theological life. As editorial board member Gayle Beebe writes, "Pascal's *Pensées* is so pivotal. It is at once an apologetic for Christian belief while giving you the basic thought forms to answer life's most enduring questions. Virtually any question I have ever faced or had myself is addressed in the book. I consider this book to be one of the great texts on our life with God, both for its intellectual acumen and its practical advice."

Pascal calls us to think about what we use to distract and divert ourselves from what he calls morbidity, thoughts about our state as humans. His pointed critique of the reasons why we are so often not content to sit quietly in our rooms, but must keep busy and entertained, feels even more stinging today, as we distract ourselves with more and more sophisticated methods of diversion.

Although Pascal's brilliant arguments present a compelling case for the reasonableness of Christianity, it is important to hear his caution that we cannot depend solely on reason. His theory of ordering still rings as true as it ever did, with its cautions about the limits of imagination and reason. We can easily see today those who are ruled by the body or the mind, rather than the heart. We can all think of those who seem to think of nothing but the way they look and what they have, or those who are so impressed by their own brilliance that they seem reluctant to admit to anyone else's authority. We can likely see at least traces of both of these characteristics in ourselves as well. It is critical that we give thought to the right ordering of our love for God, seeking to focus on submitting to God rather than to the needs of our bodies or even simply the reason of our minds. As Christians, our goals should be holiness and wisdom rather than material success or intellectual brilliance.

Finally, Pascal not only enlightens us as to our true state, a combination of God's image and that which is corrupted by sin, but he also points us clearly to the answer: Jesus. It is important to remain aware of our true state. When we think too highly of ourselves or others, we must remember the wretched part of our nature; and in turn when we find ourselves wondering if there is anything good

> Pascal's vision of Light, Life, and Love was highly ecstatic; an indescribable, incommunicable experience, which can only be suggested by his broken words of certitude and joy.
>
> —Evelyn Underhill (referencing "The Memorial" in *Pensées*)

about us, we must remember that we are created in God's image. Knowing these truths about ourselves, the only response is to submit to Jesus Christ.

How to Read *Pensées*

Written in fragments, deliberately nonlinear, and in the form of a dialogue, *Pensées* can present a challenge to the most experienced theological reader. Pascal's process was to write his thoughts and essays on long sheets of paper and later cut them up and organize them by subject, but because he died before completing the work, we will never know how exactly he envisioned the finished product. Although he did organize the first section of *Pensées,* the rest has been categorized by editors, and so the numbering and order varies from edition to edition.

Many will enjoy reading straight through the fragments, stopping and reflecting further when one is of particular interest. Others may prefer to read with a plan. If that is your preference, here is one strategy (the numbers correspond to the A. J. Krailsheimer translation published by Penguin): Start with fragment 12 for overarching purpose. Read 24, 44, and 135–137. Then read 308 to understand the three orders or levels of reality. Continue to 168–170 for the right use of reason. Then read 149 to see reason applied to the question of religious truth. Continue to 418, 449, and 918. Finish by reading 308 again, as it is the heart of the book.

No matter what approach you take to *Pensées,* there is no doubt you will find plenty of food for thought there.

EXCERPTS FROM

Pensées

12 *Order.* Men despise religion. They hate it and are afraid it may be true. The cure for this is first to show that religion is not contrary to reason, but worthy of reverence and respect.

Next make it attractive, make good men wish it were true, and then show that it is.

Worthy of reverence because it really understands human nature.

Attractive because it promises true good.

24 *Man's condition.* Inconstancy, boredom, anxiety.

149 APR* *Beginning, after explaining incomprehensibility.*

Man's greatness and wretchedness are so evident that the true religion must necessarily teach us that there is in man some great principle of greatness and some great principle of wretchedness.

It must also account for such amazing contradictions.

To make man happy it must show him that a God exists whom we are bound to love; that our true bliss is to be in him, and our sole ill to be cut off from him. It must acknowledge that we are full of darkness which prevents us from knowing and loving him, and so, with our duty obliging us to love God and our concupiscence leading us astray, we are full of unrighteousness. It must account to us for the way in which we thus

---

* It used to be thought that these initials represented an abbreviation for "At Port Royal," referring to conferences Pascal gave there, but this is no longer generally accepted, and no alternative has yet commanded assent.

go against God and our own good. It must teach us the cure for our helplessness and the means of obtaining this cure. Let us examine all the religions of the world on that point and let us see whether any but the Christian religion meets it.

Do the philosophers, who offer us nothing else for our good but the good that is within us? Have they found the cure for our ills? Is it curing man's presumption to set him up as God's equal? Have those who put us on the level of the beasts, have the Moslems, who offer nothing else for our good than earthly pleasures, even in eternity, brought us the cure for our concupiscence?

What religion, then, will teach us how to cure pride and concupiscence? What religion, in short, will teach us our true good, our duties, the weaknesses which lead us astray, the cause of these weaknesses, the treatment that can cure them, and the means of obtaining such treatment? All the other religions have failed to do so. Let us see what the wisdom of God will do.

'Men,' says his wisdom, 'do not expect either truth or consolation from men. It is I who have made you and I alone can teach you what you are.

'But you are no longer in the state in which I made you. I created man holy, innocent, perfect, I filled him with light and understanding, I showed him my glory and my wondrous works. Man's eye then beheld the majesty of God. He was not then in the darkness that now blinds his sight, nor subject to death and the miseries that afflict him.

'But he could not bear such great glory without falling into presumption. He wanted to make himself his own centre and do without my help. He withdrew from my rule, setting himself up as my equal in his desire to find happiness in himself, and I abandoned him to himself. The creatures who were subject to him I incited to revolt and made his enemies, so that today man has become like the beasts, and is so far apart from me that a barely glimmering idea of his author alone remains all of his dead or flickering knowledge. The senses, independent of reason and often its masters, have carried him off in pursuit of pleasure. All creatures either distress or tempt him, and dominate him either by forcibly subduing him or charming him with sweetness, which is a far more terrible and harmful yoke.

'That is the state in which men are today. They retain some feeble instinct from the happiness of their first nature, and are plunged into the wretchedness of their blindness and concupiscence, which has become their second nature.'

From this principle which I am disclosing to you, you can recognize the reason for the many contradictions which have amazed all mankind, and split them into such different schools of thought. Now observe all the impulses of greatness and of glory which the experience of so many miseries cannot stifle, and see whether they are not necessarily caused by another nature.

APR. *For tomorrow. Prosopopoeia.** 'Men, it is in vain that you seek within yourselves the cure for your miseries. All your intelligence can only bring you to realize that it is not within yourselves that you will find either truth or good.

'The philosophers made such promises and they have failed to keep them.

'They do not know what your true good is, nor what your true state is.

'How could they provide cures for ills which they did not even know? Your chief maladies are the pride that withdraws you from God, and the concupiscence that binds you to the earth; all they have done is to keep at least one of these maladies going. If they gave you God for object it was only to exercise your pride; they made you think that you were like him and of a similar nature. And those who saw the vanity of

---

* A term of rhetoric meaning "personification," here, of the wisdom of God, as in the Book of Proverbs.

such a pretention cast you into the other abyss, by giving you to understand that your nature was like that of the beasts, and they induced you to seek your good in concupiscence, which is the lot of the animals.

'This is not the way to cure you of the unrighteousness which these wise men failed to recognize in you. Only I can make you understand what you are.

'I do not demand of you blind faith.'

Adam, Jesus Christ.

If you are united to God, it is by grace, and not by nature.

If you are humbled, it is by penitence, not by nature.

Hence this dual capacity.

You are not in the state of your creation.

With the disclosure of these two states it is impossible for you not to recognize them.

Follow your own impulses. Observe yourself, and see if you do not find the living characteristics of these two natures.

Would so many contradictions be found in a single subject?

Incomprehensible. Everything that is incomprehensible does not cease to exist. Infinite number, an infinite space equal to the finite.

Incredible that God should unite himself to us.

This consideration derives solely from realizing our own vileness, but, if you sincerely believe it, follow it out as far as I do and recognize that we are in fact so vile that, left to ourselves, we are incapable of knowing whether his mercy may not make us capable of reaching him. For I should like to know by what right this animal, which recognizes his own weakness, measures God's mercy and keeps it within limits suggested by his own fancies. He has so little knowledge of what God is that he does not know what he is himself. Disturbed as he is by the contemplation of his own state, he dares to say that God cannot make him capable of communion with him. But I would ask him whether God demands anything but that he should love and know him, and why he thinks that God cannot enable man to know and love him, since man is naturally capable of love and knowledge. There is not doubt that he knows at least that he exists and loves something. Therefore, if he can see something in the darkness around him, and if he can find something to love among earthly things, why, if God reveals to him some spark

My Personal Top 5

KYLE STROBEL

1 *The Life of God in the Soul of Man*, Henry Scougal. Scougal's description of the Christian life as a participation in the divine nature (2 Pet 1:4)—the divine life being birthed in your own—was considered by John Wesley to be the best description in Christian literature.

2 *The Religious Affections*, Jonathan Edwards. The first time I read Edwards's *Religious Affections* I was shocked at how relevant it still is—particularly the second major section deemed the "negative signs"—and was surprised that two hundred and fifty years later we still often place our security on "signs" that prove nothing about our spiritual growth.

3 *Communion with God*, John Owen. Owen's work puts the reality of *communion* with God at the very center of the Christian life—it is, in fact, the reality of our life in the here and now that will know its fulfillment in eternity.

4 *Community and Growth*, Jean Vanier. Vanier's insights are ripe with real experiential knowledge, forged in the context of a life lived with the disabled. Rather than merely talking *about* community, Vanier brings us into the personal and existential reality of living together.

5 *Life Together*, Dietrich Bonhoeffer. For many years, this was a once-a-year read for me. *Life Together* is a pastoral work providing a rule of life for the people of God, and is full of practical and spiritual insight into the human condition.

KYLE STROBEL is the author of *Metamorpha: Jesus as a Way of Life* and is the cofounder of Meta morpha.com.

of his essence, should he not be able to know and love him in whatever way it may please God to communicate himself to us? There is thus undoubtedly an intolerable presumption in such arguments, although they seem to be based on patent humility, which is neither sincere nor reasonable unless it makes us admit that, since we do not know of ourselves what we are, we can learn it only from God....

308 The infinite distance between body and mind symbolizes the infinitely more infinite distance between mind and charity, for charity is supernatural.

All the splendour of greatness lacks lustre for those engaged in pursuits of the mind.

The greatness of intellectual people is not visible to kings, rich men, captains, who are all great in a carnal sense.

The greatness of wisdom, which is nothing if it does not come from God, is not visible to carnal or intellectual people. They are three orders differing in kind.

Great geniuses have their power, their splendour, their greatness, their victory and their lustre, and do not need carnal greatness, which has no relevance for them. They are recognized not with the eyes but with the mind, and that is enough.

Saints have their power, their splendour, their victory, their lustre, and do not need either carnal or intellectual greatness, which has no relevance for them, for it neither adds nor takes away anything. They are recognized by God and the angels, and not by bodies or by curious minds. God is enough for them.

Archimedes in obscurity would still be revered. He fought no battles visible to the eyes, but enriched every mind with his discoveries. How splendidly he shone in the minds of men!

Jesus without wealth or any outward show of knowledge has his own order of holiness. He made no discoveries; he did not reign, but he was humble, patient, thrice holy to God, terrible to devils, and without sin. With what great pomp and marvellously magnificent array he came in the eyes of the heart, which perceive wisdom!

It would have been pointless for Archimedes to play the prince in his mathematical books, prince though he was.

It would have been pointless for Our Lord Jesus Christ to come as a king with splendour in his reign of holiness, but he truly came in splendour in his own order.

It is quite absurd to be shocked at the lowliness of Jesus, as if his lowliness was of the same order as the greatness he came to reveal.

If we consider his greatness in his life, his passion, his obscurity, his death, in the way he chose his disciples, in their desertion, in his secret resurrection and all the rest, we shall see that it is so great that we have no reason to be shocked at a lowliness which has nothing to do with it.

But there are some who are only capable of admiring carnal greatness, as if there were no such thing as greatness of the mind. And others who only admire greatness of the mind, as if there were not infinitely higher greatness in wisdom.

All bodies, the firmament, the stars, the earth and its kingdoms are not worth the least of minds, for it knows them all and itself too, while bodies know nothing.

All bodies together and all minds together and all their products are not worthy the least impulse of charity. This is of an infinitely superior order.

Out of all bodies together we could not succeed in creating one little thought. It is impossible, and of a different order. Out of all bodies and minds we could not extract one impulse of true charity. It is impossible, and of a different, supernatural, order.

THE MEMORIAL

(A piece of parchment, together with a paper in almost identical terms, was found sewn into Pascal's clothing after his death, and it seems that he carried it with him at all times.)

913 The year of grace 1654

Monday, 23 November, feast of Saint Clement, Pope and Martyr, and of others in the Martyrology.

Eve of Saint Chrysogonus, Martyr and others.

From about half past ten in the evening until half past midnight.

FIRE

'God of Abraham, God of Isaac, God of Jacob,' not of philosophers and scholars.

Certainty, certainty, heartfelt, joy, peace.

God of Jesus Christ.

God of Jesus Christ.

My God and your God.

'Thy God shall be my God.'

The world forgotten, and everything except God.

He can only be found by the ways taught in the Gospels.

Greatness of the human soul.

'O righteous Father, the world had not known thee, but I have known thee.'

Joy, joy, joy, tears of joy.

I have cut myself off from him.

They have forsaken me, the fountain of living waters.

'My God wilt thou forsake me?'

Let me not be cut off from him for ever!

'And this is life eternal, that they might know thee, the only true God, and Jesus Christ whom thou hast sent.'

Jesus Christ.

Jesus Christ.

I have cut myself off from him, shunned him, denied him, crucified him.

Let me never be cut off from him!

He can only be kept by the ways taught in the Gospel.

Sweet and total renunciation.

Total submission to Jesus Christ and my director.

Everlasting joy in return for one day's effort on earth.

I will not forget thy word. Amen.[2]

A Study Guide for *Pensées*

1. What are you more often struck by, the greatness of people or the wretchedness? Why is it essential to be aware of both? How did Jesus exemplify greatness and lowliness?

2. A theme Pascal returns to many times is that of how a person's power and authority can be conveyed exclusively by his or her appearance, for example, clothing, uniform, and entourage (44). When have you been led astray by a person's appearance in this way? How else do you think your imagination prevents you from seeing what is really true?

3. How would you describe Pascal's view of humankind?

4. According to Pascal, what is diversion and from what do we need it? What form does diversion take in your life?

5. Are you ruled most often by your body, your mind, or your heart? How can you work to be less ruled by your body or your mind?

6. Pascal writes that one who is ruled by the heart will demonstrate charity. What does he mean by charity? How did Jesus demonstrate it? How is it opposed to covetousness and lust?

7. Why is Christianity the best answer to the human condition?

8. In Pascal's wager (418), he famously states that it is better to believe in God and find out that God does not exist than not to believe in God and find out that God does exist. "If you win you win everything, if you lose you lose nothing."[3] What do you think of this argument? Why do you think Pascal made it?

The Pilgrim's Progress

JOHN BUNYAN

> This book will make a traveler of thee,
>
> If by its counsel thou wilt ruled be;
>
> It will direct thee to the Holy Land,
>
> If thou wilt its directions understand
>
> Yea, it will make the slothful active be;
>
> The blind also delightful things to see.

John Bunyan's *The Pilgrim's Progress* is a biblical allegory about a man named Christian who seeks to find the way to the Celestial City, or salvation.

JOHN BUNYAN was born in Bedfordshire, England, in 1628. The son of a tinker, he seems to have received little education, eventually becoming a tinker himself. Even as a child, he was greatly troubled by a recognition of his own sinfulness, and as a young adult, he was baptized in a local nonconformist church called St. John's Church where he soon became a deacon and began preaching. But when Charles II took the throne, it became illegal to attend churches other than Anglican churches, so Bunyan was tried and jailed for years for preaching. While in jail he conceived and later wrote *The Pilgrim's Progress,* an allegorical tale of a man named Christian's faith journey. From the information in the autobiography Bunyan also published, *The Pilgrim's Progress* is believed to be largely autobiographical.

Part I of the book begins with a narrator watching a man named Christian who lives in the city of Destruction. Weighed down by a large burden on his back, Christian despairs as he reads his book because it tells him he must perish. Then he meets Evangelist, who tells him he can be saved by going through the narrow gate. He sets out on a journey, trying to follow Evangelist's instructions but gets trapped in the Slough of Despond and temporarily waylaid by Mr. Worldly Wiseman and another gentleman, Legality. He returns to Evangelist's path, however, where Goodwill opens the gate for him. He then proceeds to the Interpreter's house, who shows him several object lessons, including how only grace (like water) is adequate to remove the dust of sin, while the law only serves to stir it up. Next Christian reaches the cross, where he is finally able to give up his great burden, which falls into the sepulchre. He proceeds on his way to the Celestial City. The path is difficult, and he meets many who try to distract him or convince him to take shortcuts, but finally he reaches a Castle whose inhabitants teach him more about Jesus and give him some protective armor and a sword. Then he meets Apollyon, the prince of the city of Destruction, who fights Christian and indeed almost kills him, but Christian perseveres in the end. As he travels through the Valley of the Shadow of Death, he is comforted to hear a voice on the road in front of him reciting Psalm 23. Later he meets Faithful, the man who was talking aloud, and the two become traveling companions.

As the pair gets closer and closer to the Celestial City, the temptations grow more and more subtle. Christian runs ahead of Faithful; they meet Talkative, who speaks glibly of faith matters but does not exemplify them with his life. When Christian and Faithful enter the city of Vanity Fair, the merchants there are so offended that the pair care nothing for their worldly goods that they throw the two men into prison. They are tried, and Faithful is executed, after which he is immediately taken to the Celestial City. Christian, however, is only imprisoned and is able to escape. Soon he meets a new traveling companion named Hopeful. Now Christian is more knowledgeable and is able to offer correction to those they meet. Together the two refute and rebuff Atheist and Ignorance, who refuses to admit to his own sinfulness. They finally reach the grounds of the Celestial City, but Christian sinks deep into a river they must cross and despairs that his sins are too great. Hopeful reminds him that trials are sent by God to see if he will depend upon God to get him through it, and both enter triumphantly into the Celestial City. In Part II of *The Pilgrim's Progress,* Christian's wife, Christiana, and their children repent and follow in his footsteps to the Celestial City, facing similar trials and consolations.

Why *The Pilgrim's Progress* Is Essential

The Pilgrim's Progress has enjoyed phenomenal success for hundreds of years, after having been published in many different languages and editions. Its popularity and readership approaches that of the Bible. *The Pilgrim's Progress* has been beloved for so many years because of the drama of its narrative, the truth and reliability of its doctrine, and its absolute reliance on Scripture. Truly, *The Pilgrim's Progress* is awash in Scripture. Even where it is not directly quoted, many of the words and phrases in the text come from Jesus' sayings or parables. In addition, many of the people the pilgrims meet are minor and major biblical figures. Reading *The Pilgrim's Progress* is truly a Bible and theology lesson.

The Pilgrim's Progress is also an excellent illustration of the journey of the Christian life. Like Christian and the other pilgrims, we are on a path, charged with a goal, and are seeking to move forward, although we occasionally find ourselves erring by backtracking or standing still. And the story recognizes the challenges all Christians face on the journey, in the form of other people who jeer at us or try to steer us down a false path; rough terrain, doubt, confusion, even physical ailments. Yet starting the journey is the essential part; we cannot understand everything about it before we begin. We will gain the knowledge we need, but it comes along the way. We must start down the path, and more will be revealed as we progress, up until the very minute we reach the Celestial City.

Few works exemplify so well the struggles and temptations we will face on our journeys—not only the obvious physical struggles illustrated by Christian's fight with Apollyon, but also our struggles

The Pilgrim's Progress has great merit, both for invention, imagination, and the conduct of the story; and it has had the best evidence of its merit, the general and continued approbation of mankind. Few books, I believe, have had a more extensive sale. It is remarkable, that it begins very much like the poem of Dante; yet there was no translation of Dante when Bunyan wrote.

—Samuel Johnson

with wanting to be first, being tempted to take an easier path, or to halt all progress. Some even turn back, the details of which Christian describes to his friend Hopeful right before they reach the Celestial City: "1. They draw off their thoughts, all that they may, from the remembrance of God, death, and judgment to come. 2. Then they cast off by degrees private duties, as closet prayer, curbing their lusts, watching, sorrow for sin, and the like. 3. Then they shun the company of lively and warm Christians. 4. After that, they grow cold to public duty, as hearing, reading, godly conference, and the like. 5. They then begin to pick holes, as we say, in the coats of some of the godly, and that devilishly, that they may have a seeming color to throw religion (for the sake of some infirmities they have espied in them) behind their backs. 6. Then they begin to adhere to, and associate themselves with, carnal, loose, and wanton men. 7. Then they give way to carnal and wanton discourses in secret; and glad are they if they can see such things in any that are counted honest, that they may the more boldly do it through their example. 8. After this they begin to play with little sins openly. 9. And then, being hardened, they show themselves as they are. Thus, being launched again into the gulf of misery, unless a miracle of grace prevent it, they everlastingly perish in their own deceivings."[1]

We are to take this list as a warning and progress in the other direction, even when we face great trials. For as Hopeful says to Christian as he struggles in the deep water in the Celestial City, "My brother, you have quite forgot the text where it is said of the wicked, 'There are no bands in their death, but their strength is firm; they are not troubled as other men, neither are they plagued like other men' (Ps 73:4, 5). These troubles and distresses that you go through in these waters, are no sign that God hath forsaken you; but are sent to try you, whether you will call to mind that which heretofore you have received of his goodness, and live upon him in your distresses."[2] And as we see when Christian and Faithful compare notes, our temptations differ in particularity, but the solutions to them are the same—we call on Jesus and remember what we know to be true, and, most of all, we persevere.

How to Read *The Pilgrim's Progress*

The Pilgrim's Progress is an enjoyable read, available in many different versions, some meant for children, some in very contemporary language. Because of its numerous Bible references, a valuable method of reading it for spiritual formation might be to read with Bible at hand to look up the relevant passages. We can also, as the author challenges us in his concluding verses, try to interpret all of his symbols, but as he also points out, there is always the danger of misinterpreting, so our focus should be, as always, on "the substance of [his] matter."[3]

EXCERPTS FROM

The Pilgrim's Progress

As I walked through the wilderness of this world, I lighted on a certain place where was a den, and laid me down in that place to sleep; and as I slept, I dreamed a dream. I dreamed, and behold, I saw a man clothed with rags, standing in a certain place, with his face from his own house, a book in his hand, and a great burden upon his back (Isa 64:6; Luke 14:33; Ps 38:4). I looked and saw him open the book, and read therein; and as he read, he wept and trembled; and not being able longer to contain, he brake out with a lamentable cry, saying, "What shall I do?" (Acts 2:37; 16:30; Hab 1:2, 3).

In this plight, therefore, he went home, and restrained himself as long as he could, that his wife and children should not perceive his distress; but he could not be silent long, because that his trouble increased. Wherefore at length he brake his mind to his wife and children; and thus he began to talk to them: "O, my dear wife," said he, "and you the children of my bowels, I, your dear friend, am in myself undone by reason of a burden that lieth hard upon me; moreover, I am certainly informed that this our city will be burnt with fire from heaven; in which fearful overthrow, both myself, with thee my wife, and you my sweet babes, shall miserably come to ruin, except (the which yet I see not) some way of escape can be found whereby we may be delivered." At this his relations were sore amazed; not for that they believed that what he had said to them was true, but because they thought that some frenzy distemper had got into his head; therefore, it drawing towards night, and they hoping that sleep might settle his brains, with all haste they got him to bed. But the night was as troublesome to him as the day; wherefore, instead of sleeping, he spent it in sighs and tears. So when the morning was come, they would know how he did. He told them, "Worse and worse:" he also set to talking to them again; but they began to be hardened. They also thought to drive away his distemper by harsh and surly carriage to him; sometimes they would deride, sometimes they would chide, and sometimes they would quite neglect him. Wherefore he began to retire himself to his chamber to pray for and pity them, and also to condole his own misery; he would also walk solitarily in the fields, sometimes reading, and sometimes praying: and thus for some days he spent his time.

Now I saw, upon a time, when he was walking in the fields, that he was (as he was wont) reading in his book, and greatly distressed in his mind; and as he read, he burst out, as he had done before, crying, "What shall I do to be saved?" (Acts 16:30, 31).

I saw also that he looked this way, and that way, as if he would run; yet he stood still because (as I perceived) he could not tell which way to go. I looked then, and saw a man named Evangelist coming to him, and he asked, "Wherefore dost thou cry?"

He answered, "Sir, I perceive, by the book in my hand, that I am condemned to die, and after that to come to judgment

(Heb 9:27); and I find that I am not willing to do the first (Job 10:21, 22), nor able to do the second" (Ezek 22:14).

Then said Evangelist, "Why not willing to die, since this life is attended with so many evils?" The man answered, "Because, I fear that this burden that is upon my back will sink me lower than the grave, and I shall fall into Tophet (Isa 30:33). And Sir, if I be not fit to go to prison, I am not fit to go to judgment, and from thence to execution; and the thoughts of these things make me cry."

Then said Evangelist, "If this be thy condition, why standest thou still?" He answered, "Because I know not whither to go." Then he gave him a parchment roll, and there was written within, "Fly from the wrath to come" (Matt 3:7).

The man therefore read it, and looking upon Evangelist very carefully, said, "Whither must I fly?" Then said Evangelist (pointing with his finger over a very wide field), "Do you see yonder wicket-gate?" (Matt 7:13, 14). The man said, "No." Then said the other, "Do you see yonder shining light?" (Ps 119:105; 2 Pet 1:19). He said, "I think I do." Then said Evangelist, "Keep that light in your eye, and go up directly thereto, so shalt thou see the gate; at which, when thou knockest, it shall be told thee what thou shalt do." So I saw in my dream that the man began to run. Now he had not run far from his own door when his wife and children, perceiving it, began to cry after him to return; but the man put his fingers in his ears, and ran on crying, Life! life! eternal life! (Luke 14:26). So he looked not behind him (Gen 19:17), but fled towards the middle of the plain. . . .

. . .

Then Christian began to gird up his loins, and to address himself to his journey. So the other told him, that by that he was gone some distance from the gate, he would come to the house of the Interpreter, at whose door he should knock, and he would show him excellent things. Then Christian took his leave of his friend, and he again bid him God speed.

Then he went on till he came at the house of the Interpreter, where he knocked over and over. At last one came to the door, and asked who was there.

Christian: Sir, here is a traveller, who was bid by an acquaintance of the good man of this house to call here for my profit; I would therefore speak with the master of the house.

So he called for the master of the house, who, after a little time, came to Christian, and asked him what he would have.

Christian: Sir, said Christian, I am a man that am come from the city of Destruction, and am going to the Mount Zion; and I was told by the man that stands at the gate at the head of this way, that if I called here you would show me excellent things, such as would be helpful to me on my journey.

Interpreter: Then said Interpreter, Come in; I will show thee that which will be profitable to thee. So he commanded his man to light the candle, and bid Christian follow him; so he had him into a private room, and bid his man open a door; the which when he had done, Christian saw the picture a very grave person hang up against the wall; and this was the fashion of it: It had eyes lifted up to heaven, the best of books in his hand, the law of truth was written upon its lips, the world was behind its back; it stood as if it pleaded with men, and a crown of gold did hang over its head.

Christian: Then said Christian, What means this?

Interpreter: The man whose picture this is, is one of a thousand: he can beget children (1 Cor 4:15), travail in birth with children (Gal 4:19), and nurse them himself when they are born. And whereas thou seest him with his eyes lift up to heaven, the best of books in his hand, and the law of truth writ on his lips: it is to show thee, that his work is to know, and unfold dark things to sinners; even as also thou seest him stand as if he pleaded with men. And whereas thou seest the world as cast behind him, and that a crown hangs over his head; that is to show thee, that slighting and despising the things that are present, for the love that he hath to his Master's service, he is sure in the world that comes next, to have glory for his reward. Now, said the Interpreter, I have showed thee this picture first, because the man whose picture this is, is the only man whom the Lord of the place whither thou art going hath authorized to be thy guide in all difficult places thou mayest meet with in the way: wherefore take good heed to what I have showed thee, and bear well in thy mind what thou hast seen, lest in thy journey thou meet with some that pretend to lead thee right, but their way goes down to death.

My Personal Top 7

JAMES BRYAN SMITH

1 ***Celebration of Discipline***, Richard J. Foster

2 ***The Divine Conspiracy***, Dallas Willard

3 ***Mere Christianity***, C. S. Lewis

4 ***The Sermons of John Wesley***

5 ***A Man in Christ***, James S. Stewart

6 ***Confessions***, St. Augustine

7 ***The Imitation of Christ***, Thomas à Kempis

JAMES BRYAN SMITH is director of The Aprentis Institute, professor at Friends University, and an ordained United Methodist minister. He has written many books, including *The Apprentice* series and *A Spiritual Formation Workbook*.

Then he took him by the hand, and led him into a very large parlor that was full of dust, because never swept; the which after he had reviewed it a little while, the Interpreter called for a man to sweep. Now, when he began to sweep, the dust began so abundantly to fly about, that Christian had almost therewith been choked. Then said the Interpreter to a damsel that stood by, "Bring hither water, and sprinkle the room;" the which when she had done, it was swept and cleansed with pleasure.

Christian: Then said Christian, What means this?

Interpreter: The Interpreter answered, This parlor is the heart of a man that was never sanctified by the sweet grace of the Gospel. The dust is his original sin, and inward corruptions, that have defiled the whole man. He that began to sweep at first, is the law; but she that brought water, and did sprinkle it, is the Gospel. Now whereas thou sawest, that so soon as the first began to sweep, the dust did so fly about that the room by him could not be cleansed, but that thou wast almost choked therewith; this is to show thee, that the law, instead of cleansing the heart (by its working) from sin, doth revive (Rom 7:9), put strength into (1 Cor 15:56), and increase it in the soul (Rom 5:20), even as it doth discover and forbid it; for it doth not give power to subdue. Again, as thou sawest the damsel sprinkle the room with water, upon which it was cleansed with pleasure, this is to show thee, that when the Gospel comes in the sweet and precious influences thereof to the heart, then, I say, even as thou sawest the damsel lay the dust by sprinkling the floor with water, so is sin vanquished and subdued, and the soul made clean, through the faith of it, and consequently fit for the King of glory to inhabit (John 15:3; Eph 5:26; Acts 15:9; Rom 16:25, 26).[4]

A Study Guide for *The Pilgrim's Progress*

1. What parts of *The Pilgrim's Progress* speak most closely to your own journey?

2. Why do you think this book has spoken to so many? How does your experience reading *The Pilgrim's Progress* differ from reading the Bible itself?

3. Christian meets many enemies who wish to turn him away from the path he is following. Apollyon even physically fights him. What people have tried to turn you away from following Christ?

4. Christian must cross some rough terrain on his way. What has been the hardest ground for you to cover in your journey?

5. Christian tells Charity that his wife and children didn't want to come on the journey with him because they thought he was too righteous and denied himself things they thought were fine. When have you thought this of someone? When, if ever, has someone thought this of you? How did you respond?

6. As Christian passes through the Valley of the Shadow of Death, he is comforted to hear a voice ahead of him reciting Psalm 23, reminding him both that God is with him and that others are traveling the same path. Later he meets Faithful, who saves his life later in the story. What companions have comforted and aided you along your journey?

7. Even just outside the Celestial City, Christian sinks into the water and almost gives in to despair over his sin. Why do you think he faltered just when he was so close to his goal?

The Practice of the Presence of God

BROTHER LAWRENCE

The time of business . . . does not with me differ from the time of prayer; and in the noise and clutter of my kitchen, while several persons are at the same time calling for different things, I possess GOD in as great tranquility as if I were upon my knees at the Blessed Sacrament.

In this collection of conversations and letters, seventeenth-century monk Brother Lawrence describes how he lives with a constant sense of the immanent presence of God.

NICHOLAS HERMAN was born in the Lorraine region of France around 1614. After a conversion experience at age eighteen, he served as a soldier and a footman before entering a Carmelite monastery in Paris. Lacking the education necessary to become a cleric, he became a lay brother, taking the name Brother Lawrence. He lived and worked in this community, mostly in the kitchen, until his death in 1691. There, Brother Lawrence began his practice of seeking constantly to be aware of God's presence, while performing his kitchen duties and other tasks as well as during the community's set times of prayer. The outward effects of his practice, an "edifying countenance" marked by a "sweet and calm devotion" with an "even uninterrupted composure and tranquillity of spirit,"[1] earned the humble kitchen worker a measure of renown in his community and beyond. With visits and letters, people sought Brother Lawrence's advice as to how they could practice his method. After Brother Lawrence's death, Joseph de Beaufort, counsel to the Paris archbishop, published *The Practice of the Presence of God,* a collection of some of

Brother Lawrence's letters and four conversations between de Beaufort and Brother Lawrence.

The central message of the letters and conversations is Brother Lawrence's method of constantly sensing God's presence. He describes his frustration and lack of success with various formulaic prayer methods and how he instead sought to turn his attention to God at all times, not just during the daily prayer times of his community. At the center of his practice is his conviction that what matters is not so much what we do but why we do it. We are to do even the smallest things in life for no other reason than the love of God.

In the four conversations included in the book, Brother Lawrence recounts joining the Carmelite community as a way of punishing himself for his sins. Instead of suffering, however, he was surprised to find satisfaction. He describes his constant joy due to his practice of seeking God always and in all parts of his life, not artificially confining God to certain times of the day or practicing "trivial devotions." Instead he advises holding our faith before us as our constant rule of conduct. He advocates talking to God in plain speech, asking for help in all we do, and recounts how this practice has helped him through many difficult tasks, even helping him to overcome his aversion for kitchen work. According to Brother Lawrence, the shortest way to God is "by a continual exercise of love, and doing all things for His sake."[2]

Brother Lawrence advocates a life of simplicity, focused solely on God, and warns of trivialities that take our attention away from God. He speaks of himself as the greatest of unworthy sinners, yet he also explains how when he finds fault within himself, he simply seeks pardon and moves on without being discouraged. It is striking how even as he describes the great intimacy of his life with God, he remains humbly aware of his lowliness and God's greatness, noting that his practice has caused him to hold God in even higher esteem.

Many of the letters seem to be written in response to questions about following his practice. Brother Lawrence writes of how discouraging he found some of the prayer methods that were recommended to him and how his simple practice of seeking to constantly recall God's presence yielded the most results. Far from following some complicated program or engaging in elaborate preparations, he advises simply beginning right away. God knows whether such practice comes to us easily or not and will meet us where we are. In the third letter he gives perhaps the plainest description of his practice, when he recommends to a soldier friend that he "think of God the most he can," thus accustoming himself by degrees to this holy exercise.

In answer to what happens when his attention is drawn away from God, Brother Lawrence responds that God recalls his attention with a delightful sensation and that he simply returns his attention without punishment, remembering how miserable he felt without God. He also seems to have been frequently asked how to deal with suffering. He advises viewing it as a "favor from God." For Brother Lawrence, all things in life are opportunities to grow closer to God. No matter what the question, however, he always returns to describing the "most excellent method,"[3] the practice of the presence of God.

Why *The Practice of the Presence of God* Is Essential

For hundreds of years Brother Lawrence's letters have inspired Christians with their message of being in constant communion with God, even and especially during the most quotidian of tasks. As we read his words, it becomes clear that this humble kitchen worker is no less than a spiritual master whose life exemplifies the scriptural exhortation to pray without ceasing (1 Thess 5:17). It is estimated that in the more than three centuries since *The Practice of the Presence of God* was first published, more Christians have read it than any book other than the Bible. John Wesley and A. W. Tozer were among its many champions, Wesley including it as part of his spiritual library of recommended reading for all Christians.

Brother Lawrence's message has endured because the idea of being in constant communion with God is such a key part of spiri-

One of the purest souls ever to live on this fallen planet was Nicholas Herman, known as Brother Lawrence. He wrote very little, but what he wrote has seemed to several generations of Christians to be so rare and so beautiful as to deserve a place near the top among the world's great books of devotion. The writings of Brother Lawrence are the ultimate in simplicity; ideas woven like costly threads to make a pattern of great beauty.

—A. W. Tozer

tual formation. Unceasing prayer is an ideal to which all Christians should strive. As Richard J. Foster puts it, "My whole life, in one sense, has been an experiment in how to be a portable sanctuary—learning to practice the presence of God in the midst of the stresses and strains of contemporary life."[4] The idea of being constantly aware of God's presence is, at least on the surface, a simple message from someone who views himself as a simple man, yet anyone who has tried his method knows how difficult maintaining a constant sense of God's presence truly is and how discouraging it feels when we fail at it time and time again. Brother Lawrence not only shows us that such a practice is indeed possible, he offers advice and encouragement for continuing with the practice.

And while Brother Lawrence's method is stunning in its simplicity, it still feels as revolutionary today as it must have seemed in the seventeenth century. (We can infer from the letters that Brother Lawrence's contemporaries found his method extraordinary as well as elusive.) So many times we fall into thinking that God cares only about the big things in our lives—our jobs, our major life choices. We think in terms of big gestures or big sacrifices, that to do something for God means becoming a pastor or a missionary or giving away a substantial amount of money. To this mind-set Brother Lawrence's words are shocking: focus not so much on what you do but why you do it. Even picking up a straw from the ground can be done for the love of God. Thinking this way both frees us to seek God in our daily lives and adds the weight of additional responsibility to our shoulders—*all* that we do is to be done for the love of God.

Further, just as Brother Lawrence gently rebukes those in his own time who thought talking to God was just for certain times of the day, he would have much to say to modern Christians who tend not only to relegate God to Sunday mornings, but also to compartmentalize their entire lives into categories like work, home, and church. Brother Lawrence calls us to a true practice of the discipline of worship, but his words also call us to a messiness we might not find appealing: he exhorts us to let our faith bleed right over all the carefully drawn lines in our daily lives. His warning about distracting ourselves with frivolities and even "trivial devotions" smarts just as much today as it did in his own time, our world filled as it is with clever ways to distract ourselves from God. What better antidote for the increasing fragmentation we feel both individually and as a society than Brother Lawrence's most excellent method of being fully aware of God's presence even and most especially as we wash the dishes, go to the office, talk to friends, and do the smallest of tasks.

How to Read *The Practice of the Presence of God*

Diving into *The Practice of the Presence of God* presents few difficulties. It is a slim volume with many accessible translations. It can easily be read in one sitting, but we would recommend reading it slowly and more than once. It might be helpful to journal while reading, to record your own past and present experiences with Brother Lawrence's method. For those of us who discover that Brother Lawrence's method is more difficult than it might seem at first blush, we can take heart from his own words in the Second Letter. He writes that he struggled with the practice for ten years, that constantly forgetting and then having to recall to his mind God's presence caused him no small amount of pain and difficulties until he finally came to "a place of great peace." Ever humble, he also cautions that he has done this practice "very imperfectly" but has found great advantages to it.

Also remember that the writings that comprise *The Practice of the Presence of God* were collected and intended for several different people, so do not be put off if the writings feel at times a little disjointed or repetitive. Of course, Brother Lawrence himself was fully aware of this tendency of his to repeat. In the Ninth Letter he writes, "You will tell me that I am always saying the same thing: it is true, for this is the best and easiest method I know; and as I use no other, I advise all the world to it."[5]

The Practice of the Presence of God

I have always been governed by love without selfish views, and have resolved to make the love of God the end of all my actions. I have been well satisfied with this single motive. I am pleased when I can take a straw from the ground simply for the love of God, seeking Him only and nothing else—not even seeking His gifts.

I was long troubled by the belief that perhaps I would be damned. All the men in the world could not have persuaded me to the contrary. Then I reasoned with myself: I have engaged in a religious life only for the love of God; I have endeavored to act only for Him; whatever becomes of me, whether I be lost or saved, I will always continue to act purely for the love of God. I shall have this good at least, that till death I shall have done all that is in me to love God. That troubled state of mind had been with me for years. I had suffered much during that time; but since the time I saw this trouble arise from lack of faith, I have passed my life in perfect liberty and continual joy. I even placed my sins between myself and the Lord to tell Him that I did not deserve His favors, but He continued to bestow His favors upon me, in abundance, anyway!

In order to first form the habit of conversing with God continually and of referring all that we do to Him, we must first apply ourselves to Him with diligence. After a little such care we shall find His love inwardly excites us to His presence without any difficulty.

I expect that, after the pleasant days that God has given me, I will have my turn of pain and suffering. But I am not uneasy about this, knowing very well that since I can do nothing of myself, God will not fail to give me the strength to bear it.

On some occasions when it has been my opportunity to exercise some virtue, I have turned to God confessing, "Lord I cannot do this unless You enable me." I then received strength that was more than sufficient.

When I fail in my duty I simply admit my faults, saying to God, "I shall never do otherwise if You leave me to myself. It is You who must stop my falling and it is You who must amend that which is amiss." After such praying I allow myself no further uneasiness about my faults.

In all things we should act toward God with the greatest simplicity, speaking to Him frankly and plainly and imploring His assistance in our affairs just as they happen. God never fails to grant that assistance, as has often been my experience.

Recently I went to Burgundy to buy the wine provisions for the society which I have joined. This was a very unwelcome task for me. I have no natural business ability and, being lame, I cannot get around the boat except by rolling myself over the casks. Nonetheless, this matter gave me no uneasiness, nor did the purchase of wine. I told the Lord that it was His business that I was about. Afterwards, I found the whole thing well performed.

And so it is the same in the kitchen (a place to which I have a great natural aversion). I have accustomed myself to doing everything there for the love of God. On all occasions, with prayer, I have found His grace to do my work well, and I have found it easy during the fifteen years in which I have been employed here.

I am very well pleased with the post that I am now in but I am as ready to quit it as I was my former occupation, since in every condition I please myself by doing little things for the love of God.

My set times of prayer are not different from other times of the day. Although I do retire to pray (because it is the direction of my superior) I do not need such retirement nor do I ask for it because my greatest business does not divert me from God.

I am aware of my obligations to love God in all things and as I endeavor to do so I have no need of a director to advise me although I need a confessor to absolve me. I am keenly aware of my faults, but I am not discouraged by them. When I have confessed my faults to the Lord, I peacefully resume my usual practice of love and adoration to Him.

When I have a troubled mind I do not consult anyone. But knowing, by the light of faith, that God is with me in all things, I am content with directing all of my actions to Him. In other words, I carry out my actions with the desire to please the Lord and then let all else come as it will.

Our useless thoughts spoil everything. They are where mischief begins. We ought to reject such thoughts as soon as we perceive their impertinence to the matter at hand. We ought to reject them and return to our communion with God.

In the beginning I often passed my appointed time for prayer in simply rejecting wandering thoughts and then falling back into them. I also meditated for some time, but afterward ceased from that exercise—how exactly I cannot account for. I have never been able to regulate my devotion by certain methods, as some do.

All bodily mortification and other exercises are useless except as they serve to arrive at union with God by love. I have well considered this and found that the shortest way to God is to go straight to Him by a continual exercise of love and doing all things for His sake.

We ought to make a great difference between the acts of the understanding and those of the will. Acts in response to our own mental understanding are of comparatively little value. Action we take in response to the deep impressions of our heart are of all value. Our only business is to love and delight ourselves in God.

All kinds of mortification, no matter what they are, if they are void of the love of God, cannot erase a single sin. We ought, without any anxiety, to expect the pardon of our sins from the blood of the Lord Jesus Christ; our only endeavor should be to love Him with all our hearts. God seems to have granted the greatest favor to the greatest sinners, as more signal monuments of His mercy.

The greatest pains or pleasures of this world are not to be compared with what I have experienced of both pain and pleasure in a spiritual state. Therefore, I am careful for nothing and fear nothing, desiring only one thing of God—that I might not offend Him.

I have no scruples; for when I fail in my duty I readily acknowledge it saying, "I am used to doing so; I shall never do otherwise if I am left to myself." If I do not fail, then I give God thanks, acknowledging that the strength comes from Him.

My Personal Top 5

JONATHAN WILSON-HARTGROVE

These are the books that have been most helpful in my discipleship and growth.

1 *Fear and Trembling*, Soren Kierkegaard. Baptized at seven, I thought I had faith figured out by fifteen. When experience proved otherwise, a Danish philosopher helped me begin the journey toward figuring out what it really means to trust Jesus with my whole life.

2 *Life Together*, Dietrich Bonhoeffer. As an exchange student in Germany during high school, I stumbled across Bonhoeffer in a Christian book shop. His vision for community grabbed me and hasn't let go yet.

3 *The Rule of Benedict*, St. Benedict of Nursia. When I found my way to Christian community as a young adult, I learned that the practice of life together was harder than Bonhoeffer had made it sound. Benedict's wisdom has sustained me in community. I return to it again and again.

4 *The Wisdom of the Desert Fathers and Mothers*. Next to the Bible, this collection of sayings is the devotional guide I return to most often. Often a single line can change my whole way of thinking about something.

5 *The Seven Storey Mountain*, Thomas Merton. Writing is prayer, for me, and I don't think any single book shaped my writing more than Merton's memoir. He helped me see that prayer is a way of engaging the world with your eyes wide open.

JONATHAN WILSON-HARTGROVE is a founding member of Rutba House in Durham, North Carolina, and one of the leaders of the contemporary New Monastic movement. He is the author of *The Wisdom of Stability* and editor of *Common Prayer*.

. . .

A few days ago I was talking to a brother of piety. He told me that the spiritual life was a life of peace which was arrived at in three steps. He said there is first fear; after that, fear is changed to hope of eternal life; finally there is a consummation, that of pure love. He said that each of these three states is a different stage which eventually brings one to "that blessed consummation."

I have never followed this method. On the contrary, it was because I had myself been so discouraged by such methods that, when I finally came to the Lord, I decided just to give myself up to Him. The gift of myself was the best satisfaction I could hope to make for my sins. I realized that only out of pure love for Him could I renounce all the other concerns and interests of the world.

During my early years of seeking God I did use methods. I would set aside specific times to devote my thoughts to death, judgment, heaven, hell or my sins. I did this for years. But during the rest of the day I began doing something else. I spent the rest of my time, even in the midst of my business, carefully turning my mind to the presence of God. I always considered that His presence was with me, even *in* me!

Finally I even gave up using those set times of prayer for any type of methodical devotion which was a great delight and comfort to me. I began to use my regular times of devotion in the same way I did the rest of my time, in fixing my mind on the presence of God. This new practice revealed to me even more of the worth of my Lord. Faith alone, not a method, and certainly not fear, was able to satisfy me in coming to Him.

That was my beginning.

The next ten years were very hard, and I suffered a great deal. I was afraid I was not as devoted to God as I wanted to be; my past sins were always present in my mind; and there was the problem of the undeserved favors which God bestowed upon me! These matters were the source of my sufferings.

During this period I often fell, yet just as often I rose again. Sometimes it seemed that all creation, reason and even the Lord Himself were against me . . . and faith alone was for me. I was troubled with the thought that perhaps it was pure presumption on my part to believe I had received favor and mercy from God, and that this presumption only pretended to have taken me to a point that others arrived at only after going through many difficult stages. On occasion I even thought perhaps my simple touch with God was just a willful delusion on my part, and that I didn't even have salvation!

Amazingly, all these thoughts and fears did not diminish my trust in God but rather served to increase my faith. Finally, I came to the realization that I should put aside all the thoughts which brought about these times of trouble and unrest. Immediately I found myself changed. My soul, which had been so troubled, then felt a profound sense of inward peace and rest.

Ever since that time I have walked before God in simple faith. I have walked there with humility and love. Now I have but one thing to do: to apply myself diligently to being in God's presence, and to do nothing and say nothing that would displease Him. I hope that when I have done what I can, He will do with me whatever He pleases.

Many years have passed since that time. I have no pain and no doubt in my present state, because I have no will but God's. To that will I am so submissive that I would not take up a straw from the ground against His order, nor would I pick it up out of any other motive than purely that of love for Him.

I have given up *all forms* of devotion and set prayers other than those to which my state obliges me. My only business now is to persevere in His holy presence. I do so by a simple and loving attention to the Lord. Then I have the experience of the actual presence of God. To use another term I will call it a *secret* conversation between my soul and the Lord.

A question frequently asked me is, "What do you do about your mind wandering off on other things?" This does happen, sometimes of necessity, sometimes out of weakness. But the

Lord soon recalls me. I am recalled by an inward emotion or an inward sense so charming and delightful that I am at a loss as to know exactly how to describe it.

Do not be impressed with me because of what I am telling you. You are well aware of my weaknesses, so keep them in mind. I am utterly unworthy and ungrateful of the great favor the Lord has turned upon me.

My set times for prayer are exactly like the rest of the day to me. They are but a continuation of the same exercise of being in God's presence. Sometimes I see myself as a stone before the carver, ready to be made a statue. I present myself to God desiring Him to form His own perfect image in my soul and to make me entirely like Himself. At other times while praying, I feel my whole spirit and soul lifted up, with no effort on my part at all, to the very center and being of God.

Some people have said that this state is nothing but inactivity, delusion and self-love on my part. I agree that it is a holy inactivity, and it would be a happy self-love if the soul were capable of self-love in that state. But actually the very reverse is true. When the soul is at rest in God it does not follow its usual selfish behavior; its love is only for God.

I cannot bear, either, to regard this as "delusion." When my inner man is in the Lord's presence, enjoying Him, it desires nothing except the Lord! If this is a delusion, then it is up to God to remedy it.

Lord, do with me as You please. I desire only You, and to be wholly devoted to You.[6]

A Study Guide to *The Practice of the Presence of God*

1. What is your first reaction to Brother Lawrence's method of practicing the presence? How does it fit with your current ways of connecting with God?

2. Brother Lawrence mentions more than once how God has surprised him with blessings and joy. "I thought that perhaps [in a monastery] I would be made, in some way, to suffer for my awkwardness and for all the faults I had committed. I decided to sacrifice my life with all its pleasures to God. But He greatly disappointed me in this idea, for I have met with nothing but satisfaction in giving my life over to Him."[7] In what ways has God similarly "disappointed" you?

3. Reminding himself that he was doing the Lord's business allowed Brother Lawrence to accomplish difficult tasks and overcome his aversion to other tasks. When have you been able to accomplish tasks that made you uncomfortable by focusing on God or putting God first?

4. Brother Lawrence recommends considering sickness and suffering as "a gift from the hand of God."[8] "The worst possible afflictions and suffering appear intolerable *only* when seen in the wrong light. When we see such things as dispensed by the hand of God, when we know that it is our own loving Father who abases us and distresses us, then our sufferings lose their bitterness. Our mourning becomes all joy."[9] Have you ever viewed suffering in this way? If so, how did it help or not help? If this is a new idea for you, how might it affect the way you feel when you are in pain?

5. Brother Lawrence speaks often of the "trifles" with which we busy ourselves and how they take our attention away from God. What "trifles" absorb you? How might God look upon them?

6. Do you think it was easier for Brother Lawrence to practice the presence of God in the monastery setting than it would be for someone in "the real world"? Why or why not? In what settings or times in your life have you had the most and least success feeling connected and responsive to God? What factors do you think contributed to your success or lack thereof?

7. During what times do you currently find it most difficult to sense the presence of God? What can you learn from noticing this? How can you become aware of God's presence even in these situations?

8. Brother Lawrence's words about set prayer times may seem at best, counterintuitive, and at worst, harsh, at least for those of us who treasure these times. Among other things, he writes, "I am more united to God in my outward employments than when I leave them for devotion and retirement."[10] How do you react to this statement? Do you tend to connect to God more easily when you are engaged in outward employments or when you are devoting yourself to prayer? How might Brother Lawrence's insights help you to achieve balance?

A Serious Call to a Devout and Holy Life

WILLIAM LAW

> ↶ *And if you will here stop, and ask yourselves, why you are not as pious as the primitive Christians were, your own heart will tell you, that it is neither through ignorance nor inability, but purely because you never thoroughly intended it.*

BORN IN 1686 in Northamptonshire, England, William Law began his professional life as an academic at Cambridge. But when George I took the throne, Law, who had made public his sympathies with the rival Stuarts, lost his position and eventually became the tutor and spiritual director for Edward Gibbon and his family. For the ten years he held this position, he influenced a wide range of important men who were close to the Gibbon family, such as John and Charles Wesley. Disgusted with the excesses he saw in English society, especially among the "leisure classes" whose only concession to their professed Christian faith was church attendance, he wrote several books calling for reform, the most important of these being *A Serious Call to a Devout and Holy Life.* Then he moved back to his home at Kings Cliffe, Northamptonshire, and spent his last years living the kind of life he wrote about in *A Serious Call,* one of faith, study, and giving to others.

Law begins by defining devotion as a life given (devoted) to God. Not just our prayers but all our actions must be given over to God's will. If we do not show devotion in our way of life, the way we

William Law draws attention to the hypocrisy of those who claim to be Christians but do not bring their faith to bear upon their daily lives. He calls all Christians to make it their sincere intention to please God in all their actions, in addition to just their prayer and church attendance.

spend our time and money, then how can we call ourselves Christians? He decries the folly and hypocrisy of praying well but not offering up the rest of our lives to God, too. Just as we would not assume someone could live a holy life without prayer, how can someone pray but not live a holy life? He is especially critical of those who consider themselves Christian because they attend church, pointing out that the Gospels never command us to public worship, and frequent attendance at church is never mentioned in the New Testament. Instead all the directions of the New Testament are for the governing of daily life. "If we are to be in Christ new creatures, we must show that we are so, by having new ways of living in the world. If we are to follow Christ, it must be in our common way of spending every day."[1] Since religion does teach us how to be in the world, how we are to act toward others, how we are to use our time and money, then how can we feel that we must obey what is written about prayer and not about these matters? The Christian lifestyle is exemplified by renouncing wealth, idleness, and folly, and cultivating humility and self-denial. As Law writes, "If our common life is not a common course of humility, self-denial, renunciation of the world, poverty of spirit, and heavenly affection, we do not live the lives of Christians."[2]

Our actions fail to match up with our professions of faith because we simply lack the intention. If we but sincerely intend to please God in all our actions, our lives and world will be utterly transformed. Law is careful to say that we do not have the power to make ourselves perfect, but insists that we can be better than we are. We are capable of more, if we only capture the intention.

Next Law describes how we can live with devotion. Since all is God's, we must regard all the things of this world and all our actions this way, as belonging to God. We must seek to do all that we do for the glory of God. As an example, he gives us Calidus, who is so busy with his work that he feels he cannot take the time to pray or slow down. If those like Calidus did not feel the need to grow rich and successful and provide their families with lots of material things, they would "find themselves at leisure to live every day like Christians."[3] Above all, we must express uniformity in our piety, as much in our work and home lives as in our actions at church and in prayer.

One important way we must act with intention is in the disposal of our money, or "estate," as Law refers to it. We should use it in good works, "making ourselves friends, and fathers, and benefactors, to all our fellow-creatures, imitating the Divine love, and turning all our power into acts of generosity, care, and kindness to such as are in need of it."[4] He likens saving money ("lock[ing] it up in chests") or spending it on unnecessary expenses to locking up a spare pair of eyes and hands, the ultimate in foolish stewardship. We not only waste an opportunity to do good, but we do harm to ourselves by participating in something we must later renounce. Further, the more we spend money uselessly, the more silly and extravagant we will become. Instead, we must always exercise frugality and moderation, so as to have the most money to devote to charity and good works.

The two things that we must most carefully regulate, and through which we can be the greatest blessings to others, are our time and our money. To this end, he gives us the examples of Flavia, who attends church but wears all the latest fashions and spends much of her time in leisure, and her sister, Miranda, her opposite in every way. Law writes that Miranda would not give a poor man money to go to a puppet show, but that she applies the same logic to herself, that what should be spent on necessities and charity should not be spent on foolish entertainment. Miranda does, however, give freely of her money to others without being concerned about merit. Law reminds us that Scripture never makes merit the rule of charity but tells us simply to help those who need it. Law goes one step further by telling us that we should always wish every blessing on those we help.

The example of Miranda reveals how we should all seek to make the best use of the time and money that God has placed in our hands, as Miranda does. Law argues quite persuasively that prayers are "the smallest parts" of devotion, since it is relatively easy to worship God this way, and more difficult to honor God with the right use of our time and money and through disciplining our bodies with self-denial.

About prides, superiorities, and affronts, there's no book better than Law's *A Serious Call to a Devout and Holy Life,* where you'll find all of us pinned like butterflies on cards—the cards being little stories of typical characters in the most sober, astringent eighteenth-century prose.

—C. S. Lewis

Law also suggests proper times and hours for prayer. We are to rise early to pray in the morning; too much sleeping lulls the soul into dullness and complacency. We should start our time of devotion by chanting or singing a psalm, to "awaken all that is good and holy within you, that is to call your spirits to their proper duty, to set you in your best posture towards heaven, and tune all the powers of your soul to worship and adoration."[5] This singing awakens joy in the heart and mind, an outward action to raise an inward feeling. He recommends praying at nine o'clock in the morning, at noon, and at three o'clock and six o'clock in the afternoon, focusing on, in turn, humility, intercession, submission and conformity to God's will, and examination and confession. Such discipline and regularity in prayer aids us in achieving the true spirit of Christian perfection.

Why *A Serious Call to a Devout and Holy Life* Is Essential

Into a sea of books focused on prayer and the interior life comes William Law like a breath of fresh air. No one else writes with such practical focus on how to translate our Christian faith into actions in our lives. As editorial board member Richard J. Foster writes, "I am endlessly moved by the writings of William Law because he so obviously believed in prayer and was so utterly committed to living out his faith in the ordinary junctures of daily life."[6] Law's message of matching our actions to our professions of faith was highly influential both in his lifetime and since.

Law's book has several key formation applications for modern-day readers. First, he emphasizes intention. We must first *intend* to lead holy lives; our actions will follow. He sees intention as the missing ingredient for so many who profess Christianity but fail to make any real changes in their lives. He calls us to an earnest examination of our lives with attention to whether we truly want to live holy lives.

Although Law would never downplay the importance of prayer, he is rigorous in his stand that prayer is just a small part of what it means to be Christian. He challenges Christians to bring their faith out of church and into daily life. With example after scathing example, he points out the foolishness of professing in church to believe one thing and not carrying that focus over to our work, recreation, and home lives. "Devotion is a *life* given to God," he writes (italics added), a definition at odds with a common contemporary understanding of a devotion as a practice that we do once a day for a half hour or so. Our prayer is to be endlessly intertwined with our daily lives. Not only are the sentiments in it to be expressed in our lives, but it should affect and influence them, including how we spend our time and our money.

In his discussion of money, Law highlights the disciplines of generosity and frugality. Often we find that we are better at practicing one or the other of these disciplines, but Law offers practical advice about practicing both at the same time. We are not to waste our money by throwing it away on frivolities, clothes, and entertainment, but neither are we to waste it by saving it, locking it up in a chest, as he puts it, when we could instead use it to do good works.

Finally, from a practical standpoint, we can learn much from Law's examples, which feel almost astonishingly relevant to our times. Who among us cannot see a little of Calidus or Flavia in ourselves? Who among us does not need to strive to be more like Miranda? Open yourself to letting Law show you any areas of your life that you have not yet given over to God.

How to Read *A Serious Call to a Devout and Holy Life*

A Serious Call to a Devout and Holy Life is not a quick read. It is a long and dense book. A good strategy for reading might be to read it a chapter at a time, allowing yourself time to pause and reflect when warranted. Keep reading. As Richard J. Foster writes, "If you will stay with this book, it will do more for your spiritual development than twenty contemporary 'devotional' books."

Law's recommendations may feel overly ascetic, even off-putting. Remember that he was a reformer, trying to call people away from their excesses to lives of holiness. While reading, try to open yourself to the wonders of this life devoted to God. Put yourself in the place of the examples Law uses so cleverly. Remember that Law is not trying to prescribe exactly what our lives should look like; he is just making the point that when we give our lives over to God, we can expect to see this commitment reflected in our whole lives.

EXCERPTS FROM

A Serious Call to a Devout and Holy Life

CHAPTER I

It is very observable, that there is not one command in all the Gospel for public worship; and perhaps it is a duty that is least insisted upon in Scripture of any other. The frequent attendance at it is never so much as mentioned in all the New Testament. Whereas that religion or devotion which is to govern the ordinary actions of our life is to be found in almost every verse of Scripture. Our blessed Saviour and His Apostles are wholly taken up in doctrines that relate to common life. They call us to renounce the world, and differ in every temper and way of life, from the spirit and the way of the world: to renounce all its goods, to fear none of its evils, to reject its joys, and have no value for its happiness: to be as new-born babes, that are born into a new state of things: to live as pilgrims in spiritual watching, in holy fear, and heavenly aspiring after another life: to take up our daily cross, to deny ourselves, to profess the blessedness of mourning, to seek the blessedness of poverty of spirit: to forsake the pride and vanity of riches, to take no thought for the morrow, to live in the profoundest state of humility, to rejoice in worldly sufferings: to reject the lust of the flesh, the lust of the eyes, and the pride of life: to bear injuries, to forgive and bless our enemies, and to love mankind as God loveth them: to give up our whole hearts and affections to God, and strive to enter through the strait gate into a life of eternal glory.

This is the common devotion which our blessed Saviour taught, in order to make it the common life of all Christians. Is it not therefore exceeding strange that people should place so much piety in the attendance upon public worship, concerning which there is not one precept of our Lord's to be found, and yet neglect these common duties of our ordinary life, which are commanded in every page of the Gospel? I call these duties the devotion of our common life, because if they are to be practised, they must be made parts of our common life; they can have no place anywhere else.

If contempt of the world and heavenly affection is a necessary temper of Christians, it is necessary that this temper appear in the whole course of their lives, in their manner of using the world, because it can have no place anywhere else. If self-denial be a condition of salvation, all that would be saved must make it a part of their ordinary life. If humility be a Christian duty, then the common life of a Christian is to be a constant course of humility in all its kinds. If poverty of spirit be necessary, it must be the spirit and temper of every day of our lives. If we are to relieve the naked, the sick, and the prisoner, it must be the common charity of our lives, as far as we can render ourselves able to perform it. If we are to love our enemies, we must make our common life a visible exercise and demonstration of that love. If content and thankfulness, if the patient bearing of evil be duties to God, they are the duties of every day, and in every circumstance of our life. If we are to be wise and holy as the new-born sons of God, we can no otherwise be so, but by renouncing everything that is foolish and vain in every part of our common life. If we are to be in Christ new creatures, we must show that we are so, by having new ways of living in the world. If we are to follow Christ, it must be in our common way of spending every day.

Thus it is in all the virtues and holy tempers of Christianity; they are not ours unless they be the virtues and tempers of our ordinary life. So that Christianity is so far from leaving us to live in the common ways of life, conforming to the folly of customs, and gratifying the passions and tempers which the spirit of the world delights in, it is so far from indulging us in any of these things, that all its virtues which it makes necessary to salvation are only so many ways of living above and contrary to the world, in all the common actions of our life. If our common life is not a common course of humility, self-denial, renunciation of the world, poverty of spirit, and heavenly affection, we do not live the lives of Christians.

But yet though it is thus plain that this, and this alone, is Christianity, a uniform, open, and visible practice of all these virtues, yet it is as plain, that there is little or nothing of this to be found, even amongst the better sort of people. You see them often at Church, and pleased with fine preachers: but look into their lives, and you see them just the same sort of people as others are, that make no pretences to devotion. The difference that you find betwixt them, is only the difference of their natural tempers. They have the same taste of the world, the same worldly cares, and fears, and joys; they have the same turn of mind, equally vain in their desires. You see the same fondness for state and equipage, the same pride and vanity of dress, the same self-love and indulgence, the same foolish friendships, and groundless hatreds, the same levity of mind, and trifling spirit, the same fondness for diversions, the same idle dispositions, and vain ways of spending their time in visiting and conversation, as the rest of the world, that make no pretences to devotion.

I do not mean this comparison, betwixt people seemingly good and professed rakes, but betwixt people of sober lives. Let us take an instance in two modest women: let it be supposed that one of them is careful of times of devotion, and observes them through a sense of duty, and that the other has no hearty concern about it, but is at Church seldom or often, just as it happens. Now it is a very easy thing to see this difference betwixt these persons. But when you have seen this, can you find any farther difference betwixt them? Can you find that their common life is of a different kind? Are not the tempers, and customs, and manners of the one, of the same kind as of the other? Do they live as if they belonged to different worlds, had different views in their heads, and different rules and measures of all their actions? Have they not the same goods and evils? Are they not pleased and displeased in the same manner, and for the same things? Do they not live in the same course of life? Does one seem to be of this world, looking at the things that are temporal, and the other to be of another world, looking wholly at the things that are eternal? Does the one live in pleasure, delighting herself in show or dress, and the other live in self-denial

My Personal Top 5

EDUARDO ROSA PEDREIRA

1 *The Inner Experience*, Thomas Merton. An outstanding invitation to the inner dimension of our experience with God, this is one of the most important books for my life.

2 *Letters and Papers from Prison*, Dietrich Bonhoeffer. It is staggering to enter into the soul of this modern martyr revealed through his letters written in Tegel prison. His struggle, his joy and pain described in this writing have been an inspiration for my journey.

3 *Leap Over a Wall*, Eugene H. Peterson. Through the reflection on King David's life made in this book, I was able to make the most important travel of my life: a trip to my own heart. It was both a painful and joyful experience. This book is proof that reading can be a therapeutic and transforming experience.

4 *Streams of Living Water*, Richard J. Foster. This book holds the best systematic view of the traditions of Christian spirituality. It is not only a historical view, but goes far beyond it by giving us a holistic approach for the six dimensions of our spiritual lives, as individuals and community.

5 *A Testament of Devotion*, Thomas R. Kelly. This is a foundational book for those who want to go deeper with God, especially the chapter on the simplification of life. It is a tribute to simplicity in an era of complexity.

EDUARDO ROSA PEDREIRA is the president of Renovaré Brasil and the pastor of Comunidade Presbiteriana da Barra da Tijuca in Rio de Janeiro.

and mortification, renouncing everything that looks like vanity, either of person, dress, or carriage? Does the one follow public diversions, and trifle away her time in idle visits, and corrupt conversation, and does the other study all the arts of improving her time, living in prayer and watching, and such good works as may make all her time turn to her advantage, and be placed to her account at the last day? Is the one careless of expense, and glad to be able to adorn herself with every costly ornament of dress, and does the other consider her fortune as a talent given her by God, which is to be improved religiously, and no more to be spent on vain and needless ornaments than it is to be buried in the earth? Where must you look, to find one person of religion differing in this manner, from another that has none? And yet if they do not differ in these things which are here related, can it with any sense be said, the one is a good Christian, and the other not?

Take another instance amongst the men? Leo has a great deal of good nature, has kept what they call good company, hates everything that is false and base, is very generous and brave to his friends; but has concerned himself so little with religion that he hardly knows the difference betwixt a Jew and a Christian.

Eusebius, on the other hand, has had early impressions of religion, and buys books of devotion. He can talk of all the feasts and fasts of the Church, and knows the names of most men that have been eminent for piety. You never hear him swear, or make a loose jest; and when he talks of religion, he talks of it as of a matter of the last concern.

Here you see, that one person has religion enough, according to the way of the world, to be reckoned a pious Christian, and the other is so far from all appearance of religion, that he may fairly be reckoned a heathen; and yet if you look into their common life; if you examine their chief and ruling tempers in the greatest articles of life, or the greatest doctrines of Christianity, you will not find the least difference imaginable.

Consider them with regard to the use of the world, because that is what everybody can see.

Now to have right notions and tempers with relation to this world, is as essential to religion as to have right notions of God. And it is as possible for a man to worship a crocodile, and yet be a pious man, as to have his affections set upon this world, and yet be a good Christian.

But now if you consider Leo and Eusebius in this respect, you will find them exactly alike, seeking, using, and enjoying, all that can be got in this world in the same manner, and for the same ends. You will find that riches, prosperity, pleasures, indulgences, state equipages, and honour, are just as much the happiness of Eusebius as they are of Leo. And yet if Christianity has not changed a man's mind and temper with relation to these things, what can we say that it has done for him? For if the doctrines of Christianity were practised, they would make a man as different from other people, as to all worldly tempers, sensual pleasures, and the pride of life, as a wise man is different from a natural; it would be as easy a thing to know a Christian by his outward course of life, as it is now difficult to find anybody that lives it. For it is notorious that Christians are now not only like other men in their frailties and infirmities, this might be in some degree excusable, but the complaint is, they are like heathens in all the main and chief articles of their lives. They enjoy the world, and live every day in the same tempers, and the same designs, and the same indulgences, as they did who knew not God, nor of any happiness in another life. Everybody that is capable of any reflection, must have observed, that this is generally the state even of devout people, whether men or women. You may see them different from other people, so far as to times and places of prayer, but generally like the rest of the world in all the other parts of their lives: that is, adding Christian devotion to a heathen life. I have the authority of our blessed Saviour for this remark, where He says, "Take no thought, saying, What shall we eat? or, What shall we drink? or, Wherewithal shall

we be clothed? For after all these things do the Gentiles seek."
[Matt 6:31, 32] But if to be thus affected even with the necessary
things of this life, shows that we are not yet of a Christian spirit,
but are like the heathens, surely to enjoy the vanity and folly of
the world as they did, to be like them in the main chief tempers
of our lives, in self-love and indulgence, in sensual pleasures and
diversions, in the vanity of dress, the love of show and greatness,
or any other gaudy distinctions of fortune, is a much greater
sign of an heathen temper. And, consequently, they who add
devotion to such a life, must be said to pray as Christians, but
live as heathens.[7]

A Study Guide for

A Serious Call to a Devout and Holy Life

1. How is one generally judged to be a Christian or not a
   Christian in today's world? What would your lifestyle say
   about your faith?

2. Why do you think we often place such emphasis on church
   attendance as a measure of Christian faith?

3. Law believes that we lack sufficient intention to please God
   with our actions. He writes, "So that the fault does not lie
   here, that we desire to be good and perfect, but through the
   weakness of our nature fall short of it; but it is, because we
   have not piety enough to intend to be as good as we can, or
   to please God in all the actions of our life."[8] How have your
   intentions fallen short?

4. If, like the young man in chapter 3 of *A Serious Call,* you
   knew you were to die soon, what would you wish you had
   changed about your life? In what areas would you wish
   you had been more pious or more sensitive to God? What
   would seem of less importance to you? What would seem
   more important?

5. What do you see of yourself in Calidus, in chapter 4, who is constantly focused on his business, and therefore always in a hurry, with little time for prayer? Law writes that if Calidus and those like him were to focus more on laying up their treasures in heaven rather than on earth, they would "find themselves at leisure to live every day like Christians." What do you think he means by being at leisure to live like a Christian? Do you think of the Christian life in this way? Why or why not?

6. What areas of your life do you find the hardest to devote to God?

7. Law has harsh words for those who do not spend their money wisely. Not only are they leaving good works undone, but they are leading themselves into even more silliness and extravagance. How have you seen this exemplified in your life or the lives of others? Where do you think you err most in terms of financial stewardship? How might it change your perspective to view your money as good works undone?

8. What of yourself do you see in Flavia, the beautifully dressed lady of leisure? What of yourself do you see in her sister, Miranda, described as a "sober, reasonable Christian"?[9]

9. Law writes that indulging in expensive finery of dress is a sin because it shows "a foolish and unreasonable state of heart, that is fallen from right notions of human nature, that abuses the end of clothing, and turns the necessities of life into so many instances of pride and folly."[10] What should a right attitude toward clothing be? What is your attitude toward clothing?

10. What is Law's reason for advocating prayer on the strict schedule of upon rising, nine in the morning, noon, and three and six in the afternoon? How does this correspond to

your own prayer schedule or lack of one? If you do not pray in this way already, how do you think you might benefit from praying as he suggests?

11. How does reading Law's book affect your understanding of what it means to be a Christian?

The Way of a Pilgrim

UNKNOWN AUTHOR

> *By the grace of God I am a Christian, by my deeds a great sinner, and by my calling a homeless wanderer of humblest origin, roaming from place to place.*

A nineteenth-century Russian peasant wanders through the countryside in a quest to learn how to pray without ceasing.

THE WAY OF A PILGRIM was written in the mid-nineteenth century in Russia. No one knows for certain who wrote it or even whether the titular pilgrim was a real person or a fictional character.

The Way of a Pilgrim, and its companion volume, *The Pilgrim Continues His Way,* is the first-person narrative of a devout Russian peasant who, upon hearing the verse from 1 Thessalonians instructing Christians to pray without ceasing (5:17), sets out on a quest to find out exactly how to do that. After failing to find help from sermons and various wise people he encounters, he meets an elder on the road who commiserates with him about the lack of teaching about prayer that comes from real experience. This elder speaks of the importance of "frequent prayer" rather than ceaseless prayer because humans cannot reach purity and perfection in their prayer. He then gives the pilgrim a copy of *The Philokalia,* telling him that this book provides clear instruction as to how to do that which is mysteriously presented in the Bible. He explains that the Bible is a shining light and *The Philokalia* is the necessary glass through which to view that light. The elder shows the pilgrim the Jesus Prayer found in *The Philokalia*: "Lord Jesus Christ, have mercy on me" and advises him to begin repeating it. The pilgrim obeys his direction to great success and stays for a while at the elder's monastery, but when the elder dies, he sets off again. From his repetition of the Jesus Prayer, he feels that he has learned ceaseless prayer but would like to progress still further, to a prayer that is self-activated within his heart, not directed by him from the outside.

Throughout the rest of the book, the pilgrim wanders from place to place, reciting the Jesus Prayer and reading *The Philokalia*. Along the way he meets many fellow Christians and pilgrims who share their insights with him and whom he also teaches. We learn that this pilgrim has a crippled arm and so cannot work and that his wanderings were prompted by the loss of his livelihood and the death of his wife. Despite all the adverse circumstances in his life, the pilgrim maintains a steadfast faith and hope in God. At one point during his wanderings he is robbed and mourns the loss of his Bible and copy of *The Philokalia*. In a dream the elder tells him that this trial is to teach him detachment from material things. He then runs into an officer who has apprehended the men who robbed him and is able to get his books back, to his great delight. After more wandering, the pilgrim meets a man who tells him of a hut where he can live for a few months, fulfilling his great desire to have a place to stay in order to focus on *The Philokalia*. Yet when the pilgrim is finally able to read *The Philokalia* in its entirety, he finds himself unable to reconcile all the ideas about interior prayer presented there. That night his elder appears to him again in a dream and prescribes a course of study in *The Philokalia*. When he awakes, he finds those passages marked in his book in charcoal.

When he must leave the hut, he wanders again, eventually settling for a time as the watchman of a small chapel. But on his way out of town, he runs into a peasant girl who begs him to save her from marriage to a schismatic. When men looking for the girl find the two together, the pilgrim is jailed and beaten. He praises God for being able to suffer in God's name.

In the companion book, *The Pilgrim Continues His Way,* the pilgrim returns to his spiritual father a year later with stories of the year that has passed. Although he was unable to reach Jerusalem, he had encounters with other wanderers, including a fellow pilgrim who teaches him about what the Gospels say about prayer. This man, later identified as a professor, directs him to Matthew 6—its teaching about prayer with pure motivation in a quiet place, and how prayer is to precede action—and then to the Gospel of John and what it teaches about interior prayer.

The last section of the book is comprised of two conversations between the professor, the pilgrim, his spiritual father/elder, and various friends of the elder. A monk reads an article about constancy of prayer, and during their discussion the professor states that those who have professions cannot practice unceasing prayer, but the monk takes exception to this argument and cites John Chrysostom, who said that we can erect an altar to God everywhere in our hearts by way of prayer. And to the question of the priest as to whether it is not better to pray less often but with our hearts, the monk responds that the vocal Jesus Prayer is essential even when we do not feel it is so. He compares it to a child learning his ABCs who may wonder whether his time would not be better spent fishing with his father since he does not understand what learning the ABCs will bring him eventually. In the final conversation, a hermit advises the professor, pilgrim, and elder that although it is advisable to have a spiritual director, if we do not have such a formal teacher, we can take counsel from those around us if we have faith and good intention.

The Way of a Pilgrim gives us a sense of the mystical depth of Christianity in the Orthodox tradition. It's almost to live in the poetry of God instead of in the doctrine of God. But I think the greatest benefit to Western Christians is to expand our minds with the vastness of God and how all our enculturated experiences have to come together to make that unity.

—Phyllis Tickle

Why *The Way of a Pilgrim* Is Essential

The Way of a Pilgrim is an enduring spiritual classic of the Eastern Orthodox tradition. Since it was first discovered by a monk and published in 1884, the pilgrim's journey has inspired and instructed Christians both East and West. *The Way of a Pilgrim* takes us into the mystical depths of the interior life, in contrast to the emphasis on morality, doctrine, and rules we more commonly find in Western/Latin Christianity. As the author himself writes in reference to a sect that has rejected Orthodoxy, "The Old Believers are preoccupied with the external aspects of worship and they don't seem to be aware of the interior man, while we are careless about the externals."[1] For those of us who learned a faith that focuses on externals, it is essential to recover some of this focus on the soul and the spirit.

The Way of a Pilgrim offers a concrete way to learn to maintain a constant inner sense of the presence of God—the Jesus Prayer that is so beloved by the narrator. And while *The Philokalia* also deals with interior prayer, the narrative form of *The Way of a Pilgrim* is a helpful and accessible way to learn about the Jesus Prayer. This focus on the Jesus Prayer with a concrete example of how it is practiced is probably *The Way of a Pilgrim*'s most enduring contribution to the Christian canon. As editorial board member Frederica Mathewes-Green writes, "The Jesus Prayer has proved to be a very helpful way of learning to maintain a constant inner sense of the presence of God. This book distills that wisdom into a narrative form that readers new to the Jesus Prayer will find accessible." The story shows some concrete ways the Jesus Prayer has changed the pilgrim; not only has it enabled him to maintain this sense of the presence of God, but it has also taught him in other ways. At one point the head of a devout family with whom the pilgrim is visiting asks the pilgrim if he is not a nobleman in disguise, due to his ability to read, write, and reason. The pilgrim responds that he has been given these gifts by his practice of interior prayer, and that such gifts are available to all through this path: "My ignorance has been enlightened by interior prayer, which is the result of God's grace and the teachings of my late elder. What I have, every man can have."[2] Prayer, the ability to seek God, is available to all.

The Way of a Pilgrim offers a beautiful illustration of life as a journey. The pilgrim's journey itself is as much the point as the spiritual place in which the pilgrim finds himself at the story's end. And indeed, this less-than-definitive ending only underscores the lesson that the journey continues throughout our lives and beyond. We see in the story that the itinerant wanderer was not an uncommon phenomenon in that era in Russia. The people whom the pilgrim meets most often treat him with kindness, even reverence at times.

Most seem to respect what he is doing. Jack Kerouac aside, there is no real equivalent in Western society. A Western response to such a person might be to wonder why he doesn't do something with his life. What would the pilgrim reply to this? He would likely say that he is doing the most important thing one can do, giving himself over entirely to God. Our postmodern era has gained new appreciation for this expression of life as a journey, but it is still helpful to reflect on the wisdom that we do not always have to have a plan or to know what is coming next to be of value to God.

The pilgrim presents an inspiring example of the discipline of simplicity in action. Truly he has placed himself in God's hands, relinquishing the hold of all material possessions except his Bible and *The Philokalia*. More important to him than anything in the world is his journey to God, aided by his recitation of the Jesus Prayer. We can all learn from such single-minded focus and the simplicity that results.

How to Read *The Way of a Pilgrim*

Although we cannot know if this story is the autobiography of a pilgrim, the story of an amalgamation of pilgrims, or a creative work of spiritual fiction, *The Way of a Pilgrim* is still first and foremost a story and meant to be read that way. We put ourselves in the place of the pilgrim. For some of us, it might be hard to give ourselves over to this wanderer and his somewhat rambling story. Yet the aimless sense of the narrative is rather the point. The pilgrim is a rootless wanderer, jobless, without a family. We can all relate in some way to his rudderlessness, to his search for a sense of purpose, to not knowing exactly what will happen next. He allows himself to be an itinerant, in much the same way that Jesus was. We may not be able to drop the commitments of our everyday lives and wander like Jesus and the pilgrim, but we can give ourselves over to the story and learn from the way the pilgrim devotes his every waking minute to Jesus.

The Way of a Pilgrim

By the grace of God I am a Christian, by my deeds a great sinner, and by my calling a homeless wanderer of humblest origin, roaming from place to place. My possessions consist of a knapsack with dry crusts of bread on my back and in my bosom the Holy Bible. This is all!

On the twenty-fourth Sunday after Pentecost I came to church to attend the Liturgy and entered just as the epistle was being read. The reading was from Paul's First Letter to the Thessalonians, which says in part, "Pray constantly." These words made a deep impression on me, and I started thinking of how it could be possible for man to pray without ceasing when the practical necessities of life demand so much attention. I checked my Bible and saw with my own eyes exactly what I had heard, that it is necessary to pray continuously (1 Thess 5:17); to pray in the Spirit on every possible occasion (Eph 6:18); in every place to lift your hands reverently in prayer (1 Tim 2:8). I thought and thought about these words, but no understanding came to me.

What shall I do? I thought. Where can I find a person who will explain this mystery to me? I will go to the various churches where there are good preachers and perhaps I will obtain an explanation from them. And so I went. I heard many very good homilies on prayer, but they were all instructions about prayer in general: what is prayer, the necessity of prayer, and the fruits of prayer, but no one spoke of the way to succeed in prayer. I did hear a sermon on interior prayer and ceaseless prayer but nothing about attaining that form of prayer. Inasmuch as listening to public sermons had not given me any satisfaction, I stopped attending them and decided, with the grace of God, to look for an experienced and learned person who would satisfy my ardent desire and explain ceaseless prayer to me. . . .

Toward the evening of the fifth day an old man caught up with me who looked like the member of some religious community.

To my question he answered that he was a monk and that his hermitage was about ten versts from the main road, and he invited me to visit the hermitage. "We receive pilgrims and strangers and give them food and lodging in our guesthouse," he said.

Since I had no inclination to stop there, I replied, "My peace does not depend on a place to stay but on spiritual direction. I am not looking for food, as I have enough bread in my knapsack."

"And what manner of direction are you looking for; what seems to be puzzling you? Come, come dear brother, visit us; we have experienced elders who can give spiritual nourishment and direct one on the path of truth according to the word of God and the writings of the holy Fathers."

"You see, Father, about a year ago while I was at a Liturgy I heard the following admonition from the Apostle Paul: 'Pray constantly.' Not being able to understand this I began to read the Bible, where in many places I found God's precept that it is necessary to pray continuously, to pray always, at all times and in all places, not only while working, not only when awake but also in one's sleep. 'I sleep but my heart is awake' (Song of Sol 5:2). I was very surprised by this and could not understand how this could be possible and by what means it could be accomplished. A strong desire and curiosity took hold of me and day and night it did not leave me. For this reason I went from church to church to listen to sermons on prayer; and though I have heard very many of them, I did not receive the desired instruction, how to pray without ceasing. The homilies I heard were about the preparation for prayer or the fruits of prayer and similar things, but I did not learn how to pray without ceasing or what is the meaning of such prayer. I kept reading the Bible and in this way I tested what I had heard. But I could not find the desired knowledge, and so to this day I am left bewildered and without peace."

The elder blessed himself and began to speak: "Thank God, dear brother, for this insatiable desire to understand ceaseless mental prayer. Recognize in it a call from God and be at peace. Believe that up to this time your seeking was in accordance with God's will and you were given to understand that heavenly light regarding continuous prayer is not reached by worldly wisdom and superficial curiosity. On the contrary, it is discovered in the spirit of poverty and simplicity of heart through active experience. Therefore, it is not surprising that you did not hear about the essential act of prayer and learn how to carry it on without ceasing.

"The truth is that, though there is neither a shortage of sermons or of treatises of various writers about prayer, for the most part these discourses are based on mental analysis and on natural considerations rather than on active experience. For this reason they teach more about the external character of prayer than the essence of prayer. One speaks beautifully about the necessity of prayer, another about its power and its benefits, and still another of the means and conditions for its accomplishment: that is, zeal, attention, warmth of heart, purity of thought, reconciliation with the enemies, humility, contrition, and so on.

"And what is prayer? And how does one learn to pray? To these primary and most fundamental questions one seldom finds an accurate explanation in the homilies of our time. These basic questions are more difficult to understand than the above-mentioned discourses and they require mystical perception in addition to academic learning. What is most unfortunate is that worldly wisdom compels these spiritual teachers to measure God's ways by human standards. Many approach prayer with a misunderstanding and think that the preparatory means and acts produce prayer. They do not see that prayer is the source of all good actions and virtue. They look upon the fruits and results of prayer as means and methods and in this way depreciate the power of prayer." . . .

The course of this conversation brought us close to the hermitage. In order not to let this wise man go, and to quickly receive my heart's desire, I hurried to ask him, "Please, be gracious, Reverend Father, and explain the meaning of ceaseless mental prayer to me and show me how I can learn to practice it.

....

My Personal Top 5

SCOT MCKNIGHT

1 *The Cost of Discipleship* and *Life Together*, Dietrich Bonhoeffer. I first read both of these as a college student and, while I "got" it, I was a long way from a comprehension of Bonhoeffer's vision. I've since read both books several times, and consider both to be brilliant expositions of both the individual and ecclesial life for the follower of Jesus.

2 *Confessions*, St. Augustine. Because of a professor's recommendation, I read *Confessions* in college but when I read it through a second time in my forties it was a stunning experience—in hindsight we find how God was at work in Augustine drawing him and molding him into the man who thirsted for God and who found one supreme joy.

3 *I and Thou*, Martin Buber. Relationality is at the heart of life, and no one has plumbed it more analytically and self-consciously and existentially than Buber. There are statements in Buber that peel back deeper realities that are at times so deep all he can give is a glimpse, and the glimpse is all we can know or handle.

4 *Mere Christianity*, C. S. Lewis. I read two to three pages of this book before any writing day begins—the prose, the posture, and the plots of chapters are brilliant examples of how to communicate, and his grasp of the great tradition and capacity to make it understandable make this book what it is.

5 *Everything That Rises Must Converge*, Flannery O'Connor. A friend recommended I read Flannery, and I am now a convert. I've read all her letters and most of her short stories, but this one is my favorite—and my favorite story is "Parker's Back." Through her grotesque imagery she paints the heart of humans before God and alongside others.

SCOT MCKNIGHT is a religion professor at North Park University. He is a widely recognized authority on the New Testament, early Christianity, and the historical Jesus, and is the author of *The Jesus Creed* and other books.

....

I can see that you are both well versed and experienced in this matter."

The elder received my plea lovingly and invited me to visit him in his cell: "Come, stop by and I will give you a book of the holy Fathers from which, with the help of God, you can learn all about prayer and understand it clearly and in detail." When we entered his cell, the elder said, "The ceaseless Jesus Prayer is a continuous, uninterrupted call on the holy name of Jesus Christ with the lips, mind and heart; and in the awareness of His abiding presence it is a plea for His blessing in all undertakings, in all places, at all times, even in sleep. The words of the Prayer are, 'Lord Jesus Christ, have mercy on me!' Anyone who becomes accustomed to this Prayer will experience great comfort as well as the need to say it continuously. He will become accustomed to it to such a degree that he will not be able to do without it and eventually the Prayer will of itself flow in him."

"Now do you understand what ceaseless prayer is?" he asked me.

"Very clearly, dear Father. For the love of God please tell me how to make it my own," I exclaimed in joy.

"To learn about this prayer we will read from a book called *The Philokalia*. This book, which was compiled by twenty-five holy Fathers, contains complete and detailed instructions about ceaseless prayer. The content of this book is of such depth and usefulness that it is considered to be the primary teacher of contemplative life, and as the Venerable Nicephorus says, 'It leads one to salvation without labor and sweat.'"

"Is it then more important than the Holy Bible?" I asked.

"No, it is neither more important nor holier than the Bible, but it contains clear exposition of the ideas that are mysteriously presented in the Bible and are not easy for our finite mind to understand. I will give you an illustration. The sun—a great, shining, and magnificent light—cannot be contemplated and looked at directly with the naked eye. An artificial glass, a million times smaller and dimmer than the sun, is needed to look at the great king of lights to be enraptured by its fiery ways. In a similar way the Holy Bible is a shining light and the *Philokalia* is the necessary glass."[3]

A Study Guide for *The Way of a Pilgrim*

1. What do you think awakened this burning desire in the wanderer to learn how to pray without ceasing? Have you ever been so driven to find the answer to a similar question?

2. The elder whom the pilgrim meets early in his journey gives him *The Philokalia,* explaining that it is a tool to help him better see the Bible, which he describes as too great and magnificent to see with the naked eye. What or who has helped you to better see the blinding light that is the Bible?

3. The elder tells the pilgrim that without the guidance of a spiritual director it is not very profitable to study the interior life. Do you agree? What have your experiences been with formal or informal spiritual direction?

4. How does the Jesus Prayer differ from other types of prayer? Why is the element of repetition so important?

5. After the pilgrim has recited the Jesus Prayer thousands of times a day, he finds that he experiences joy and longing for the prayer. The elder tells him that the discipline of his practice has made him like an oiled machine, ready to work. "Ah, how indescribably wonderful it is when God deigns to purify a soul from passion and grants to it the gift of self-activating interior prayer."[4] How have you experienced the joy that comes from a disciplined practice? What do you think is meant by self-activating prayer? Have you ever experienced it?

6. The wanderer does not ever seem to wish for stability, security, a home, or a family; he seems to long only for a

quiet place to study and contemplate *The Philokalia*. What about his journey is difficult for you to understand? What can you relate to? What is your innermost desire?

7. The pilgrim and the priest who hires him to watch over the chapel debate about whether the pilgrim should seek solitude or remain among people. The pilgrim tells the priest that each person has his gift from God—some to be preachers and others to be hermits. To which lifestyle do you find yourself attracted? Is it the same one you find yourself living? Why or why not? Are there any hermits in our day, in our culture?

8. Throughout the story, people show the pilgrim great generosity and hospitality—from hosting him at their homes to giving him bread and salt. The pilgrim, too, recalls how he was admonished by his grandfather at a young age to give to the church and to the poor. Do you think the wanderer for God or pilgrim has a place in your culture? If so, how? How do you see generosity and hospitality practiced in your culture?

9. Despite the fact that he teaches many of the people he encounters during his travels, the pilgrim remains ever humble and open to the teachings of others. What do you learn from his attitude?

The Brothers Karamazov

FYODOR DOSTOEVSKY

> *I'm a Karamazov. For when I do leap into the pit, I go headlong with my heels up, and am pleased to be falling in that degrading attitude, and pride myself upon it. And in the very depths of that degradation I begin a hymn of praise. Let me be accursed. Let me be vile and base, only let me kiss the hem of the veil in which my God is shrouded. Though I may be following the devil, I am Thy son, O Lord, and I love Thee, and I feel the joy without which the world cannot stand.*

FYODOR DOSTOEVSKY was born in Moscow in 1821. He experienced literary success at a young age with his first novel, *Poor Folk,* and continued to write novels exploring nineteenth-century Russian society. At the age of twenty-eight he was sentenced to four years hard labor in Siberia for his membership in an underground intellectual group. During his prison term, he experienced a conversion to Christianity, specifically to the Russian Orthodox Church. Both spiritual and anti-Western themes dominated many of his later works, such as *The Idiot* and *Crime and Punishment.* He spent three years writing *The Brothers Karamazov,* his last novel. It was intended to be a trilogy titled *The Life of a Great Sinner,* but Dostoevsky died shortly after the book was published.

The Brothers Karamazov is the story of Fyodor Pavlovich Karamazov, an unabashed sensualist, and his three sons, Dmitri, also a sensualist; Ivan, an atheist intellectual; and Alexei, a Christian who is a novice at a local monastery. Alexei, most often called

Fyodor Dostoevsky's last novel is the expansive spiritual drama of three Russian brothers—Dmitri, Ivan, and Alexei Karamazov—and their father, Fyodor Pavlovich Karamazov. Through the story of Fyodor's murder and his eldest son, Dmitri's, accusation and trial amid numerous subplots, Dostoevsky weaves in themes of morality, love, faith, doubt, reason, family, and redemption.

Alyosha, is the heart of the story; Dostoevsky refers to him as the story's hero. Alyosha tries to care for and bring to faith his father and both brothers, but his father is too proud of his own debauchery, Dmitri is convinced he is too like his father, and Ivan is too troubled by intellectual questions about human suffering and free will. Fyodor himself is a hard man to love, taking pride in his own buffoonery. Dmitri and his father are both in love with the same woman, known as Grushenka. Because of their bitter rivalry, when the elder Karamazov is found murdered, Dmitri is arrested and tried for the crime. In the course of the trial, it is revealed that there is a fourth brother—Smerdyakov, Fyodor's servant and illegitimate son. The archetypes of the son are central to the plot; Dostoevsky said that each represented a stage of his own faith journey.

In the conversations between the brothers, the women they love, between Alyosha and his elder, Zossima, and also in the narrative asides from Dostoevsky himself, we become privy to Dostoevsky's thoughts on a wide variety of topics, including morality, class, human suffering, and redemption. Arguably the most famous theological passage is a story Ivan tells Alyosha, called "The Grand Inquisitor." In it the Grand Inquisitor, a Jesuit priest in Spain, questions Christ about his actions here on earth, concluding that free will was a mistake. The Grand Inquisitor tells Jesus that he and his fellow Jesuits have done what Christ should have done, namely, provide bread for the people and rule over them, all the while lying to them about a heaven that awaits them. According to the Grand Inquisitor, he and his fellow rulers will be the only unhappy ones in the situation, since they will take on the sins of the masses and they alone will know the truth: that there is nothing after life but death.

Alyosha rejects his brother's story, saying that there is one who was and is willing to take on all the sins of the masses—Jesus Christ. But Alyosha's own faith is soon tested when his beloved elder dies. Local superstition had dictated that the body of such a holy man would not decay, and when Zossima's body starts to decompose even more quickly than a normal body, Alyosha starts to question all that he has believed. In the end, all three brothers and the women their lives are intertwined with, Grushenka and Katerina Ivanovna, Dmitri's betrothed, move toward redemption.

Why *The Brothers Karamazov* Is Essential

The Brothers Karamazov is considered one of the greatest works of literature ever written, by critics as varied as Sigmund Freud, Kurt Vonnegut, and Ludwig Wittgenstein, not least because of the dizzying number of theological questions it tackles—the quest for God, the problem of human suffering and evil, doubt, reason, the monastic life, murder, and morality, to name but a few. As editorial board member Michael G. Maudlin writes, "Reading *The Brothers Karamazov* showed how abstract and vague my thinking was about the Christian life. Through the three Karamazov brothers, Dmitri, Ivan, and Alyosha, I encountered three-dimensional portraits of lust, doubt, love, faithfulness, suffering, longing, hope, gentleness, anger, healing, and many other virtues and vices, not to mention how a powerful providence is at work in us. Dostoevsky is a wonderful antidote to shallow thinking about spirituality."

As many have commented, the entire book may be viewed as a work of the Holy Spirit. And one of the central messages is that the Holy Spirit is working in everything. As a novel, *The Brothers Karamazov* is uniquely positioned to drive home this message that God is not just found in our Bibles or our churches or our relationships with other Christians; God is everywhere in this messy and complicated life of ours. God cannot be contained in one or another aspect of our lives, and to try to live our lives as though our faith is only relevant to some parts is the height of foolishness.

From the words and story of Zossima, Alyosha's mentor, and the various debates between the three brothers to the very movement of the plot toward redemption, *The Brothers Karamazov* contains an incredible amount of theological insight. Zossima's final words to his fellow monks constitute a spiritual-formation primer in themselves—his advice about being servants to our servants, treating

[*The Brothers Karamazov*] is digressive and sprawling, many too many characters in it, much too long, whatever comes up to enter, is entered here and there by maybe nothing less than the Holy Spirit itself, thereby becoming, as far as I'm concerned . . . a novel less *about* the religious experience than a novel the reading of which *is* a religious experience: of God, both in his subterranean presence and in his appalling absence.

—Frederick Buechner

all with loving humility, loving all, and remembering that we are working for the whole. In the complex interlacing of all the characters and subplots, we see one of Dostoevsky's central messages—our salvation is not a purely individual matter; it is as tied in with those around us as Alyosha is connected to his father and brothers. Just as each of Fyodor's sons feels in some way responsible for his father's death, we are all responsible in some measure for the sins and holiness of those around us. Zossima understood this message. On his deathbed he tells Alyosha and the other monks that unless you can accept that you are just as responsible for the crime being tried before you, you cannot be a good judge. He reminds them that they have to keep the whole of humanity in their hearts.

This love for others, and the earthiness it implies, is what sets Zossima apart from his fellow monk Father Ferapont, who takes pride in his ascetic achievements but has no love to show for it, only a kind of madness that appeals to the crowd hungry for miracles after Father Zossima's dead body betrays his humanness by decomposing. But, of course, Zossima's connection to his body and his love for the other embodied souls around him is part of what makes him such a great and holy man. As he tells those gathered at his deathbed, "There is only one means of salvation, then take yourself and make yourself responsible for all men's sins, that is the truth, you know, friends, for as soon as you sincerely make yourself responsible for everything and for all men, you will see at once that it is really so, and that you are to blame for everyone and for all things."[1]

How to Read *The Brothers Karamazov*

Fiction affords us a unique opportunity for spiritual reading. We can allow ourselves to inhabit the characters and see the issues through their eyes, affording us new insights into our own lives. Just as Dostoevsky saw one of the stages of his faith journey in each of the brothers, we, too, can put ourselves into the story and let it speak to our own experience.

Like many Russian novels, *The Brothers Karamazov* is long and boasts a dizzying array of characters and subplots. It might be helpful to jot down the different character names and even their nicknames and a brief description on a piece of paper and then use this paper as a bookmark.

EXCERPTS FROM

The Brothers Karamazov

THE GRAND INQUISITOR

[Ivan said to Alyosha,] "My story is laid in Spain, in Seville, in the most terrible time of the Inquisition, when fires were lighted every day to the glory of God, and 'in the splendid auto da fe the wicked heretics were burnt.' Oh, of course, this was not the coming in which He will appear, according to His promise, at the end of time in all His heavenly glory, and which will be sudden 'as lightning flashing from east to west.' No, He visited His children only for a moment, and there where the flames were crackling round the heretics. In His infinite mercy He came once more among men in that human shape in which He walked among men for thirty-three years fifteen centuries ago. He came down to the 'hot pavements' of the southern town in which on the day before almost a hundred heretics had, ad majorem gloriam Dei, been burnt by the cardinal, the Grand Inquisitor, in a magnificent auto da fe, in the presence of the king, the court, the knights, the cardinals, the most charming ladies of the court, and the whole population of Seville.

"He came softly, unobserved, and yet, strange to say, everyone recognised Him. That might be one of the best passages in the poem. I mean, why they recognised Him. The people are irresistibly drawn to Him, they surround Him, they flock about Him, follow Him. He moves silently in their midst with a gentle smile of infinite compassion. The sun of love burns in His heart, and power shines from His eyes, and their radiance, shed on the people, stirs their hearts with responsive love. He holds out His hands to them, blesses them, and a healing virtue comes from contact with Him, even with His garments. An old man in the crowd, blind from childhood, cries out, 'O Lord, heal me and I shall see Thee!' and, as it were, scales fall from his eyes and the blind man sees Him. The crowd weeps and kisses the earth under His feet. Children throw flowers before Him, sing, and cry hosannah. 'It is He—it is He!' repeat. 'It must be He, it can be no one but Him!' He stops at the steps of the Seville cathedral at the moment when the weeping mourners are bringing in a little open white coffin. In it lies a child of seven, the only daughter of a prominent citizen. The dead child lies hidden in flowers. 'He will raise your child,' the crowd shouts to the weeping mother. The priest, coming to meet the coffin, looks perplexed, and frowns, but the mother of the dead child throws herself at His feet with a wail. 'If it is Thou, raise my child!' she cries, holding out her hands to Him. The procession halts, the coffin is laid on the steps at His feet. He looks with compassion, and His lips once more softly pronounce, 'Maiden, arise!' and the maiden arises. The little girl sits up in the coffin and looks round, smiling with wide-open wondering eyes, holding a bunch of white roses they had put in her hand.

"There are cries, sobs, confusion among the people, and at that moment the cardinal himself, the Grand Inquisitor, passes by the cathedral. He is an old man, almost ninety, tall and erect, with a withered face and sunken eyes, in which there is still a gleam of light. He is not dressed in his gorgeous cardinal's robes, as he was the day before, when he was burning the enemies of the Roman Church—at this moment he is wearing his coarse, old, monk's cassock. At a distance behind him come his gloomy assistants and slaves and the 'holy guard.' He stops at the sight of the crowd and watches it from a distance. He sees everything; he sees them set the coffin down at His feet, sees the child rise up, and his face darkens. He knits his thick grey brows and his eyes gleam with a sinister fire. He holds out his finger and bids the guards take Him. And such is his power, so completely are the people cowed into submission and trembling obedience to him, that the crowd immediately makes way for the guards, and in the midst of deathlike silence they lay hands on Him and lead him away. The crowd instantly bows down to the earth, like one man, before the old Inquisitor. He blesses the people in silence and passes on. The guards lead their prisoner to the close, gloomy vaulted prison—in the ancient palace of the Holy, inquisition and shut him in it. The day passes and is followed by the dark, burning, 'breathless' night of Seville. The air is 'fragrant with laurel and lemon.' In the pitch darkness the iron door of the prison is suddenly opened and the Grand Inquisitor himself comes in with a light in his hand. He is alone; the door is closed at once behind him. He stands in the doorway and for a minute or two gazes into His face. At last he goes up slowly, sets the light on the table and speaks. 'Is it Thou? Thou?' but receiving no answer, he adds at once. 'Don't answer, be silent. What canst Thou say, indeed? I know too well what Thou wouldst say. And Thou hast no right to add anything to what Thou hadst said of old. Why, then, art Thou come to hinder us? For Thou hast come to hinder us, and Thou knowest that. But dost thou know what will be to-morrow? I know not who Thou art and care not to know whether it is Thou or only a semblance of Him, but to-morrow I shall condemn Thee and burn Thee at the stake as the worst of heretics. And the very people who have to-day kissed Thy feet, to-morrow at the faintest sign from me will rush to heap up the embers of Thy fire. Knowest Thou that? Yes, maybe Thou knowest it,' he added with thoughtful penetration, never for a moment taking his eyes off the Prisoner."

"I don't quite understand, Ivan. What does it mean?" Alyosha, who had been listening in silence, said with a smile. "Is it simply a wild fantasy, or a mistake on the part of the old man—some impossible quid pro quo?"

"Take it as the last," said Ivan, laughing, "if you are so corrupted by modern realism and can't stand anything fantastic. If you like it to be a case of mistaken identity, let it be so. It is true," he went on, laughing, "the old man was ninety, and he might well be crazy over his set idea. He might have been struck by the appearance of the Prisoner. It might, in fact, be simply his ravings, the delusion of an old man of ninety, over-excited by the auto da fe of a hundred heretics the day before. But does it matter to us after all whether it was a mistake of identity or a wild fantasy? All that matters is that the old man should speak out, that he should speak openly of what he has thought in silence for ninety years."

"And the Prisoner too is silent? Does He look at him and not say a word?"

"That's inevitable in any case," Ivan laughed again. "The old man has told Him He hasn't the right to add anything to what He has said of old. One may say it is the most fundamental feature of Roman Catholicism, in my opinion at least. 'All has been given by Thee to the Pope,' they say, 'and all, therefore, is still in the Pope's hands, and there is no need for Thee to come now at all. Thou must not meddle for the time, at least.' That's how they speak and write too—the Jesuits, at any rate. I have read it myself in the works of their theologians. 'Hast Thou the right to reveal to us one of the mysteries of that world from which Thou hast come?' my old man asks Him, and answers the question for Him. 'No, Thou hast not; that Thou mayest not add to what has been said of old, and mayest not take from men the freedom which Thou didst exalt when Thou wast on earth. Whatsoever Thou revealest anew will encroach on men's freedom of faith; for it will be manifest as a miracle, and the freedom of their faith was dearer to Thee than anything in those days fifteen hundred years ago. Didst Thou not often say then, "I will make you free"? But now Thou hast seen these "free" men,' the old man adds suddenly, with a pensive smile. 'Yes, we've paid dearly for it,' he goes on, looking sternly at Him, 'but at last we have completed that work in Thy name. For fifteen centuries we have been wrestling with Thy freedom, but now it is ended and over for good. Dost Thou not believe that it's over for good? Thou lookest meekly at me and deignest not even to be wroth with me. But let me tell Thee that now, to-day, people are more persuaded than ever that they have perfect freedom, yet they have brought their freedom to us and laid it humbly at our feet. But that has been our doing. Was this what Thou didst? Was this Thy freedom?'"

My Personal Top 5

TONY CAMPOLO

1 *The Imitation of Christ*, Thomas à Kempis. I am convinced, after reading à Kempis, that meekness should be at the top of my list of spiritual virtues for development. My fragmented soul requires the kind of devotional meditations that will make me into an intense, passionate lover of Christ. If this becomes my reality, I will reach out to others in a non-manipulative way and I will be enabled, through the indwelling presence of his Holy Spirit, to enter into the sufferings of others and to exercise true compassion.

2 *Confessions*, St. Augustine. This book of meditations speaks to me directly, for the weaknesses of the flesh so evident in St. Augustine are weaknesses that I perceive in myself.

3 *A Day in Your Presence: A 40-Day Journey in the Company of Francis of Assisi*. The Church must consider the lifestyle of St. Francis if it is to embrace responsible lifestyles in an age wherein we all must live more simply if others are to simply live.

4 *John Wesley's Journal*. What can be found in Wesley's *Journal* is the evidence that theology must flow out of experience and without experience theology is nothing more than that which may have the form of godliness, but denies the power thereof.

5 *A Testament of Devotion*, Thomas R. Kelly. Though he died in 1941, Kelly spoke to the twenty-first century, and to the Church of our era, and admonished us to recognize that there is a divine presence in every one of us waiting to be awakened and listened to, and from that spirit find direction in our confusing world.

TONY CAMPOLO is the author of many books, including *The Kingdom of God Is a Party,* a widely traveled speaker, and a longtime professor at Eastern University.

"I don't understand again." Alyosha broke in. "Is he ironical, is he jesting?"

"Not a bit of it! He claims it as a merit for himself and his Church that at last they have vanquished freedom and have done so to make men happy. 'For now' (he is speaking of the Inquisition, of course) 'for the first time it has become possible to think of the happiness of men. Man was created a rebel; and how can rebels be happy? Thou wast warned,' he says to Him. 'Thou hast had no lack of admonitions and warnings, but Thou didst not listen to those warnings; Thou didst reject the only way by which men might be made happy. But, fortunately, departing Thou didst hand on the work to us. Thou hast promised, Thou hast established by Thy word, Thou hast given to us the right to bind and to unbind, and now, of course, Thou canst not think of taking it away. Why, then, hast Thou come to hinder us?' ". . . .

[Says the Grand Inquisitor:] " 'Hadst Thou taken the world and Caesar's purple, Thou wouldst have founded the universal state and have given universal peace. For who can rule men if not he who holds their conscience and their bread in his hands? We have taken the sword of Caesar, and in taking it, of course, have rejected Thee and followed him. Oh, ages are yet to come of the confusion of free thought, of their science and cannibalism. For having begun to build their tower of Babel without us, they will end, of course, with cannibalism. But then the beast will crawl to us and lick our feet and spatter them with tears of blood. And we shall sit upon the beast and raise the cup, and on it will be written, "Mystery." But then, and only then, the reign of peace and happiness will come for men. Thou art proud of Thine elect, but Thou hast only the elect, while we give rest to all. And besides, how many of those elect, those mighty ones who could become elect, have grown weary waiting for Thee, and have transferred and will transfer the powers of their spirit and the warmth of their heart to the other camp, and end by raising their free banner against Thee. Thou didst Thyself lift up that banner. But with us all will be happy and will no more rebel nor destroy one another as under Thy freedom. Oh, we shall persuade them that they will only become free when they renounce their freedom to us and submit to us. And shall we be right or shall we be lying? They will be convinced that we are right, for they will remember the horrors of slavery and confusion to which Thy freedom brought them. Freedom, free thought, and science will lead them into such straits and will bring them face to face with such marvels and insoluble mysteries, that some of them, the fierce and rebellious, will destroy themselves, others, rebellious but weak, will destroy one another, while the rest, weak and unhappy, will crawl fawning to our feet and whine to us: "Yes, you were right, you alone possess His mystery, and we come back to you, save us from ourselves!'"

" 'Receiving bread from us, they will see clearly that we take the bread made by their hands from them, to give it to them, without any miracle. They will see that we do not change the stones to bread, but in truth they will be more thankful for taking it from our hands than for the bread itself! For they will remember only too well that in old days, without our help, even the bread they made turned to stones in their hands, while since they have come back to us, the very stones have turned to bread in their hands. Too, too well will they know the value of complete submission! And until men know that, they will be unhappy. Who is most to blame for their not knowing it?—speak! Who scattered the flock and sent it astray on unknown paths? But the flock will come together again and will submit once more, and then it will be once for all. Then we shall give them the quiet humble happiness of weak creatures such as they are by nature. Oh, we shall persuade them at last not to be proud, for Thou didst lift them up and thereby taught them to be proud. We shall show them that they are weak, that they are only pitiful children, but that childlike happiness is the sweetest of all. They will become timid and will look to us and huddle close to us in fear, as chicks to the hen. They will marvel at us and will be awe-stricken before us, and will be proud at our being so powerful and clever that we have been able to subdue such a turbulent flock of thousands of millions. They will tremble impotently before our wrath, their minds will grow fearful, they will be quick to shed tears like women and children, but they will be just as ready at a sign from us to pass to laughter and rejoicing, to happy mirth and childish song. Yes, we shall set them to work, but in their leisure hours we shall make their life like a child's game, with children's songs and innocent dance. Oh, we shall allow them even sin, they are weak and helpless, and they will love us like children because we allow them to sin. We shall tell them that every sin will be expiated, if it is done with our permission, that we allow them to sin because we love them, and the punishment for these sins we take upon ourselves. And we shall take it upon ourselves, and they will adore us as their saviours who have taken on themselves their sins before God. And they will have no secrets from us. We shall allow or forbid them to live with their wives and mistresses, to have or not to have children according to whether they have been obedient or disobedient—and they will submit to us gladly and cheerfully. The most painful secrets of their conscience, all, all they will bring to us, and we shall have an answer for all. And they will be glad to believe our answer, for it will save them from the great anxiety and terrible agony they endure at present in making a free decision for themselves. And all will be happy, all the millions of creatures except the hundred thousand who rule over them. For only we, we who guard the mystery, shall be unhappy. There will be thousands of millions of happy babes, and a hundred thousand sufferers who have taken upon themselves the curse of the knowledge of good and evil. Peacefully they will die, peacefully they will expire in Thy name, and beyond the grave they will find nothing but death. But we shall keep the secret, and for their happiness we shall allure them with the reward of heaven and eternity. Though if there were anything in the other world, it certainly would not be for such as they. It is prophesied that Thou wilt come again in victory, Thou wilt come with Thy chosen, the proud and strong, but we will say that they have only saved themselves, but we have saved all. We are told that the harlot who sits upon the beast, and holds in her hands the mystery, shall be put to shame, that the weak will rise up again, and will rend her royal purple and will strip naked her loath-some body. But then I will stand up and point out to Thee the thousand millions of happy children who have known no sin. And we who have taken their sins upon us for their happiness will stand up before Thee and say: "Judge us if Thou canst and darest." Know that I fear Thee not. Know that I too have been in the wilderness, I too have lived on roots and locusts, I too prized the freedom with which Thou hast blessed men, and I too was striving to stand among Thy elect, among the strong and powerful, thirsting "to make up the number." But I awakened and would not serve madness. I turned back and joined the ranks of those who have corrected Thy work. I left the proud and went back to the humble, for the happiness of the humble. What I say to Thee will come to pass, and our dominion will be built up. I repeat, to-morrow Thou shalt see that obedient flock who at a sign from me will hasten to heap up the hot cinders about the pile on which I shall burn Thee for coming to hinder us. For if anyone has ever deserved our fires, it is Thou. To-morrow I shall burn Thee.' "[2]

A Study Guide for *The Brothers Karamazov*

1. Dostoevsky's characters are all symbolic of larger personality types. Of what type are Fyodor Pavlovich Karamazov and Dmitri? How do you see yourself in these men? What are some modern examples of a Fyodor or a Dmitri? What type is Ivan? How do you see yourself in him? Finally, of what type of person is Alyosha symbolic? How do you see yourself typified in him? To which brother or other character do you most relate? Why?

2. Elder Zossima has a tremendous influence on Alyosha's life. Indeed Dostoevsky describes an elder as "one who took your soul, your will, into his soul and his will. When you choose an elder, you renounce your own will and yield it to him in complete submission, complete self-abnegation. This novitiate, this terrible school of abnegation, is undertaken voluntarily, in the hope of self-conquest, of self-mastery, in order, after a life of obedience, to attain perfect freedom, that is, from self; to escape the lot of those who have lived their whole life without finding their true selves in themselves."[3] Is there a Western parallel to this sort of relationship? Would you ever apprentice yourself this way? Why or why not? Why do you think it was so painful for Alyosha and the other monks who viewed Zossima as their elder when Zossima's body decomposes so quickly? What do you think Dostoevsky was trying to say with this subplot?

3. When Lise's mother, Mrs. Khokhlakov, confesses to Zossima that she struggled with the idea of life after death, he instructs her to love her neighbors. The more she loves them, he tells her, the more she will be convinced of the existence of God and of the immortality of her own soul. How have you experienced this in your life? How have you experienced what the elder speaks of next, how it is easy to love mankind generally but hard to love specific people?

4. Ivan tells Alyosha that he cannot make peace with the idea of human suffering, most of all that of children. How can you relate to his feelings and his desire to see justice done?

5. What point is Ivan trying to make with his poem, "The Grand Inquisitor"? How would you have responded to him?

6. In Zossima's story, he recounts how he came to the realization that everyone is responsible for everyone else. How does the sweep of Dostoevsky's story reflect this belief?

7. In his dying words, Zossima instructs his fellow monks to take care of the peasant, to educate him and guard his heart, "for the peasant has God in his heart." Why are they to focus their efforts on the peasants rather than the upper class? What if we all took his advice to be servants to our servants?

8. Where do you see anti-Western sentiments in *The Brothers Karamazov*? Which of these critiques strike you as the most accurate and/or insightful? Why?

9. How does the life and sins of their father affect each of the sons? What is the author's overall message about family and redemption?

Orthodoxy

G. K. CHESTERTON

People have fallen into a foolish habit of speaking of orthodoxy as something heavy, humdrum, and safe. There never was anything so perilous or so exciting as orthodoxy.

GILBERT KEITH CHESTERTON was born in England in 1874. He was one of the most prolific writers of the early twentieth century, renowned for his essays, novels, plays, and many other literary works. *Orthodoxy* is his self-described "slovenly autobiography" of his intellectual search for a meaningful and true philosophy and its fulfillment in traditional Christianity. He begins with the analogy of a yachtsman who sets out on an adventure and, believing he has discovered a new land, realizes he has landed on his native English soil. Chesterton compares this to his own discovery that after having carefully crafted a life philosophy that he believed to be ahead of his late nineteenth-century times, he realizes that it is actually 1800 years behind the times, that it is, in fact, Christianity, or what Chesterton terms orthodoxy, by which he means Christianity as expressed by the Apostles' Creed.

Chesterton compares Christianity to various philosophies of his time, including materialism, determinism, and reason, concluding that Christianity holds a freedom that the others lack. Christianity's freedom is tied mainly to its mystery and mysticism, and its acceptance of paradox. As Chesterton writes, "Mysticism keeps men sane. As long as you have mystery you have health; when you destroy mystery you create morbidity. The ordinary man has always been sane because the ordinary man has always been a mystic. He has permitted the twilight. He has always had one foot in earth and the other in fairyland. He has always left himself free to doubt his gods; but (unlike the agnostic of to-day) free also to believe in them. He has always cared more for truth than for consistency. If he saw two truths that seemed to contradict each other, he would take the two truths and the contradiction along with them. . . . It is exactly this balance of apparent contradictions that has been the whole buoyancy of the healthy man."[1] He goes on to denounce the setting up of reason and faith as opposites by pointing out that to believe in reason requires faith. Chesterton also points out the shortcomings of skepticism as a philosophy. What is the use of being skeptical of everything and believing in nothing?

Chesterton expounds on the wisdom of tradition. Far from being opposed to democracy, he writes, tradition is actually "democracy extended through time. It is trusting to a consensus of common human voices rather than to some isolated or arbitrary record."[2] Those who reject tradition for the words of one modern theologian are, in essence, snobs appealing to the aristocracy. In his chapter "The Ethics of Elfland" he describes what he learned from fairy tales. We like fairy tales, he writes, because they remind us of the touch of fantastic, the miraculous, within us. We have forgotten who we really are, and "All that we call spirit and art and ecstacy [sic] only means that for one awful instant we remember that we forgot."[3] Fairy tales taught us that "life was as precious as it was puzzling. It was an ecstacy [sic] because it was an adventure; it was an adventure because it was an opportunity. The goodness of the fairy tale was not affected by the fact that there might be more dragons than princesses; it was good to be in a fairy tale. . . . The world was a shock, but it was not merely shocking; existence was a surprise, but it was a pleasant surprise."[4] To Chesterton, existence itself is so amazing and strange that one cannot complain of some limitations, analogous to having to leave the ball at midnight. One who complains of monogamy, he writes, does not appreciate the strange, unexpected gift of sex.

To his surprise Chesterton finds himself attracted to Christianity because of its transcendent and distinctive deity, and most of all, by the Christian notion that although God made the world and then set it free for us, we do not fit in the world. This viewpoint allows Chesterton to fulfill his instinct to love the world but not trust it. Moreover, it fulfills the promise of the beliefs he intuits from fairy tales.

But Chesterton finds himself struggling with the conflicting and contradictory claims of Christianity's critics—that the Church is at once too rich and too poor, weak and war-mongering, for women and antiwoman, for example. It seems to him that Christianity is accused of every vice and beaten with every stick. Finally, he concludes that in order for it to be accused of such contradictory things, it must in actuality represent a middle, or balance. Yet he soon realizes that this balance itself is found in paradox. Those critics are right, but they miss the point. Christianity's greatness is that in it humans are both chief of the creatures and chief sinners. In charity, Christians both love the sin and hate the sinner. These endless paradoxes all help Christianity to remain balanced, to allow two passionate sides—those of just war and pacifism, for example—to live side by side, without ousting each other. In fact, Chesterton defines Christianity as "a superhuman paradox whereby two opposite passions may blaze beside each other."[5]

Christianity also provides a fixed ideal, an eternal test, to which we all should strive. For if we believe (incorrectly) that progress is incremental and inevitable, we will not work toward it. The problem of Chesterton's age, he believes, is that the ideal to be achieved keeps changing, preventing any real progress. Christianity provides this eternal test, one created artistically by a creator, and, further, one that provides a sense of equality. The doctrine of the Fall addresses the fact that progress tends to lead to things getting worse and that no one among us, including and especially the rich, can be fully trusted to lead us to good. Even the democratic ideal of everyone's right to vote is Christian, in that it seeks to gain the opinion of those who are too humble or modest to otherwise offer it.

Up until this point, Chesterton has only been arguing for the health and social good of Christianity, but in the last chapter he seeks to prove its truth, to argue why it is important to believe the

Orthodoxy is about what motivates us and what we most value and how living in accordance with the teachings of Christianity makes true human flourishing possible.

—Charles Colson

doctrine and not just borrow its moral and social teachings. He describes a supernatural life that has buoyed historic Christendom, allowing Christian society to constantly resurrect itself. "All other societies die finally and with dignity," he writes. "We die daily. We are always being born again with almost indecent obstetrics."[6]

His most compelling reason, however, for submitting to Christianity as a faith is that it is a living teacher that continues to enlighten him. Even in the case of those doctrines about which he still has personal doubts, such as celibacy, Chesterton trusts to the greater authority of the Church and believes that someday he will be taught about this idea's particular good. He concludes by describing joy as the "gigantic secret of the Christian."[7] While pagans can rejoice in the small things, they must feel sad about the bigger things of life and death. Christians, in contrast, have their priorities right side up. As Chesterton writes, "Christianity satisfies suddenly and perfectly man's ancestral instinct for being the right way up; it satisfies it supremely in this; that by its creed joy becomes something gigantic and sadness something special and small."[8]

Why *Orthodoxy* Is Essential

There are not many books like *Orthodoxy*. Often described as Chesterton's journey to faith, focusing as it does on his progression of ideas rather than his life story, it is more of a work of apologetics with a little spiritual autobiography thrown in. Chesterton's book was extremely well received in his time and influenced such notable Christians as C. S. Lewis, whose own work of apologetics, *Mere Christianity,* also resides on our list.

As with the other memoirs on our list, we can read Chesterton's story, in all its quirkiness, for parallels to our own. As John Wilson, editorial board member and editor of *Books & Culture* writes, "*Orthodoxy* begins with the notion of a man setting out on a voyage— and 'discovering' his own country. Chesterton prompts us to do the same. More than a century after the book was written, the provocation remains fresh." Many among us will be able to relate to his attraction to some of the prevailing philosophies of his time, most of which are still prevalent—Nature worship, an emphasis on logic and reason above all else, and materialism, to name but a few. His sifting through and ultimate rejection of the claims of these traditions is thoughtful, helpful, and often surprising.

Perhaps the most important element of his book for modern readers is his central argument for the importance of tradition. Chesterton's defense of tradition as "democracy extended through time," as a consensus of human voices, is strongly compelling. It is refreshing and humbling to read such a defense of the voice of the common person from someone with such obvious intellectual gifts. His words speak volumes to those of us in many modern churches who may dismiss tradition for being out of date and/or view ourselves as more intelligent or enlightened as anyone who came before. He offers a corrective to any hasty concepts of reform. In addition to absorbing his thoughtful and well-articulated arguments for faith, we can also ask ourselves how open we are to this great tradition and to the living Church who seeks to teach us today and every day.

In the end, this rollicking adventure of a book is a call to the discipline of celebration. Chesterton's sense of excitement and joy in his journey is contagious. As he tells us, for Christians sadness becomes something small since we know that we can feel joyful about the larger questions in life, such as our origin and our eternal nature. Chesterton invites us to share in his joy, that "gigantic secret" of every Christian.

How to Read *Orthodoxy*

Chesterton refers to the "chaos" of his book in the last chapter, and reading his book can feel a bit like the adventure he describes as orthodoxy as he veers wildly from topic to topic, name-drops, and quotes from a wide variety of sources (seemingly off the top of his head, since his quotations are notoriously ever-so-slightly inaccurate). As a well-known journalist and writer of his times, he engaged in many public feuds in newspapers over various ideas and often made reference to the people with whom he debated. His writing is peppered with names and places that may not be familiar to a modern reader, but most editions contain footnotes that explain such references. Do not allow yourself to get hung up on such minutiae, but keep going.

Chesterton's book was written more than one hundred years ago, so it is noteworthy that so few of his ideas feel outdated. One egregious exception is his offensive words about "Negro slaves."[9] But his wit remains as effervescent as ever. For example, his thoughts on Nature: "So one elephant having a trunk was odd; but all elephants having trunks looked like a plot."[10] And on the size of the universe: "I was frightfully fond of the universe and wanted to address it by a diminutive. I often did so; and it never seemed to mind."[11] Despite his occasionally chaotic proliferation of ideas, Chesterton's humor, clarity, and effortless command of the language make *Orthodoxy* an enjoyable read.

EXCERPTS FROM

Orthodoxy

I have often had a fancy for writing a romance about an English yachtsman who slightly miscalculated his course and discovered England under the impression that it was a new island in the South Seas. I always find, however, that I am either too busy or too lazy to write this fine work, so I may as well give it away for the purposes of philosophical illustration. There will probably be a general impression that the man who landed (armed to the teeth and talking by signs) to plant the British flag on that barbaric temple which turned out to be the Pavilion at Brighton, felt rather a fool. I am not here concerned to deny that he looked a fool. But if you imagine that he felt a fool, or at any rate that the sense of folly was his sole or his dominant emotion, then you have not studied with sufficient delicacy the rich romantic nature of the hero of this tale. His mistake was really a most enviable mistake; and he knew it, if he was the man I take him for. What could be more delightful than to have in the same few minutes all the fascinating terrors of going abroad combined with all the humane security of coming home again? What could be better than to have all the fun of discovering South Africa without the disgusting necessity of landing there? What could be more glorious than to brace one's self up to discover New South Wales and then realize, with a gush of happy tears, that it was really old South Wales. This at least seems to me the main problem for philosophers, and is in a manner the main problem of this book. How can we contrive to be at once astonished at the world and yet at home in it? How can this queer cosmic town, with its many-legged citizens, with its monstrous and ancient lamps, how can this world give us at once the fascination of a strange town and the comfort and honour of being our own town?

To show that a faith or a philosophy is true from every standpoint would be too big an undertaking even for a much bigger book than this; it is necessary to follow one path of argument; and this is the path that I here propose to follow. I wish to set forth my faith as particularly answering this double spiritual need, the need for that mixture of the familiar and the unfamiliar which Christendom has rightly named romance. For the very word "romance" has in it the mystery and ancient meaning of Rome. Any one setting out to dispute anything ought always to begin by saying what he does not dispute. Beyond stating what he proposes to prove he should always state what he does not propose to prove. The thing I do not propose to prove, the thing I propose to take as common ground between myself and any average reader, is this desirability of an active and imaginative life, picturesque and full of a poetical curiosity, a life such as western man at any rate always seems to have desired. If a man says that extinction is better than existence or blank existence better than variety and adventure, then he is not one of the ordinary people to whom I am talking. If a man prefers nothing I can give him nothing. But nearly all people I have ever met in this western society in which I live would agree to the general proposition that we need this life of practical romance; the combination of something that is strange with something that is secure. We need so to view the world as to combine an idea of wonder and an idea of welcome. We need to be happy in this wonderland without once being merely comfortable. It is *this* achievement of my creed that I shall chiefly pursue in these pages.

But I have a peculiar reason for mentioning the man in a yacht, who discovered England. For I am that man in a yacht. I discovered England. I do not see how this book can avoid being egotistical; and I do not quite see (to tell the truth) how it can avoid being dull. Dulness will, however, free me from the charge which I most lament; the charge of being flippant. Mere light sophistry is the thing that I happen to despise most of all things, and it is perhaps a wholesome fact that this is the thing of which I am generally accused. I know nothing so contemptible as a mere paradox; a mere ingenious defence of the indefensible. If it were true (as has been said) that Mr. Bernard Shaw lived upon paradox, then he ought to be a mere common millionaire; for a man of his mental activity could invent a sophistry every six minutes. It is as easy as lying; because it is lying. The truth is, of course, that Mr. Shaw is cruelly hampered by the fact that he cannot tell any lie unless he thinks it is the truth. I find myself under the same intolerable bondage. I never in my life said anything merely because I thought it funny; though of course, I have had ordinary human vainglory, and may have thought it funny because I had said it. It is one thing to describe an interview with a gorgon or a griffin, a creature who does not exist. It is another thing to discover that the rhinoceros does exist and then take pleasure in the fact that he looks as if he didn't. One searches for truth, but it may be that one pursues instinctively the more extraordinary truths. And I offer this book with the heartiest sentiments to all the jolly people who hate what I write, and regard it (very justly, for all I know), as a piece of poor clowning or a single tiresome joke.

For if this book is a joke it is a joke against me. I am the man who with the utmost daring discovered what had been discovered before. If there is an element of farce in what follows, the farce is at my own expense; for this book explains how I fancied I was the first to set foot in Brighton and then found I was the last. It recounts my elephantine adventures in pursuit of the obvious. No one can think my case more ludicrous than I think it myself; no reader can accuse me here of trying to make a fool of him: I am the fool of this story, and no rebel shall hurl me from my throne. I freely confess all the idiotic ambitions of the end of the nineteenth century. I did, like all other solemn little boys, try to be in advance of the age. Like them I tried to be some ten minutes in advance of the truth. And I found that I was eighteen hundred years behind it. I did strain my voice with a painfully juvenile exaggeration in uttering my truths. And I was punished in the fittest and funniest way, for I have kept my truths: but I have discovered, not that they were not truths, but simply that they were not mine. When I fancied that I stood alone I was really in the ridiculous position of being backed up by all Christendom. It may be, Heaven forgive me, that I did try to be original; but I only succeeded in inventing all by myself an inferior copy of the existing traditions of civilized religion. The man from the yacht thought he was the first to find England; I thought I was the first to find Europe. I did try to found a heresy of my own; and when I had put the last touches to it, I discovered that it was orthodoxy.

. . .

I have another far more solid and central ground for submitting to [Christianity] as a faith, instead of merely picking up hints from it as a scheme. And that is this: that the Christian

Church in its practical relation to my soul is a living teacher, not a dead one. It not only certainly taught me yesterday, but will almost certainly teach me to-morrow. Once I saw suddenly the meaning of the shape of the cross; some day I may see suddenly the meaning of the shape of the mitre. One fine morning I saw why windows were pointed; some fine morning I may see why priests were shaven. Plato has told you a truth; but Plato is dead. Shakespeare has startled you with an image; but Shakespeare will not startle you with any more. But imagine what it would be to live with such men still living, to know that Plato might break out with an original lecture to-morrow, or that at any moment Shakespeare might shatter everything with a single song. The man who lives in contact with what he believes to be a living Church is a man always expecting to meet Plato and Shakespeare to-morrow at breakfast. He is always expecting to see some truth that he has never seen before. . . .

This, therefore, is, in conclusion, my reason for accepting the religion and not merely the scattered and secular truths out of the religion. I do it because the thing has not merely told this truth or that truth, but has revealed itself as a truth-telling thing. All other philosophies say the things that plainly seem to be true; only this philosophy has again and again said the thing that does not seem to be true, but is true. Alone of all creeds it is convincing where it is not attractive; it turns out to be right, like my father in the garden. Theosophists for instance will preach an obviously attractive idea like re-incarnation; but if we wait for its logical results, they are spiritual superciliousness and the cruelty of caste. For if a man is a beggar by his own pre-natal sins, people will tend to despise the beggar. But Christianity preaches an obviously unattractive idea, such as original sin; but when we wait for its results, they are pathos and brotherhood, and a thunder of laughter and pity; for only with original sin we can at once pity the beggar and distrust the king. Men of science offer us health, an obvious benefit; it is only afterwards that we discover that by health, they mean bodily slavery and spiritual tedium. Orthodoxy makes us jump by the sudden brink of hell;

it is only afterwards that we realise that jumping was an athletic exercise highly beneficial to our health. It is only afterwards that we realise that this danger is the root of all drama and romance. The strongest argument for the divine grace is simply its ungraciousness. The unpopular parts of Christianity turn out when examined to be the very props of the people. The outer ring of Christianity is a rigid guard of ethical abnegations and professional priests; but inside that inhuman guard you will find the old human life dancing like children, and drinking wine like men; for Christianity is the only frame for pagan freedom. But in the modern philosophy the case is opposite; it is its outer ring that is obviously artistic and emancipated; its despair is within.

My Personal Top 5

RON SIDER

1 *Miracles*, C. S. Lewis. Decades ago, this book helped me realize that belief in historic Christianity's acceptance of miracles is quite defensible for a modern thinker in our scientific world. I still use it as a text.

2 *Surprised by Resurrection*, N. T. Wright. This short statement of what this superb New Testament scholar develops in numerous books is an excellent summary of Jesus' gospel of the kingdom and our eschatological hope.

3 *The Politics of Jesus*, John Howard Yoder. I do not agree with every argument in this enormously influential book, but I believe most of his central claims are biblical and important.

4 *Celebration of Discipline*, Richard J. Foster. Perhaps the best book on the inward journey written in the last century.

5 *Discovering Biblical Equality: Complementarity Without Hierarchy*, Ronald W. Pierce (Editor), Rebecca Merrill Groothuis (Editor), Gordon D. Fee (Editor). This is probably the best place to find a solidly biblical, comprehensive argument for the full equality of women and men.

RON SIDER is the founder and president of Evangelicals for Social Action. He is the author of *Rich Christians in an Age of Hunger* and numerous other books and is a longtime professor at Palmer Theological Seminary at Eastern University.

And its despair is this, that it does not really believe that there is any meaning in the universe; therefore it cannot hope to find any romance; its romances will have no plots. A man cannot expect any adventures in the land of anarchy. But a man can expect any number of adventures if he goes travelling in the land of authority. One can find no meanings in a jungle of scepticism; but the man will find more and more meanings who walks through a forest of doctrine and design. Here everything has a story tied to its tail, like the tools or pictures in my father's house; for it is my father's house. I end where I began—at the right end. I have entered at last the gate of all good philosophy. I have come into my second childhood.[12]

A Study Guide for *Orthodoxy*

1. Chesterton believes that Christianity's mystic qualities are what sets it apart—the freedom that its adherents have to accept mystery and paradox. Do you agree? Why or why not? What contradictions have gone hand in hand with your faith?

2. What do you think of upon hearing the word *tradition*? If your thoughts are not all positive, do Chesterton's arguments (that tradition is democracy extended through time, for example) help to reclaim the idea of tradition for you? Why or why not?

3. Chesterton writes, "The fairy tales founded in me two convictions; first, that this world is a wild and startling place, which might have been quite different, but which is quite delightful; second, that before this wildness and delight one may well be modest and submit to the queerest limitations of so queer a kindness."[13] Is the modern world opposed to such ideas? Do you share them? Explain.

4. Chesterton vigorously denies the notion that some creeds are appropriate for one century and not for the next. Why does he disagree? Are there any parts of Christian faith according to the Apostles' Creed that you find outdated or otherwise inappropriate for modern times? If so, why?

5. How can you relate to Chesterton's journey toward Christianity as he puzzles through various critics' contradictory claims about Christianity, i.e., that it is both too weak and too violent, too focused on the family and too antifamily, too pessimistic and too optimistic?

6. Have you ever been bothered by any of the paradoxes within Christianity? If so, how did you resolve your way of thinking? Have you ever seen such paradoxes, as Chesterton does, as Christianity's strength?

7. Chesterton writes, "The Christian Church in its practical relation to my soul is a living teacher, not a dead one. . . . The man who lives in contact with what he believes to be a living Church is always expecting to meet Plato and Shakespeare tomorrow at breakfast. He is always expecting to see some truth that he has never seen before."[14] How has the Church been a living teacher for you? Do you live with this sense of expectancy to see new truth revealed? If not, how might doing so change your life?

8. Chesterton writes that celibacy is one of the doctrines he accepts as good because "the best human experience is against me"[15] due to its long tradition in the Church and even in other cultures, but for which he has not yet been personally taught the good of. What such doctrines are you still questioning? How might it change your mind to see it as something which you have not yet been taught?

The Poetry of
Gerard Manley Hopkins

Nineteenth-century British poet and Jesuit priest Gerard Manley Hopkins expressed his love for God and the unique characteristics of God's creatures through the striking imagery of his poetry.

SUMMA

The best ideal is the true

And other truth is none.

All glory be ascribèd to

The holy Three in One.

BORN TO A WELL-TO-DO and artistic family in Stratford, England, in 1844, Gerard Manley Hopkins began composing poetry at age ten. As a young man studying at Oxford, he converted to Catholicism and then became a Jesuit priest. Concerned that his poetry was preventing him from concentrating fully on his faith, he burned his poems and stopped writing poetry entirely for seven years. But in 1875, when he was studying theology at a Jesuit house in Wales, his superior asked him to write a poem commemorating the near sinking of the German liner *Deutschland,* in which 157 people died, including five nuns fleeing Germany's harsh anti-Catholic laws. This poem, several stanzas of which appear in the excerpt included here, expresses Hopkins's dismay at the disaster but ends on a note of adoration, reconciling the horrible events with God's ultimate goodness. He submitted the poem to a Jesuit publication, where it was accepted but not published, compounding his confusion about his poetry. He continued to write, however, completing two collections of sonnets, "God's Grandeur" and "The Windhover," before he was ordained. He wrote poetry throughout his life, but his latter sonnets reflected his depression as he struggled to find success as a teacher and continued to try to reconcile his ideas about being true to his faith with his talent as a poet. It was only after his death that his poetry became well known and started to enjoy the critical and popular accolades that it continues to receive today.

Hopkins was known for his complicated use of rhythm, a technique he called sprung rhythm, and for his concept of "inscape." By inscape Hopkins meant the particular set of attributes that make each thing unique. The concept was inherently religious; something's inscape was a glimpse as to why God created it. In fact, Hopkins believed the purpose of poetry was to convey inscape. It is little wonder, then, that nature is one of Hopkins's most pervasive themes. From "The Windhover" to "Spring" to "Pied Beauty," he expresses the beauty of nature in lovely and surprising ways. In "Pied Beauty" he describes with lush language the beauty of several of God's creatures but also admires man-made things such as "gear and tackle and trim." In "God's Grandeur" he writes of how nature remains fresh, infused with the Holy Spirit, despite being trodden on by generations of humankind. But Hopkins sees beauty in people as well as in creatures and nature. In "As Kingfishers Catch Fire, Dragonflies Draw Flame," he writes of Christ's playing "in ten thousand places," dwelling in the features of men.

Why the Poetry of Gerard Manley Hopkins Is Essential

Hopkins's poetry stands out for many literary reasons, but his devotional focus has influenced countless Christians. Thomas Merton had an abiding love of Hopkins's poetry and was reading a biography of Hopkins when he made the decision to become a Catholic. Poetry can provide us with a powerful avenue into God's presence, and Hopkins's poems exude joy and prayer in every line. From his overtly theological focus to the pleasure he obviously takes in describing the beauty of nature, Hopkins's poems are uniquely suited to prayer. As editorial board member Emilie Griffin writes, "I use his poetry as prayer. You can take a single line and allow it to lead you into the presence of God." For some this way of meeting God has been somewhat lost or set aside. In today's culture many of us only experience poetry through popular songs, at least in mainstream life. With Hopkins, we can experience the music of God, the mystery of God, the melody of God's creation. With poetry such as Hopkins's, nothing gets in the way of our seeking to encounter God through his words.

Hopkins offers us an opportunity to practice the discipline of meditation on the written word, a practice Richard J. Foster describes for us in *Celebration of Discipline:* "Take a . . . few verses, or even a single word and allow it to take root in you. Seek to live the experience, remembering the encouragement of Ignatius of Loyola to apply all our senses to our task. Smell the sea. Hear the lap of water along the shore. See the crowd. Feel the sun on your head and the hunger in your stomach. Taste the salt in the air. . . . Our task is not so much to study the passage as it is to be initiated into the reality of which the passage speaks."[1] One of the roles of poetry is to help us to look at something familiar in a new way. Like all good poets, Hopkins can help us get past ourselves and take a moment to exclaim over the goodness of God and the beauty of life.

The "inscape" we see in Hopkins's poetry captures the beauty of ordinary things and helps us to see them in a new way, a way that gives glory both to God and to creation. It also emphasizes for us the wonderful gift we have in nature and the responsibility we share as its stewards. For this focus, Hopkins has been called an early environmentalist. As we see in many of Hopkins's poems, such as "God's Grandeur," he mourned the destruction of nature caused by nineteenth-century practices of industrialization, using words like "smudge" and "smear" and "blear" to make clear just how industrialization affected God's creation. He portrays so clearly the loveliness of nature, the beauty that it has in and of itself, that we cannot help but mourn with him the loss and alteration of so much of God's creation and vow to take better care of that with which God has entrusted us.

Hopkins first discovered and employed so fully the holy and beautiful uses of distortion . . . verbal, syntactical, and imagistic distortion. He suggested God with passion and exposed God to us by setting things just enough a-kilter so we can see Him in the space beyond the stage set we call reality.

—Phyllis Tickle

How to Read the Poetry of
Gerard Manley Hopkins

Like most verse, Hopkins's poems are meant to be read aloud. Try reading them both silently, so that your heart can hear the words, and aloud, so that your ears can hear what the heart is vocalizing. Or ask someone to read them to you and then reciprocate.

Sometimes it can be hard to discern the meaning in poetry, and Hopkins's poetry is no exception. "The Wreck of the Deutschland" in particular has a reputation for being difficult. It may help to read it keeping in mind Hopkins's own advice to his friend and publisher, Robert Bridges—not to bother too much with the meaning but to "pay attention to the best and most intelligible stanzas."[2] Hopkins also commented, "Granted that it needs study and is obscure, for indeed I was not over-desirous that the meaning of all should be quite clear, at least unmistakeable, you might, without the effort that to make it all out would seem to have required, have nevertheless read it so that lines and stanzas should be left in the memory and superficial impressions deepened, and have liked some without exhausting all."[3]

So, with the permission of the poet, take it line by line, stopping with those lines and stanzas that hold particular appeal to you. And most important, try reading his poetry as you would a prayer. Offer it to God. Open yourself to it, word by word, and let it take you to a new place of understanding.

The Poetry of Gerard Manley Hopkins

STANZAS 32–35 FROM "THE WRECK OF THE DEUTSCHLAND"

32

      I admire thee, master of the tides,
        Of the Yore-flood, of the year's fall;
    The recurb and the recovery of the gulf's sides,
        The girth of it and the wharf of it and the wall;
  Stanching, quenching ocean of a motionable mind;
  Ground of being, and granite of it: past all
      Grasp God, throned behind
Death with a sovereignty that heeds but hides, bodes but
    abides;

33

      With a mercy that outrides
        The all of water, an ark
    For the listener; for the lingerer with a love glides
        Lower than death and the dark;
  A vein for the visiting of the past-prayer, pent in prison,
  The-last-breath penitent spirits—the uttermost mark
      Our passion-plungèd giant risen,
The Christ of the Father compassionate, fetched in the storm
    of his strides.

34

      Now burn, new born to the world,
        Doubled-naturèd name,
    The heaven-flung, heart-fleshed, maiden-furled
        Miracle-in-Mary-of-flame,

Mid-numbered He in three of the thunder-throne!
Not a dooms-day dazzle in his coming nor dark as he
   came;
   Kind, but royally reclaiming his own;
A released shower, let flash to the shire, not a lightning of fire
   hard-hurled.

35
      Dame, at our door
      Drowned, and among our shoals,
   Remember us in the roads, the heaven-haven of the
      Reward:
      Our King back, oh, upon English souls!
   Let him easter in us, be a dayspring to the dimness of us,
      be a crimson-cresseted east,
   More brightening her, rare-dear Britain, as his reign rolls,
      Pride, rose, prince, hero of us, high-priest,
Our hearts' charity's hearth's fire, our thoughts' chivalry's
   throng's Lord.[4]

"PIED BEAUTY"

Glory be to God for dappled things—
   For skies of couple-colour as a brinded cow;
      For rose-moles all in stipple upon trout that swim;
Fresh-firecoal chestnut-falls; finches' wings;
   Landscape plotted and pieced-fold, fallow, and plough;
      And áll trádes, their gear and tackle and trim.

All things counter, original, spare, strange;
   Whatever is fickle, freckled (who knows how?)
      With swift, slow; sweet, sour; adazzle, dim;
He fathers-forth whose beauty is past change:
      Praise him.[5]

"GOD'S GRANDEUR"

The world is charged with the grandeur of God.
   It will flame out, like shining from shook foil;

It gathers to a greatness, like the ooze of oil
Crushed. Why do men then now not reck his rod?
Generations have trod, have trod, have trod;
  And all is seared with trade; bleared, smeared with toil;
  And wears man's smudge and shares man's smell: the
    soil
Is bare now, nor can foot feel, being shod.

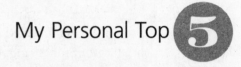

My Personal Top 5

TOM SMITH

1 ***The Return of the Prodigal Son***, Henri Nouwen. I read Nouwen when my faith was almost lost. In a time where I needed to find my identity he reminded me of my "belovedness" and invited me to make this "belovedness" the bedrock of my search for who I am.

2 ***Life Together***, Dietrich Bonhoeffer. Whenever I am discouraged and disillusioned with church life and Christians' "life together," I turn to the timeless exhortations of Bonhoeffer. He challenges motives and gives practical advice on how to live as a community together.

3 ***The Divine Conspiracy***, Dallas Willard. This book messed me up—in the best of ways. It opened up the vast panorama of God's kingdom and the invitation to live as an apprentice of Jesus. I have read this book every year since its publication and must confess that I still don't get it all.

4 ***Surprised by Hope***, N. T. Wright. Heaven never really excited me and was a hindrance of me wanting to follow Jesus. Who wants to sing for an eternity? Wright's book reclaims the importance of the physical body and life *after* life after death. This book, as the title suggests, surprised me with its hope.

5 ***Signposts to Spirituality***, Trevor Hudson. This book gave me a beautiful picture of who God is and pointed to the ways in which I can respond. It is down-to-earth and very practical. The author uses everyday stories that I can relate to. *Signposts* has been a lifesaver in the minefield of spiritual technology.

TOM SMITH is the convener of an aspiring Renovaré expression in South Africa and a member of Claypot community in Johannesburg.

And for all this, nature is never spent;
    There lives the dearest freshness deep down things;
And though the last lights off the black West went
      Oh, morning, at the brown brink eastward, springs—
Because the Holy Ghost over the bent
      World broods with warm breast and with ah! bright
          wings.[6]

"AS KINGFISHERS CATCH FIRE,
DRAGONFLIES DRÁW FLÁME"

As kingfishers catch fire, dragonflies dráw fláme;
As tumbled over rim in roundy wells
Stones ring; like each tucked string tells, each hung bell's
Bow swung finds tongue to fling out broad its name;
Each mortal thing does one thing and the same:
Deals out that being indoors each one dwells;
Selves—goes itself; *myself* it speaks and spells,
Crying *Whát I do is me: for that I came.*

Í say móre: the just man justices;
Kéeps gráce: thát keeps all his goings graces;
Acts in God's eye what in God's eye he is—
Chríst—for Christ plays in ten thousand places,
Lovely in limbs, and lovely in eyes not his
To the Father through the features of men's faces.[7]

A Study Guide for the Poetry of
Gerard Manley Hopkins

1. Have you ever tried to use poetry as prayer? If so, what was
   the result?

2. Hopkins was haunted by the wreck of the *Deutschland*
   and seemed to work through his feelings by writing his
   beautiful poem about the tragedy. When has some kind

of tragedy challenged your faith? How did you work through it? Did writing help, or in hindsight do you think it might have?

3. What do you think is meant by the phrase "Let him easter in us"?

4. What image from "Pied Beauty" most stands out to you?

5. In "Pied Beauty" Hopkins offers glory to God for created things such as cows and trout, but also for human-made things such as "gear and tackle and trim." What do you think of his offering glory for both? What unusual things do you wish to praise God for?

6. In "God's Grandeur" Hopkins describes how "nature is never spent" despite being "seared with trade" and "smeared with soil." What do you learn from reflecting on this poem? What does it say about the relationship between humankind and the earth?

7. What do you think Hopkins is trying to convey with the images in the first stanza of "As kingfishers catch fire, dragonflies dráw fláme"?

8. Reflect on the line about Christ's playing in ten thousand places. What does this mean to you? How does this stanza affect the way you think God sees you?

The Cost of Discipleship

DIETRICH BONHOEFFER

Cheap grace is the preaching of forgiveness without re- quiring repentance, baptism without church discipline, Communion without confession, absolution without per- sonal confession. Cheap grace is grace without disciple- ship, grace without the cross, grace without Jesus Christ, living and incarnate. Costly grace is . . . the call of Jesus Christ at which the disciple leaves his nets and follows him. . . . Such grace is costly *because it calls us to follow, and it is* grace *because it calls us to follow Jesus Christ. It is costly because it costs a man his life, and it is grace because it gives a man the only true life.*

> Bonhoeffer calls us to submit wholeheartedly to "the kindly yoke of Jesus Christ."

DIETRICH BONHOEFFER was born in Breslau, Ger- many, in 1906 to a well-connected and highly edu- cated family. He knew by the age of fourteen that he wanted to study theology, and at twenty-one he presented his doctoral thesis, an examination of Christ as commu- nity. After pastoring and briefly studying in the United States, he returned to Germany to serve as a university lecturer in 1931, just as Adolf Hitler was rising to power. Bonhoeffer publicly expressed his concerns about the power German society was giving to this "mis- leader" and the anti-Semitism he was promoting. After a radio ad- dress Bonhoeffer gave in 1933 criticizing Hitler was cut off midway, he left the country to pastor two German congregations in Lon- don. Meanwhile, in the late 1930s, pro-Nazi pastors took over all the bishop positions in the official German Church, which became known as the Reich Church. Within Germany, those who refused to accept anti-Semitism as official church policy started a dissenting "Confessing Church," which Hitler and his forces persecuted. Bonhoeffer was asked to lead a new seminary for the Confessing Church and immediately returned to Germany to do so. Many times afterward he could have left Germany for safety abroad, but Bonhoeffer believed that Christianity was not about being shut up prayerfully in a room but serving visibly in the world as a part of the Church, the active body of Christ. To him, Christianity meant being prepared for martyrdom and death. After the seminary was shut down by the Nazis two years later, Bonhoeffer became involved in a covert military plot to assassinate Hitler. Imprisoned in April 1943 for his role in a plan to smuggle Jews out of Germany, Bonhoeffer was eventually implicated in the coup d'état following a July 1944 failed assassination attempt on Hitler. Bonhoeffer was executed on April 9, 1945, at the concentration camp at Flossenbürg. "This is the end—for me, the beginning of life," he said.

Bonhoeffer wrote *The Cost of Discipleship* in direct opposition to the Nazi regime. He begins the book with a stinging indictment of the churches of his day for not offering enough Jesus. Instead they are preaching yet another man-made dogma to lay over the top of people's already overburdened shoulders. The Church, he asserts, has forgotten the idea of discipleship. Instead we offer cheap grace. Cheap grace is coming to church for an hour once a week to receive forgiveness, to live just like the rest of the world, without changing anything about our lives from the way they were before we were baptized. "Cheap grace is the preaching of forgiveness without requiring repentance, baptism without church discipline, Communion without confession, absolution without personal confession. Cheap grace is grace without discipleship, grace without the cross, grace without Jesus Christ, living and incarnate."[1] When acting under cheap grace, we try to submit while simultaneously resisting in favor of our own wills. Such submission is hard, if not impossible. In contrast, submitting wholeheartedly to the "kindly yoke of Jesus Christ" is easy.[2] Such obedience is costly grace. It is dropping everything to follow Jesus Christ. It costs us our lives as we knew them, but it gives us life as we were meant to have it. This grace comes not from us, but from Christ. And it is not just for the spiritual elite, but for everyone. As Luther realized, we are all called to this life of costly grace, not just a select few in monasteries and convents. In fact, our justification from sin compels us to act in the world out of gratitude and response. Bonhoeffer minces no words in condemning the theology of cheap grace, saying that it has resulted in "millions of spiritual corpses"[3] and that "the word of cheap grace has been the ruin of more Christians than any commandment of works."[4]

The discipleship Bonhoeffer describes is radical. To be true disciples means to follow Jesus, to give ourselves completely over to him. And that means that only Jesus knows where our journeys end. It is not possible to give ourselves over to the living Christ without obedience and giving up our own ways. We must leave all behind and enter a new existence through obedience. Only those who obey can be said to believe. We are not to take the time to think it over; we are simply to obey. This obedience is quite literal, and it involves taking up our crosses and following Jesus—in others words, participating in his suffering and rejection. But even as we suffer, we, paradoxically, do not, since suffering is being cut off from God and when we are in communion with him, we cannot suffer. As Bonhoeffer writes, "Hence while it is still true that suffering means being cut off from God, yet within the fellowship of Christ's suffering, suffering is overcome by suffering, and becomes the way to communion with God."[5]

In an extended meditation on the Sermon on the Mount, Bonhoeffer casts the Beatitudes as a description of the characteristics of those who are obedient to Christ. He has no patience for those who want to explain away Jesus' words or spend a lot of time analyzing what each means in each particular situation. He writes, "The object of Jesus' command is always the same—to evoke wholehearted faith, to make us love God and our neighbor with all our heart and soul. This is the only unequivocal feature in his command."[6] And if we want to know what Jesus would have us do in any concrete situation, we have the Holy Spirit to help us. Bonhoeffer interprets the entire Sermon in the light of unreserved love, spelling out, in

A man destined to fail, hanged as a thirty-nine-year-old, has now deeply influenced—perhaps troubled—Christianity for half a century.

—Eberhard Bethge

the paradoxes of which he is fond, how we are called to publicly save the world and also remain hidden in our devotion, coming to God unself-consciously, like children.

Finally, he reminds us of the vital role of the Church and its sacraments. Here is where we can find Christ. In baptism we die to our old lives and are reborn in our new lives of obedience to Christ. Baptism grants us entry into Christ's body, and the Lord's Supper gives us fellowship with one another and communion with Christ himself.

Why *The Cost of Discipleship* Is Essential

Bonhoeffer was a respected and established theologian before his untimely death, but the incredible witness he provided with his life and martyrdom helped bring his message to a global audience. His life exemplified what he urged everyone to in *The Cost of Discipleship*—complete obedience to Christ. Far from those who attend church for one hour each week and call themselves Christians without any discernible impact on their lives, Bonhoeffer calls us to a discipleship that is radical and life changing. His message calls each of us to evaluate our own level of commitment and obedience to Christ. As editorial board member Lyle SmithGraybeal writes, "Often I am reminded in *The Cost of Discipleship* of Bonhoeffer's injunction that we are to both believe and obey. No matter how much we by nature break it down to manage it, a life of following Jesus is all of one cloth. Jesus is to be our Savior and our Lord and as a consequence, as Bonhoeffer shows us, our Life." Have we renounced everything to take up our crosses and follow Christ? Have we slipped on the easy, kind yoke of Christ, or are we still struggling to be yoked to both Christ and our own self-interest? Have we wholeheartedly accepted that we no longer control our futures or know how our lives will end or what direction they will take? If we cannot answer yes to these questions, Bonhoeffer tells us that we have not truly become disciples and, further, we cannot truly be said to believe since obedience and faith are two sides of the same coin.

Bonhoeffer emphasizes a commitment to action rather than knowledge, a powerful message coming from someone so theologically and exegetically gifted. Using the evidence of the story of the rich young man and of the Pharisee who asked Jesus who his neighbor was, Bonhoeffer makes it clear we are not to sit around parsing abstract concepts or asking a lot of questions to avoid commitment. We obey, and we do it immediately, or else we cannot be obedient at all. We are called to action in the world; indeed we have a great responsibility to the world, a responsibility that requires us to act publicly and visibly. We are the light of the world, Jesus tells us in the Sermon on the Mount. *We,* not Jesus. Yet, at the same time, this discipleship that Bonhoeffer describes is one that shuns worldly recognition. In contrast to a culture of individualism, Bonhoeffer prescribes the discipline of secrecy, for Jesus tells us that the light that shines is that of our good works, not that of the disciples who perform them. He also instructs that prayer and almsgiving are to be done in secret. How do we accomplish this? To Bonhoeffer, spontaneity is the key. As much as possible our good works are to be unmeditated to such an extent that we are hardly aware of them, what Bonhoeffer calls a "voluntary blindness."[7]

And finally, Bonhoeffer brings us, quite simply, a no-holds-barred focus on what matters—Jesus, the Bible, and the Church. In the radical discipleship and obedience Bonhoeffer describes, Jesus is the mediator in front of whom we stand, naked and alone. We can have no true relationship with another person except through Jesus. In addition to his focus on Jesus, Bonhoeffer emphasizes the primacy of Scripture. His writing is adorned not with personal anecdotes or humorous stories, but with Bible references. It is an important reminder to us that, as helpful as other references and experiences may be, our foundation must always be the Bible. The Sermon on the Mount, for Bonhoeffer, is particularly important as a roadmap to discipleship.

And, finally, Bonhoeffer reminds us of the importance of the Church as Christ's body and of the sacraments of baptism and Communion. To any of us who might be tempted to try to practice a solo Christianity, Bonhoeffer reminds us that Jesus brings us a new fellowship, that of the Church. We are indeed Christ's visible body, and it is in this capacity that we are called to a frontal assault on the world.

How to Read *The Cost of Discipleship*

The Cost of Discipleship is a work of theology, and it differs from many more contemporary writings in that Bonhoeffer uses no personal stories or anecdotes; he is drawing upon the Bible rather than his life. But despite the lack of personal stories in the text, the details of Bonhoeffer's life overlay the entire book. Here is no hypocrite calling others to a radical form of taking up their crosses that he does not himself adhere to. We know that Bonhoeffer lived out his words to the fullest extent. So if we find his tone harsh at times and feel overwhelmed at the height of his standards, we remember that Bonhoeffer is trying to help us. He has no patience for excuses and theological debate unconnected to life; he wants us to know what it is to truly follow Christ. And to do that, we have to get out there and get on with it.

EXCERPTS FROM

The Cost of Discipleship

COSTLY GRACE

Cheap grace is the deadly enemy of our Church. We are fighting to-day for costly grace.

Cheap grace means grace sold on the market like cheapjacks' wares. The sacraments, the forgiveness of sin, and the consolations of religion are thrown away at cut prices. Grace is represented as the Church's inexhaustible treasury, from which she showers blessings with generous hands, without asking questions or fixing limits. Grace without price; grace without cost! The essence of grace, we suppose, is that the account has been paid in advance; and, because it has been paid, everything can be had for nothing. Since the cost was infinite, the possibilities of using and spending it are infinite. What would grace be if it were not cheap?

Cheap grace means grace as a doctrine, a principle, a system. It means forgiveness of sins proclaimed as a general truth, the love of God taught as the Christian "conception" of God. An intellectual assent to that idea is held to be of itself sufficient to secure remission of sins. The Church which holds the correct doctrine of grace has, it is supposed, *ipso facto* a part in that grace. In such a Church the world finds a cheap covering for its sins; no contrition is required, still less any real desire to be delivered from sin. Cheap grace therefore amounts to a denial of the living Word of God, in fact, a denial of the Incarnation of the Word of God.

Cheap grace means the justification of sin without the justification of the sinner. Grace alone does everything, they say, and so everything can remain as it was before. "All for sin could not atone." The world goes on the same old way, and we are still sinners "even in the best life" as Luther said. Well, then, let the Christian live like the rest of the world, let him model himself on the world's standards in every sphere of life, and not presumptuously aspire to live a different life under grace from his old life under sin. That was the heresy of the enthusiasts, the Anabaptists and their kind. Let the Christian beware of rebelling against the free and boundless grace of God and desecrating it. Let him not attempt to erect a new religion of the letter by endeavouring to live a life of obedience to the commandments of Jesus Christ! The world has been justified by grace. The Christian knows that, and takes it seriously. He knows he must not strive against this indispensable grace. Therefore—let him live like the rest of the world! Of course he would like to go and do something extraordinary, and it does demand a good deal of self-restraint to refrain from the attempt and content himself with living as the world lives. Yet it is imperative for the Christian to achieve renunciation, to practise self-effacement, to distinguish his life from the life of the world. He must let grace be grace indeed, otherwise he will destroy the world's faith in the free gift of grace. Let the Christian rest content with his worldliness and with this renunciation of any higher standard than the world. He is doing it for the sake of the world rather than for the sake of grace. Let him be comforted and rest assured in his possession of this grace—for grace alone does everything. Instead of following Christ, let the Christian enjoy the consolations of his grace! That is what we mean by cheap grace, the grace which amounts to the justification of sin without the justification of the repentant sinner who departs from sin and from whom sin departs. Cheap grace is not the kind of forgiveness of sin which frees us from the toils of sin. Cheap grace is the grace we bestow upon ourselves.

Cheap grace is the preaching of forgiveness without requiring repentance, baptism without church discipline, Communion without confession, absolution without personal confession. Cheap grace is grace without discipleship, grace without the cross, grace without Jesus Christ, living and incarnate.

Costly grace is the treasure hidden in the field; for the sake of it a man will gladly go and sell all that he has. It is the pearl of great price to buy which the merchant will sell all his goods. It is the kingly rule of Christ, for whose sake a man will pluck out the eye which causes him to stumble; it is the call of Jesus Christ at which the disciple leaves his nets and follows him.

Costly grace is the gospel which must be *sought* again and again, the gift which must be *asked* for, the door at which a man must *knock*.

Such grace is *costly* because it calls us to follow, and it is *grace* because it calls us to follow *Jesus Christ*. It is costly because it costs a man his life, and it is grace because it gives a man the only true life. It is costly because it condemns sin, and grace because it justifies the sinner. Above all, it is *costly* because it cost God the life of his Son: "ye were bought at a price," and what has cost God much cannot be cheap for us. Above all, it is *grace* because God did not reckon his Son too dear a price to pay for our life, but delivered him up for us. Costly grace is the Incarnation of God.

Costly grace is the sanctuary of God; it has to be protected from the world, and not thrown to the dogs. It is therefore the living word, the Word of God, which he speaks as it pleases him. Costly grace confronts us as a gracious call to follow Jesus, it comes as a word of forgiveness to the broken spirit and the contrite heart. Grace is costly because it compels a man to submit to the yoke of Christ and follow him; it is grace because Jesus says: "My yoke is easy and my burden is light."

THE IMAGE OF CHRIST

To be conformed to the image of Christ is not an ideal to be striven after. It is not as though we had to imitate him as well as we could. We cannot transform ourselves into his image; it is rather the form of Christ which seeks to be formed in us (Gal 4:19), and to be manifested in us. Christ's work in us is not finished until he has perfected his own form in us. We must be assimilated to the form of Christ in its entirety, the form of Christ incarnate, crucified and glorified.

Christ took upon himself this human form of ours. He became Man even as we are men. In his humanity and in his lowliness we recognize our own form. He has become like a man, so that men should be like him. And in the Incarnation the whole human race recovers the dignity of the image of God. Henceforth, any attack even on the least of men is an attack on Christ, who took the form of man, and in his own Person restored the image of God in all that bears a human form. Through fellowship and communion with the incarnate Lord, we recover our true humanity, and at the same time we are delivered from that individualism which is the consequence of sin, and retrieve our solidarity with the whole human race. By being partakers of Christ incarnate, we are partakers in the whole humanity which he bore. We now know that we have been taken up and borne in the humanity of Jesus, and therefore that new nature we now enjoy means that we too must bear the sins and sorrows of others. The incarnate Lord makes his followers the brothers of all mankind. The "philanthropy" of God (Titus 3:4) revealed in the Incarnation is the ground of Christian love toward all on earth that bears the name of man. The form of Christ incarnate makes the Church into the Body of Christ. All the sorrows of mankind fall upon that form, and only through that form can they be borne.

The earthly form of Christ is the form that died on the cross. The image of God is the image of Christ crucified. It is to this image that the life of the disciples must be conformed; in other words, they must be conformed to his death (Phil 3:10; Rom 6:4f). The Christian life is a life of crucifixion (Gal 2:19). In baptism the form of Christ's death is impressed upon his own. They are dead to the flesh and to sin, they are dead to the world, and the world is dead to them (Gal 6:14). Anybody living in the strength of Christ's baptism lives in the strength of Christ's death. Their life is marked by a daily dying in the war between the flesh and the spirit, and in the mortal agony the devil inflicts upon them day by day. This is the suffering of Christ which all his disciples on earth must undergo. A few, but only a few, of his followers are accounted worthy of the closest fellowship with his sufferings—the blessed martyrs. No other Christian is so closely identified with the form of Christ crucified. When Christians are exposed to public insult, when they suffer and die for his sake, Christ takes on visible form in his Church. Here we see the divine image created anew through the power of Christ crucified. But throughout the Christian life, from baptism to martyrdom, it is the same suffering and the same death.

If we are conformed to his image in his Incarnation and crucifixion, we shall also share the glory of his resurrection. "We shall also bear the image of the heavenly" (1 Cor 15:49). "We shall be like him, for we shall see him even as he is" (1 John 3:2). If we contemplate the image of the glorified Christ, we shall be made like unto it, just as by contemplating the image of Christ crucified we are conformed to his death. We shall be drawn into his image, and identified with his form, and become a reflection of him. That reflection of his glory will shine forth in us even in this life, even as we share his agony and bear his cross. Our life will then be a progress from knowledge to knowledge, from glory to glory, to an ever closer conformity with the image of the Son of God. "But we all, with unveiled face reflecting as a mirror the glory of the Lord, are transformed into the same image from glory to glory" (2 Cor 3:18).

My Personal Top 5

BRIAN MCLAREN

When I think of spiritual influences on my life today, I go to authors first, then books.

1 Barbara Brown Taylor writes in prose, but her books work on me like spiritual poetry. **An Altar in This World**, her most recent, is probably my favorite.

2 I have come back to Paul Tournier's **The Adventure of Living** again and again. His magnanimous approach to faith, people, and God captured my heart when I was in college.

3 Leonardo Boff's **Cry of the Earth, Cry of the Poor** captures his vision and spirit. He communicates a spirituality that engages with the world.

4 Few books have broadened and deepened me theologically more than Kwame Bediako's **Theology and Identity**, and the impact of his point of view on my own spiritual development continues. Bediako wrote theology from an African perspective, something we in the West desperately need.

5 As an articulator of Christian faith in the contemporary world, I think of Wendell Berry (along with Walker Percy) as America's C. S. Lewis. It's hard to choose between Berry's nonfiction (like **Sex, Economy, Freedom, and Community**), his fiction (like **Jayber Crow** or **Hannah Coulter**), and his poetry, but for spiritual nourishment, I'd have to go with his poetry, with **A Timbered Choir** being my favorite. If one can't be outdoors, communing with God in the wordless poetry of God's own creation, reading Wendell Berry might be the next best thing.

BRIAN MCLAREN is the author of *A New Kind of Christianity* and *Naked Spirituality*.

This is what we mean when we speak of Christ dwelling in our hearts. His life on earth is not finished yet, for he continues to live in the lives of his followers. Indeed it is wrong to speak of the Christian life: we should speak rather of Christ living in us. "I live, and yet no longer I, but Christ liveth in me" (Gal 2:20). Jesus Christ, incarnate, crucified and glorified, has entered my life and taken charge. "To me to live is Christ" (Phil 1:21). And where Christ lives, there the Father also lives, and both Father and Son through the Holy Ghost. The Holy Trinity himself has made his dwelling in the Christian heart, filling his whole being, and transforming him into the divine image. Christ, incarnate, crucified and glorified is formed in every Christian soul, for all are members of his Body, the Church. The Church bears the human form, the form of Christ in his death and resurrection. The Church in the first place is his image, and through the Church all her members have been refashioned in his image too. In the Body of Christ we are become "like Christ."

Now we can understand why the New Testament always speaks of our becoming "like Christ" (καθώς Χριστός). We have been transformed into the image of Christ, and are therefore destined to be like him. He is the only pattern we must follow. And because he really lives his life in us, we too can "walk even as he walked" (1 John 2:6), and "do as he has done" (John 13:15), "love as he has loved" (Eph 5:2; John 13:34; 15:12), "forgive as he forgave" (Col 3:13), "have this mind, which was also in Christ Jesus" (Phil 2:5), and therefore we are able to follow the example he has left us (1 Pet 2:21), lay down our lives for the brethren as he did (1 John 3:16). It is only because he became like us that we can become like him. It is only because we are identified with him that we can become like him. By being transformed into his image, we are enabled to model our lives on his. Now at last deeds are performed and life is lived in single-minded discipleship in the image of Christ, and his words find unquestioning obedience. We pay no attention to our own lives or the new image which we bear, for then we should at once have forfeited it, since it is only to serve as a mirror for the image of Christ on whom our gaze is fixed. The disciple looks solely at his Master. But when a man follows Jesus Christ and bears the image of the incarnate, crucified and risen Lord, when he has become the image of God, we may at last say that he has been called to be the "imitator of God." The follower of Jesus is the imitator of God. "Be ye therefore imitators of God, as beloved children" (Eph 5:1).[8]

A Study Guide for *The Cost of Discipleship*

1. How have you seen costly and cheap grace exemplified? In what ways have you been guilty of cheapening grace?

2. How does grace compel us to act in the world? How has it compelled you? What is the distinction Bonhoeffer draws between "justification of sin" and "justification of the sinner"?[9]

3. Following Jesus means we give up control and that only he knows the end of our journeys. How has the uncertainty inherent in following Jesus affected or manifested itself in your life?

4. How does Bonhoeffer's personal story affect your understanding of costly discipleship?

5. Bonhoeffer emphasizes that Jesus calls us to take up our crosses and thus to be rejected and suffer, yet he promises that God suffers with us and also that suffering is the only way to overcome suffering. In other words, "suffering has to be endured in order that it may pass away."[10] What does this mean to you? How have you experienced this?

6. In front of Jesus we stand alone. He is the mediator between us and every person in our lives, dividing us from them, but also uniting us since the only true connection we can

have to another person is through him. How have you seen Jesus as the mediator in your relationships? Are there any relationships in which you have not allowed Jesus to serve as mediator?

7. Jesus calls us to secrecy, in our works and our prayers. To do this, he recommends a sort of "voluntary blindness" in which we act with such spontaneity that we remain almost unaware of our good actions. How have you been able to practice secrecy in your life? What challenges have you faced?

8. What is the difference between striving after the image of Christ and the form of Christ seeking to be formed in us? How can we tell if our lives exemplify the former or the latter?

A Testament of Devotion

THOMAS R. KELLY

⟶ *I find that a life of little whispered words of adoration, of praise, of prayer, of worship can be breathed all through the day. One can have a very busy day, outwardly speaking, and yet be steadily in the holy Presence.*

A Testament of Devotion calls us to center our lives in God, with inner peace, stillness, and quiet as the result.

Born in Ohio in 1893 into a devout Quaker family, Thomas R. Kelly received a Ph.D. before serving as a missionary in post–World War I Germany with his wife, Lael. He returned home to a career in academia, teaching at Earlham College in Indiana, Harvard University, the University of Hawaii, and, finally, Haverford College in Pennsylvania. Throughout his career he longed for academic recognition and publishing success, which he never received. But in the last years of his life, at Haverford, he seemed to come to peace with his life as it was, speaking to friends about his newfound focus on God's presence within him. After he died suddenly at the age of forty-seven, several essays on which he had been working were published as *A Testament of Devotion*.

In the first essay, "The Light Within," Kelly guides us to the Divine Center, which he describes with a number of terms—the Divine Light, the Slumbering Christ, the Light Within. In short, it is God's presence within us. With regular visits to this inner sanctuary, we can, he promises, bring "the sanctuary frame of mind" with us into the outside world. This inward orientation was not only the secret of Jesus' inner life but also the inner life he expected each of his followers to have, regardless of whether they were cloistered in religious communities or in the world.

Kelly offers specific advice: "Walk and talk and work and laugh with your friends. But behind the scenes, keep up the life of simple prayer and inward worship. Keep it up throughout the day. Let inward prayer be your last act before you fall asleep and the first act when you awake. And in time you will find, as did Brother Lawrence, that 'those who have the gale of the Holy Spirit go forward even in sleep.'"[1] He urges us to have patience and to forgive ourselves when we forget God for long periods of time. At first we will alternate between the outer and inner worlds, but our goal is simultaneous awareness of both. We will know we have begun to reach such a goal when, even when we forget about God for a time, we realize that we have not entirely forgotten but that God has only become more vivid to us as we return with our whole attention. And always we must remember that though we feel as though we are the initiators of such secret prayer, really it is God who meets, tutors, and disciplines us. The result of such a heavenly orientation is that we become less attached to the things of the world and at the same time are given a great love and concern for the world.

In Book 2: "Holy Obedience," Kelly urges us to commit our lives in unreserved obedience to God—"not as a lovely ideal, a charming pattern to aim at hopefully, but as a serious, concrete program of life, to be lived here and now, in industrial America, by you and by me."[2] Although some are brought to obedience by mystical experiences that convince them once and for all that God is real and life must be lived in relation to this reality, most of us are brought to obedience by a slow process of subjecting our wills piece by piece to the divine will. To begin this process, Kelly recommends offering ourselves in obedience continually, behind the scenes of our outer lives. As we submit, we will see our need for purity and holiness, leading us to yet another contradiction of the spiritual life, in which as God's holiness takes hold of us, we see at the same time just how black our souls are. As Kelly writes, "For humility and holiness are twins in the astonishing birth of obedience in the heart of men."[3] Living in total obedience does not mean living a life free of suffering, for indeed as we grow more obedient, we grow ever sensitive to the great needs and pain of the world around us, but it does mean a life of simplicity, characterized by great joy and trust.

In Book 3: "The Blessed Community," Kelly describes the reordering of our friendships that occurs when we grow closer to the Divine Center, how we grow closer to those in whom we see the same focus. When our lives are immersed in God, we are related to one another through God. In this Holy Fellowship we reach past theological differences, whether perceived or actual, to our common experience of God. As Kelly writes, "Holy Fellowship, freely tolerant of these important yet more superficial clarifications, lives in the Center and rejoices in the unity of His love."[4] Kelly pushes us to even more: "Can we make *all* our relations to our fellows relations which pass *through Him?*"[5]

Where once the Church was too concerned about focusing on eternity (nonworldly things) to the point of excluding those who had real material needs for sustenance and shelter, now the pendulum has swung too far in the other direction so much so that we are only concerned with what changes things in the now, Kelly writes in Book 4, "The Eternal Now and Social Concern." Focus on the Divine Presence allows us to focus both on time and eternity. Our normal perspective is that of time as a ribbon, as we live fearfully in the now, carefully weighing the past in preparation for the all-important future. But, "In the immediate experience of the Presence, the Now is no mere nodal point between the past and the future. It is the seat and region of the Divine Presence itself. No longer is the ribbon spread out with equal vividness before one, for the past matters less and the future matters less, for the Now contains all that is needed for the absolute satisfaction of our deepest cravings."[6] This experience of the Holy Now brings joy, a sense of the love of God, and peace. But it also lays upon us a concern, a particularization of our responsibility, as Kelly puts it. He writes, "The Loving Presence does not burden us equally with all things, but considerately puts upon each of us just a few central tasks, as emphatic responsibilities. For each of us these special undertakings are our share in the joyous burdens of love."[7] Our

> *A Testament of Devotion* has been the single most helpful written resource for the most important endeavor of my life: practicing God's presence.
> —Gerald G. May

life is wonderfully simplified when we dedicate it to those few concerns to which we are truly called.

This simplification is the focus of Book 5. The reason that so many of us complain of a chaotic, overly busy existence is not due, as we most often think, to the external demands upon us, but to our inner conflicts as we try to listen to the cacophony of voices inside us. Because we want to be the best at everything, because we care about outward results and what people think about us, we never say no. Cultivating an interior focus will teach us to say no when necessary, to do only that to which we are called. This listening to God frees us from our frantic busyness. As Kelly writes, "I find He never guides us into an intolerable scramble of panting feverishness."[8] Instead, God leads us to peace.

Why *A Testament of Devotion* Is Essential

There is no shortage of books, even books recommended here, that focus on interior prayer. But Thomas R. Kelly's book is different. Unlike so many other classics of the interior life, *A Testament of Devotion* was written by a person involved in the exterior world, for those of us who are also in the world. As Richard J. Foster writes, "One of the greatest gifts that Thomas Kelly brings to us is an ability to see the Holy in the most common of places and the most unexpected of events. . . . Each time I leaf through the pages of this book, I know I am in the presence of a giant soul. I am the better for the encounter."[9] As much insight as we can glean from contemplative books written by and for those who live the cloistered life, here is a book that recognizes and offers solutions to the problems so many of us share with trying to translate an interior focus to a life lived in the busy, noisy modern world.

And oh how we need that focus. As Kelly himself points out, while in the past many of those in the Church may have focused too much on the interior world to the point of not addressing social problems in the exterior world, today most of us have the opposite problem of focusing too little on the interior. With specific and practical advice, Kelly offers us a method of cultivating an awareness of the interior world that we can carry with us into our busy lives. He draws us away from focusing on results, to a deeper, more contemplative way of life. But we do not need to retire to a monastery or spend hours each day in silence in order to achieve this interior awareness. Like Brother Lawrence before him, Kelly tells us that even during our daily activities with others, we can be constantly engaged with God, whispering, adoring, listening, all the hours of our day. Kelly describes for us just exactly how this process can take place, how it will begin with alternation between exterior and interior, and how often at first we will forget about God, but then also how we will know when we are starting to achieve the simultaneity of living on both levels at once.

But, of course, the corollary of his lesson is that our busy lives will no longer look the same. Once we submit to the Presence within us, our busy lives will also undergo evaluation. First, Kelly suggests that we need to bring everything from the exterior world down into the Presence and "resee" it. He calls us to reorient everything in our lives according to God. As part of this process, he also presents the liberating idea that each of us has only a few central tasks to which we ourselves are particularly burdened. Such a concept is wisdom to a world in which, today even more than in Kelly's time, so many of us feel we must excel at everything, be everything to everyone. This mind-set is a selfish one. It assumes that we are the only ones at work in the world. It ignores God's role. If we can attune ourselves to God's voice within us, we will know to say no to those things to which we are not particularly called. Kelly tells us in no uncertain terms: the frantic rush and hurry in our lives is not of God. The life to which God calls us is one of peace and serenity.

How to Read *A Testament of Devotion*

Written in clear twentieth-century prose, *A Testament of Devotion* should present few problems for reading. It is a short book and could be read from cover to cover quickly. We urge you *not* to read it this way. It is a devotional book and so lends itself to being read slowly with lots of pauses for reflection. One strategy might be to read a small portion each day and journal about it. Another strategy might be to read and reflect on each essay separately.

A Testament of Devotion

THE LIGHT WITHIN

There is a way of ordering our mental life on more than one level at once. On one level we may be thinking, discussing, seeing, calculating, meeting all the demands of external affairs. But deep within, behind the scenes at a profounder level, we may also be in prayer and adoration, song and worship and a gentle receptiveness to divine breathings.

The secular world of today values and cultivates only the first level, assured that *there* is where the real business of mankind is done, and scorns, or smiles in tolerant amusement, at the cultivation of the second level—a luxury enterprise, a vestige of superstition, an occupation for special temperaments. But in a deeply religious culture men know that the deep level of prayer and of divine attendance is the most important thing in the world. It is at this deep level that the real business of life is determined. The secular mind is an abbreviated, fragmentary mind, building only upon a part of man's nature and neglecting a part—the most glorious part—of man's nature, powers, and resources. The religious mind involves the whole of man, embraces his relations with time within their true ground and setting in the Eternal Lover. It ever keeps close to the fountains of divine creativity. In lowliness it knows joys and stabilities, peace and assurances, that are utterly incomprehensible to the secular mind. It lives in resources and powers that make individuals radiant and triumphant, groups tolerant and bonded together in mutual concern, and is bestirred to an outward life of unremitting labor.

Between the two levels is fruitful interplay, but ever the accent must be upon the deeper level, where the soul ever dwells in the presence of the Holy One. For the religious man is forever bringing all affairs of the first level down into the Light, holding them there in the Presence, reseeing them and the whole of the world of men and things in a new and overturning way, and responding to them in spontaneous, incisive, and simple ways of love and faith. Facts remain facts, when brought into the Presence in the deeper level, but their value, their significance, is wholly realigned. Much apparent wheat becomes utter chaff, and some chaff becomes wheat. Imposing powers? They are out of the Life, and must crumble. Lost causes? If God be for them, who can be against them? Rationally plausible futures? They are weakened or certified in the dynamic Life and Light. Tragic suffering? Already He is there, and we actively move, in His tenderness, toward the sufferers. Hopeless debauchees? These are children of God, His concern and ours. Inexorable laws of nature? The dependable framework for divine reconstruction. The fall of a sparrow? The Father's love. For faith and hope and love for all things are engendered in the soul, as we practice their submission and our own to the Light Within, as we humbly see all things, even darkly and as through a glass, yet through the eye of God. . . .

How, then, shall we lay hold of that Life and Power, and live the life of prayer without ceasing? By quiet, persistent practice in turning of all our being, day and night, in prayer and inward worship and surrender, toward Him who calls in the deeps of our souls. Mental habits of inward orientation must be established. An inner, secret turning to God can be made fairly steady, after weeks and months and years of practice and lapses and failures and returns. It is as simple an art as Brother Lawrence found it, but it may be long before we achieve any steadiness in the process. Begin now, as you read these words, as you sit in your chair, to offer your whole selves, utterly and in joyful abandon, in quiet, glad surrender to Him who is within. In secret ejaculations of praise, turn in humble wonder to the Light, faint though it may be. Keep contact with the outer world of sense and meanings. Here is no discipline in absent-mindedness. Walk and talk and work and laugh with your friends. But behind the scenes, keep up the life of simple prayer and inward worship. Keep it up throughout the day. Let inward prayer be your last act before you fall asleep and the first act when you awake. And in time you will find, as did Brother Lawrence, that "those who have the gale of the Holy Spirit go forward even in sleep."

The first days and weeks and months are awkward and painful, but enormously rewarding. Awkward, because it takes constant vigilance and effort and reassertions of the will, at the first level. Painful, because our lapses are so frequent, the intervals when we forget Him so long. Rewarding, because we have begun to live. But these weeks and months and perhaps even years must be passed through before He gives us greater and easier stayedness upon Himself.

Lapses and forgettings are so frequent. Our surroundings grow so exciting. Our occupations are so exacting. But when you catch yourself again, lose no time in self-recriminations, but breathe a silent prayer for forgiveness and begin again, just where you are. Offer *this* broken worship up to Him and say: "This is what I am except Thou aid me." Admit no discouragement, but ever return quietly to Him and wait in His Presence.

At first the practice of inward prayer is a process of alternation of attention between outer things and the Inner Light. Preoccupation with either brings the loss of the other. Yet what is sought is not alternation, but simultaneity, worship undergirding every moment, living prayer, the continuous current and background of all moments of life. Long practice indeed is needed before alternation yields to concurrent immersion in both levels at once. The "plateaus in the learning curve" are so long, and many falter and give up, assenting to alternation as the best that they can do. And no doubt in His graciousness God gives us His gifts, even in intermittent communion, and touches us into flame, far beyond our achievements and deserts. But the hunger of the committed one is for unbroken communion and adoration, and we may be sure He longs for us to find it and supplements our weakness. For our quest is one of His initiation, and is carried forward in His tender power and completed by His grace.

The first signs of simultaneity are given when at the moment of recovery from a period of forgetting there is a certain sense that we have not completely forgotten Him. It is as though we are only coming back into a state of vividness which had endured in dim and tenuous form throughout. What takes place now is not reinstatement of a broken prayer but return to liveliness of that which had endured, but mildly. The currents of His love have been flowing, but whereas we had been drifting in Him, now we swim. It is like the background of a picture which extends all the way across behind a tree in the foreground. It is not that we merely know intellectually that the background of the picture has unbroken extension; we experience aesthetically that it *does* extend across. Again, it is like waking from sleep yet knowing, not by inference but by immediate awareness, that we have lived even while we were asleep. For sole preoccupation with the world is sleep, but immersion in Him is life.

But periods of dawning simultaneity and steadfast prayer may come and go, lapsing into alternation for long periods and returning in glorious power. And we learn to submit to the inner discipline of withdrawing of His gifts. For if the least taint of spiritual pride in our prayer-growth has come, it is well that He humble us until we are worthy of greater trust. For though we begin the practice of secret prayer with a strong sense that we are the initiators and that by our wills we are establishing our habits, maturing experience brings awareness of being met and tutored, purged and disciplined, simplified and made pliant in His holy will by a power waiting within us. For God Himself works in our souls, in their deepest depths, taking increasing control as we are progressively willing to be prepared for His wonder. We cease trying to make ourselves the dictators and God the listener, and become the joyful listeners to him, the Master who does all things well.

The Simplification of Life

There is a way of life so hid with Christ in God that in the midst of the day's business one is inwardly lifting brief prayers, short ejaculations of praise, subdued whispers of adoration and of tender love to the Beyond that is within. No one need know about it. I only speak to you because it is a sacred trust, not mine but to be given to others. One can live in a well-nigh continuous state of unworded prayer, directed toward God, directed toward people and the enterprises we have on our heart. There is no hurry about it at all; it is a life unspeakable and full of glory, an inner world of splendor within which we, unworthy, may live. Some of you know it and live in it; others of you may wistfully long for it; it can be yours.

Now out from such a holy Center come the commissions of life. Our fellowship with God issues in world-concern. We cannot keep the love of God to ourselves. It spills over. It quickens us. It makes us see the world's needs anew. We love people and we grieve to see them blind when they might be seeing, asleep with all the world's comforts when they ought to be awake and living sacrificially, accepting the world's goods as their right when they really hold them only in temporary trust. It is because from this holy Center we relove people, relove our neighbors as ourselves, that we are bestirred to be means of their awakening.

The deepest need of men is not food and clothing and shelter, important as they are. It is God. We have mistaken the nature of poverty, and thought it was economic poverty. No, it is poverty of soul, deprivation of God's recreating, loving peace. Peer into poverty and see if we are really getting down to the deepest needs, in our economic salvation schemes. These are important. But they lie farther along the road, secondary steps toward world reconstruction. The primary step is a holy life, transformed and radiant in the glory of God.

This love of people is well-nigh as amazing as the love of God. Do we want to help people because we feel sorry for them, or because we genuinely love them? The world needs some-

My Personal Top 5

MINDY CALIGUIRE

1 *Good to Great*, Jim Collins. Collins's groundbreaking and extensive research identifies a completely new category of effective leadership. "Level Five" leaders, unlike most conventional thinking about success, display two distinguishing characteristics: deep personal humility and fierce resolve. Actually developing those characteristics in the soul of a leader is not the scope of his research, but it points out to me the great potential in engaging leaders in a process of spiritual formation—against the norm of convention, into the image of Christ.

2 *A Testament of Devotion*, Thomas R. Kelly. Kelly was one of the first writers who wrote in a way that connected to my growing experience of and capacity for openness to God. While I had already experienced prayer, simplicity, and community in a busy life and leadership context, this book moved me further into living into a more surrendered and yielded life.

3 *Connecting*, Larry Crabb. Crabb's vision for how the Holy Spirit works through ordinary connections between people opened both my mind and imagination, and ultimately my willingness, enough to venture into the rough but healing waters of transformation-minded relationships.

4 *Boundaries*, Henry Cloud and John Townsend. Cloud and Townsend messed with my head! But oh what a beautiful mess. Through their writing, I learned a biblically and psychologically valid way of sensing and ultimately navigating the brokenness in my own life and in the lives of others.

5 *Renovation of the Heart*, Dallas Willard. While I had a hunch that my whole self—spirit, mind, body, social environment, and soul—by default is integrated and works together, Dallas actually explained it. While I'm still learning, this work provided much-needed understanding for my own growth and, most important, in helping others and other ministries.

MINDY CALIGUIRE is the founder of Soul Care (www.soulcare.com), the author of *Discovering Soul Care* (InterVarsity Press) and other books, and the director of transformation ministry for the Willow Creek Association.

thing deeper than pity; it needs love. (How trite that sounds, how real it is!) But in our love of people are we to be excitedly hurried, sweeping all men and tasks into our loving concern? No, that is God's function. But He, working within us, portions out His vast concern into bundles, and lays on each of us our portion. These become our tasks. Life from the Center is a heaven-directed life.

Much of our acceptance of multitudes of obligations is due to our inability to say No. We calculated that that task had to be done, and we saw no one ready to undertake it. We calculated the need, and then we calculated our time, and decided maybe we could squeeze it in somewhere. But the decision was a heady decision, not made within the sanctuary of our soul. When we say Yes or No to calls for service on the basis of heady decisions, we have to give reasons, to ourselves and to others. But when we say Yes or No to calls on the basis of inner guidance and whispered promptings of encouragement from the Center of our life, or on the basis of a lack of any inward "rising" of that Life to encourage us in the call, we have no reason to give, except one—the will of God as we discern it. Then we have begun to live in guidance. And I find He never guides us into an intolerable scramble of panting feverishness. The Cosmic Patience becomes, in part, our patience, for after all God is at work in the world. It is not we alone who are at work in the world, frantically finishing a work to be offered to God.

Life from the Center is a life of unhurried peace and power. It is simple. It is serene. It is amazing. It is triumphant. It is radiant. It takes no time, but it occupies all our time. And it makes our life programs new and overcoming. We need not get frantic. He is at the helm. And when our little day is done we lie down quietly in peace, for all is well.[10]

A Study Guide for *A Testament of Devotion*

1. What does Kelly mean by inward orientation? How does it differ from religious theory or outward deeds?

2. How have you become aware of the two levels of existence—the first level of our external world and the second level of our inward life? How does your experience in one affect the other?

3. Kelly describes the beginnings of "simultaneity"—being aware of your inner life with God even while actively engaged in your outer life—as, among other things, a feeling that we are now swimming in a current in which before we were only drifting. When have you experienced this simultaneity?

4. In Book 2: "Holy Obedience," Kelly urges us to commit our lives in unreserved obedience to God—"not as a lovely ideal, a charming pattern to aim at hopefully, but as a serious, concrete program of life, to be lived here and now, in industrial America, by you and by me."[11] Have you thought of the idea of obedience to God at something "to aim at hopefully"? How does this concept differ from what Kelly calls us to?

5. Kelly describes how as we grow closer to the Divine Center, we will experience a reordering of our friends, in which we will suddenly long for the fellowship of those who were once merely acquaintances but whom we now sense are also in tune with the Divine Center. We will also be forced to relegate to the level of acquaintance some of those whom we currently count as close friends. Have you ever experienced such a realignment? How did you deal with it?

6. Kelly writes that we don't create fellowship deliberately, but "we find it and we find ourselves increasingly within it as

we find ourselves increasingly within Him."[12] How has your faith led you to fellowship?

7. Kelly describes many religious people as living uncertainly in the now, while we weigh the past and consider the future. Experiencing the Divine Presence, however, causes us to value the now over the past and the future. How have you experienced such a time with God that it caused you to be wholly present in the Holy Now?

8. Kelly contends that so many Western Christians feel stressed because of the state of their inner lives rather than their exterior obligations and culture. Do you agree? How has such a feeling manifested itself in your life?

9. How well do you feel you listen for inner guidance to know when to say yes, or no, to obligations?

10. Kelly writes, "I find that He never guides us into an intolerable scramble of panting feverishness."[13] When in your life have you experienced this kind of "panting feverishness"? How did you or could you leave this behind?

The Seven Storey Mountain

THOMAS MERTON

I looked straight at the Host, and I knew, now, Who it was that I was looking at, and I said:

"Yes, I want to be a priest, with all my heart I want it. If it is Your will, make me a priest—make me a priest."

When I had said them, I realized in some measure what I had done with those last four words, what power I had put into motion on my behalf, and what a union had been sealed between me and that power by my decision.

THOMAS MERTON (1915–1968) was one of the twentieth century's most prominent Catholics, despite having chosen a life of withdrawal into the art of prayer and contemplation. The immense popularity of his writings gained him international renown, starting with the publication in 1948 of *The Seven Storey Mountain,* the story of a young man's long journey to peace.

Thomas Merton was born in Prades, France, in 1915 to American parents. He lost his mother at a young age and was raised primarily by his father in the United States, France, and then England. His father practiced a quiet faith, but Merton grew up without any real religious instruction. He went through what he calls a religious phase as a schoolboy in England, but after his father died from a brain tumor during Merton's teen years, Merton writes that "the hard crust of my dry soul finally squeezed out all the last traces of religion that had ever been in it. There was no room for any God in that empty temple full of dust and rubbish which I was now so

In this eloquent spiritual autobiography, Thomas Merton describes his journey from the glimpses of God he received as a child to his subsequent conversion to Catholicism and decision to enter a Trappist monastery.

jealously to guard against all intruders, in order to devote it to the worship of my own stupid will."[1]

Before university, however, Merton traveled to Italy and found himself very attracted to the Byzantine mosaics in the churches he visited. He also felt drawn to the sense of peace he felt in the churches. He began reading the Gospels and other Christian writings. One night he had a powerful experience of feeling the presence of his deceased father and then seeing with clarity the deplorable state of his own soul. As he writes, "The whole thing passed in a flash, but in that flash, instantly, I was overwhelmed with a sudden and profound insight into the misery and corruption of my own soul, and I was pierced deeply with a light that made me realize something of the condition I was in, and I was filled with horror at what I saw, and my whole being rose up in revolt against what was within me, and my soul desired escape and liberation and freedom from all this with an intensity and an urgency unlike anything I had ever known before. And now I think for the first time I really began to pray—praying not with my lips and with my intellect and my imagination, but praying out of the very roots of my life and of my being, and praying to the God I had never known, to reach down towards me out of His darkness and to help me to get free of the thousand terrible things that held my will in their slavery."[2]

But Merton tells us that "this real but temporary religious fervor cooled down and disappeared"[3] aided by his disappointing experiences in some churches he visited. Through his university years at Cambridge and then Columbia in New York, he studied poetry, philosophy, and literature and flirted with Communism. One day, when he was in graduate school, he finally obeyed a strong urge to attend Mass, where he was deeply moved by the sermon. From that day forward, he writes, "All I know is that I walked in a new world."[4] Soon after, he decided to become a Catholic. After the rush and excitement of catechism training and finally baptism, confession, and communion, Merton writes that "after receiving the immense grace of Baptism, after all the struggles of persuasion and conversion, and after all the long way I had come, through so much of the no-man's land that lies around the confines of hell, instead of becoming a strong and ardent and generous Catholic, I simply slipped into the ranks of the millions of tepid and dull and sluggish and indifferent Christians who live a life that is still half animal, and who barely put up a struggle to keep the breath of grace alive in their souls."[5] Thinking that he could live much the same life he had before, as long as he tried to avoid mortal sin, he struggled with trying to translate knowledge and belief into action as he pursued his Ph.D. and dreamed of a career as a writer.

Then one day the idea came to him. He was going to be a priest. For years, even before becoming a Catholic, he had toyed with the idea of entering the priesthood. But that day, he went to Mass at a church he had never before visited and committed to the idea. Next, attracted to the simplicity, informality, and commitment to poverty of the Franciscan order, he applied to be a Franciscan novice. While he was waiting to enter the novitiate, Merton began to practice the Ignatian spiritual exercises and attend Mass each day and found himself in a place of peace. But soon he came to the uncomfortable realization that God had not called him to be a Franciscan. He had chosen it because he thought it would suit him, and he realized, "God was not going to let me walk out of the miseries of the world into a refuge of my own choosing."[6] When he went to the Franciscan with whom he had applied for the novitiate and explained his qualms and what a short time he had been a Catholic, the father agreed and helped him withdraw his application. Merton was devastated. Since God had kept him out of the cloister, he believed, he would try his best to be a lay contemplative. He took a job teaching English at a Catholic university, St. Bonaventure's, and resolved to say the Breviary, the canonical Office, each day. In the meantime, World War II raged on in Europe, and Merton and his friends lived with the constant knowledge that they could be called to fight at any time. He was greatly relieved to be rejected from the draft because he'd had so many teeth pulled.

After teaching for a short time, he decided to make a retreat at Gethsemani, a Trappist monastery in Kentucky. As soon as he started to research the Trappists, he felt an immediate connection to them and their way of life—their poverty, silence, and commit-

It is a rare pleasure to read an autobiography with a pattern and meaning valid for all of us. *The Steven Storey Mountain* is a book one reads with a pencil so as to make it one's own.

—Graham Greene

ment to working with their hands. During his retreat, Merton was deeply moved by the rhythm of the celebration of the divine Office and his sense that, opposite to the world, at the monastery they were the greatest who stood out the least. Before Merton left, he prayed to receive a vocation to come to the monastery, but upon returning home, he still doubted whether it was the right path for him. After much soul-searching, he finally decided to enter the monastery. At the same time, he received a summons for another army medical examination for the draft. But as he headed to the monastery, he found himself no longer troubled by whether he would have to join the army. "I was free," he wrote. "I had recovered my liberty. I belonged to God, not to myself: and to belong to Him is to be free, free of all the anxieties and worries and sorrows that belong to this earth, and the love of the things that are in it. What was the difference between one place and another, one habit and another, if your life belonged to God, and if you placed yourself completely in His hands?"[7] And so he entered what he termed "the four walls of my new freedom."[8] In Gethsemani, Merton found his lifelong home, and within those four walls he would finally pursue his dreams of practicing a contemplative lifestyle and, also, of becoming a writer.

Why *The Seven Storey Mountain* Is Essential

The Seven Storey Mountain is notable not least for its literary success. It earned the distinction of being the first religious book ever to hit the *New York Times* bestseller list, in 1949. Merton's brilliance and writing talent is evident on every page. His vivid descriptions of his search for the peace he finally found in the Trappist monastery are so compelling that his book is credited with inspiring a flood of new converts to the monastic lifestyle. Although by no means a new idea—Augustine's *Confessions* provided inspiration for Merton—Merton's book is emblematic of the modern spiritual biography. First-person spiritual narratives such as this one offer many opportunities for spiritual formation. Reading Merton's description of his own faith journey challenges us to sketch our own.

As editorial board member Richard Rohr says, "Merton is a writer par excellence. You can identify with his sinfulness, his brokenness, his immaturity, and you can see him go through the stages. A masterpiece." Merton, a gifted writer, explains concepts in a way we ourselves might not be able to. Not only can we reflect on the places where God made decisive changes in our lives, but we can also become better attuned to the subtle ways in which God has touched our lives. God spoke to Merton in many ways—through other people, through books, through Church tradition. *The Seven Storey Mountain* calls us to consider the different ways God has reached out and continues to reach out to us.

Finally, one of the most important insights we can glean from Merton's book is about the process of conversion. Far from a one-time occurrence, for Merton and for many of us, conversion is more like a chronology of growth. Just as Merton had a number of experiences that caused him to become closer and more committed to God, so, too, we continually experience the conversion of growing ever closer to God, ever more conformed to God's will.

How to Read *The Seven Storey Mountain*

Merton's writing presents little in the way of obstacles to reading. Quite the opposite, it is an exceptionally well-written narrative. Some may struggle, however, with his critical views of the Protestant Church. It may be helpful to remember that when Merton wrote this book, he was still in what might be termed his "honeymoon phase" with the Catholic Church. Later in life, he moderated many of his critical views of other Christian denominations. Indeed, in 1958, he wrote in his journal about an experience he had standing on a street corner in Louisville, Kentucky, in which he realized "that I loved all the people and that none of them were or could be totally alien to me. As if waking from a dream—a dream of my separateness, of the 'special' vocation to be different. My vocation does not really make me different from the rest of men or put me in a special category except artificially, juridically. I am still a member of the human race, and what more glorious destiny is there for man, since the Word was made flesh and became, too, a member of the Human Race! Thank God! Thank God! I am only another member of the human race, like all the rest of them, I have the immense joy of being man, a member of a race in which God Himself became incarnate. As if the sorrows and stupidities of the human condition could overwhelm me, now that I realize what we all are. And if only everybody could realize this! But it cannot be explained. There is no way of telling people that they are all walking around shining like the sun."[9]

The Seven Storey Mountain

So far, however, there had been no deep movement of my will, nothing that amounted to a conversion, nothing to shake the iron tyranny of moral corruption that held my whole nature in fetters. But that also was to come. It came in a strange way, suddenly, a way that I will not attempt to explain.

I was in my room. It was night. The light was on. Suddenly it seemed to me that Father, who had now been dead more than a year, was there with me. The sense of his presence was as vivid and as real and as startling as if he had touched my arm or spoken to me. The whole thing passed in a flash, but in that flash, instantly, I was overwhelmed with a sudden and profound insight into the misery and corruption of my own soul, and I was pierced deeply with a light that made me realize something of the condition I was in, and I was filled with horror at what I saw, and my whole being rose up in revolt against what was within me, and my soul desired escape and liberation and freedom from all this with an intensity and an urgency unlike anything I had ever known before. And now I think for the first time in my whole life I really began to pray—praying not with my lips and with my intellect and my imagination, but praying out of the very roots of my life and of my being, and praying to the God I had never known, to reach down towards me out of His darkness and to help me to get free of the thousand terrible things that held my will in their slavery. . . .

How do I know it was not merely my own imagination, or something that could be traced to a purely natural, psychological cause—I mean the part about my father? It is impossible to say. I do not offer any explanation. And I have always had a great antipathy for everything that smells of necromancy— table-turning and communications with the dead—and I would never deliberately try to enter in to any such thing. But whether it was imagination or nerves or whatever else it may have been, I can truly say that I did feel, most vividly, as if my father were present there, and the consequences that I have described followed from this, as though he had communicated to me without words an interior light from God, about the condition of my own soul—although I wasn't even sure I had a soul.

The one thing that seems to me morally certain is that this was really a grace, and a great grace. If I had only followed it through, my life might have been very different and much less miserable for the years that were to come.

Before now I had never prayed in the churches I had visited. But I remember the morning that followed this experience. I remember how I climbed the deserted Aventine, in the spring sun, with my soul broken up with contrition, but broken and clean, painful but sanitary like a lanced abscess, like a bone broken and re-set. And it was true contrition, too, for I don't think I was capable of mere attrition, since I did not believe in hell. I went to the Dominicans' church, Santa Sabina. And it was a very definite experience, something that amounted to a capitulation, a surrender, a conversion, not without struggle, even now, to walk deliberately into the church with no other purpose than to kneel down and pray to God. Ordinarily, I never knelt in these churches, and never paid any formal or official attention to Whose house it was. But now I took holy water at the door and went straight up to the altar rail and knelt down and said, slowly, with all the belief I had in me, the Our Father.

It seems almost unbelievable to me that I did no more than this, for the memory remains in me as that of such an experience that it would seem to have implied at least a half hour of impassioned prayer and tears. The thing to remember is that I had not prayed at all for some years.

Another thing which Catholics do not realize about converts is the tremendous, agonizing embarrassment and self-consciousness which they feel about praying publicly in a Catholic Church. The effort it takes to overcome all the strange imaginary fears that everyone is looking at you, and that they all think you are crazy or ridiculous, is something that costs a tremendous effort. And that day in Santa Sabina, although the church was almost entirely empty, I walked across the stone floor mortally afraid that a poor devout old Italian woman was following me with suspicious eyes. As I knelt to pray, I wondered if she would run out and accuse me at once to the priests, with scandalous horror, for coming and praying in their church—as if Catholics were perfectly content to have a lot of heretic tourists walking around their churches with complete indifference and irreverence, and would get angry if one of them so far acknowledged God's presence there as to go on his knees for a few seconds and say a prayer!

However, I prayed, then I looked about the church, and went into a room where there was a picture by Sassoferrato, and stuck my face out a door into a tiny, simple cloister, where the sun shone down on an orange tree. After that I walked out into the open feeling as if I had been reborn, and crossed the street, and strolled through the suburban fields to another deserted church where I did not pray, being scared by some carpenters and scaffolding. I sat outside, in the sun, on a wall, and tasted the joy of my own inner peace, and turned over in my mind how my life was now going to change, and how I would become better.

. . .

There were still about three weeks left until Easter. Thinking more and more about the Trappist monastery where I was going to spend Holy Week, I went to the library one day and took down the *Catholic Encyclopaedia* to read about the Trappists. I found out that the Trappists were Cistercians, and then, in looking up Cistercians, I also came across the Carthusians, and a great big picture of the hermitages of the Camaldolese.

What I saw on those pages pierced me to the heart like a knife.

What wonderful happiness there was, then, in the world! There were still men on this miserable, noisy, cruel earth, who tasted the marvelous joy of silence and solitude, who dwelt in forgotten mountain cells, in secluded monasteries, where the news and desires and appetites and conflicts of the world no longer reached them.

They were free from the burden of the flesh's tyranny, and their clear vision, clean of the world's smoke and of its bitter sting, were raised to heaven and penetrated into the deeps of heaven's infinite and healing light.

They were poor, they had nothing, and therefore they were free and possessed everything, and everything they touched struck off something of the fire of divinity. And they worked with their hands, silently ploughing and harrowing the earth, and sowing seed in obscurity, and reaping their small harvests to feed themselves and the other poor. They built their own houses and made, with their own hands, their own furniture and their own coarse clothing, and everything around them was simple and primitive and poor, because they were the least and the last of men, they had made themselves outcasts, seeking, outside the walls of the world, Christ poor and rejected of men.

Above all, they had found Christ, and they knew the power and the sweetness and the depth and the infinity of His love, living and working in them. In Him, hidden in Him, they had become the "Poor Brothers of God." And for His love, they had thrown away everything, and concealed themselves in the Secret of His Face. Yet because they had nothing, they were the richest men in the world, possessing everything because in proportion as grace emptied their hearts of created desire, the Spirit of God entered in and filled the place that had been made for God. And the Poor Brothers of God, in their cells, they tasted within them the secret glory, the hidden manna, the infinite nourishment and strength of the Presence of God. They tasted the sweet exultancy of the fear of God, which is the first intimate touch of the reality of God, known and experienced on earth, the beginning of heaven. The fear of the Lord is the beginning of heaven. And all day long, God spoke to them: the clean voice of God, in His tremendous peacefulness, spending truth within them as simply and directly as water wells up in a spring. And grace was in them, suddenly, always in more and more abundance, they knew not from where, and the coming of this grace to them occupied them altogether, and filled them with love, and with freedom.

And grace, overflowing in all their acts and movements, made everything they did an act of love, glorifying God not by drama, not by gesture, not by outward show, but by the very simplicity and economy of utter perfection, so utter that it escapes notice entirely.

Outside in the world were holy men who were holy in the sense that they went about with portraits of all the possible situations in which they could show their love of God displayed about them: and they were always conscious of all these possibilities. But these other hidden men had come so close to God in their hiddenness that they no longer saw anyone but Him. They themselves were lost in the picture: there was no comparison between them receiving and God giving, because the distance by which such comparison could be measured had dwindled to nothing. They were in Him. They had dwindled down to nothing and had been transformed into Him by the pure and absolute humility of their hearts.

And the love of Christ overflowing in those clean hearts made them children and made them eternal. Old men with limbs like the roots of trees had the eyes of children and lived, under their grey woolen cowls, eternal. And all of them, the young and the old, were ageless, the little brothers of God, the little children for whom was made the Kingdom of Heaven.

Day after day the round of the canonical hours brought them together and the love that was in them became songs as austere

----

My Personal Top 5

JULIA L. ROLLER

These books are the ones that have most profoundly affected my life, listed in the order I encountered them.

1 **The Works of Madeleine L'Engle**. I was captivated by her young adult fiction as a child and then by her journals and theological writings as an adult. More than anyone else, L'Engle showed me the path I wanted to emulate. Her work is a beautiful example of imagination employed for God and kingdom living.

2 *A Theology of Liberation*, Gustavo Gutiérrez. I first encountered the ideas of liberation theology in college, and its social teachings have forever altered the way I see the world and my role in it. Nothing I've read before or since has presented such a challenge to my comfortable Christianity.

3 *Celebration of Discipline*, Richard J. Foster. Despite studying theology for years, I felt stuck in a cycle of failing to live the spiritual life I wanted, with very little understanding of why. Foster's book both relieved and burdened me. How wonderful to realize that there were concrete practices to help me progress spiritually, yet how dismaying to realize how little I had understood and experienced them. No book other than the Bible has had more impact on my spiritual practice.

4 *The Practice of the Presence of God*, Brother Lawrence. Brother Lawrence showed me the legitimacy of the way I was already trying to pray. Such a simple concept, so hard to put into practice the way Brother Lawrence does.

5 *Revelations of Divine Love*, Julian of Norwich. Her message of the goodness of God is one I can never hear enough. I long for her peacefulness, her ability to rest in the arms of God, and I admire and learn from her comfort with paradox and ambiguity.

JULIA L. ROLLER is a writer and editor whose recent projects include *A Year with God* and *A Year with Aslan*.

as granite and as sweet as wine. And they stood and they bowed in their long, solemn psalmody. Their prayer flexed its strong sinews and relaxed again into silence, and suddenly flared up again in a hymn, the color of flame, and died into silence: and you could barely hear the weak, ancient voice saying the final prayer. The whisper of the *amens* ran around the stones like sighs, and the monks broke up their ranks and half emptied the choir, some remaining to pray.

And in the night they also rose, and filled the darkness with the strong, patient anguish of their supplication to God: and the strength of their prayer (the Spirit of Christ concealing His strength in the words their voices uttered) amazingly held back the arm of God from striking and breaking at last the foul world full of greed and avarice and murder and lust and all sin.

The thought of those monasteries, those remote choirs, those cells, those hermitages, those cloisters, those men in their cowls, the poor monks, the men who had become nothing, shattered my heart.

In an instant the desire of those solitudes was wide open within me like a wound.[10]

A Study Guide for *The Seven Storey Mountain*

1. Merton writes that as a young adult he referred mockingly to the two years in school where he rather unquestioningly believed and attended church with his fellow students as his "religious phase." He goes on to say that almost everyone does, in fact, have such a phase, but that it is, sadly, only a phase for the majority. Did you experience such a religious phase as a youth? If so, how did it develop or not into a lasting faith? He goes on to write, "If the impulse to worship God and to adore Him in truth by the goodness and order of our own lives is nothing more than a transitory and emotional thing, that is our own fault. It is so only because we make it so, and because we take what

is substantially a deep and powerful and lasting moral impetus, supernatural in its origin and in its direction, and reduce it to the level of our own weak and unstable and futile fancies and desires."[11] Do you agree? Why or why not?

2. Of his father, dying of a brain tumor, Merton writes: "Souls are like athletes, that need opponents worthy of them, if they are to be tried and extended and pushed to the full use of their powers, and rewarded according to their capacity. And my father was in a fight with this tumor, and none of us understood the battle. We thought he was done for, but it was making him great."[12] Do you agree with Merton's view of souls as needing worthy opponents? What challenges have you faced that have tried and extended you?

3. One night Merton receives a powerful insight into the terrible state of his own soul, and it leads him to pray for what he thinks is probably the first real time. Later he writes, "For in my greatest misery He would shed, into my soul, enough light to see how miserable I was, and to admit that it was my own fault and my own work. . . . The mere realization of one's own unhappiness is not salvation: it may be the occasion of salvation, or it may be the door to a deeper pit in Hell, and I had much deeper to go than I realized. But now, at least, I realized where I was, and I was beginning to try to get out."[13] Have you had such an experience where you viewed your soul as God might see it? If so, how did it affect you? How could such an experience be either the occasion of salvation or the door to a deeper pit in hell?

4. Merton recounts his feeling of discomfort and awkwardness praying in the Catholic church for the first time, as if someone might get upset or report him to the priest. When have you felt uncomfortable in a place of worship? Did this

feeling prevent you from praying or worshipping? Why or why not? Where do you think such a feeling comes from?

5. After the rush and excitement of catechism training and finally baptism, confession, and Communion, Merton writes that "instead of becoming a strong and ardent and generous Catholic, I simply slipped into the ranks of the millions of tepid and dull and sluggish and indifferent Christians who live a life that is still half animal, and who barely put up a struggle to keep the breath of grace alive in their souls."[14] Do you see any of yourself in this statement? What do you think allows people to fall into the sluggishness he describes? What could have helped him to lead a more ardent Christian life?

6. When Merton realizes God has not called him to enter the Franciscan novitiate as he had planned, all the peace he had felt since making the decision leaves him; he is devastated, describing himself as "once more out in the cold and naked and alone."[15] Has God ever changed your plans in this way? If so, what do you think was the reason?

7. Once Merton has entered the monastery, he realizes that one of the most important tests to whether he could remain there was whether he could accept life in close community with other imperfect humans. He writes, "The imperfections are much smaller and more trivial than the defects and vices of people outside in the world: and yet somehow you tend to notice them more and feel them more, because they get to be so greatly magnified by the responsibilities and ideals of the religious state, through which you cannot help looking at them. People even lose their vocations because they find out that a man can spend forty or fifty or sixty years in a monastery and still have a bad temper."[16] Why does monastery life make one notice each person's shortcomings even more? When have you struggled with your faith or your commitment to your

religious community because of the imperfections of those in the community?

8. Merton clearly prefers the contemplative lifestyle to an active or combined active-contemplative lifestyle. To which are you most drawn? Which are you currently living? If it is not the one to which you are drawn, what can you do to introduce more elements of that lifestyle?

Mere Christianity

C. S. LEWIS

The real Son of God is at your side. He is beginning to turn you into the same kind of thing as Himself. He is beginning, so to speak, to "inject" His kind of life and thought, His Zoe, into you; beginning to turn the tin soldier into a live man. The part of you that does not like it is the part that is still tin.

Mere Christianity is Lewis's explanation of the basics of Christian faith, what "all Christians agree on." Widely considered a modern classic of Christian apologetics, it is also a passionate invitation to the challenge and the adventure that is the Christian life.

CLIVE STAPLES LEWIS was born in 1898 in Belfast, Northern Ireland. Recognized as an intellectual at a young age, he studied and later taught at Oxford. He considered himself an atheist for years, a belief supported by his experiences fighting in World War I. But he was intellectually attracted to Christianity, and in 1931, prompted by a late-night talk with his Oxford colleagues J. R. R. Tolkien and Hugo Dyson, Lewis experienced a dramatic conversion. He famously describes getting into the sidecar of his brother's motorcycle for a trip to the zoo, saying, "When we set out I did not believe that Jesus is the Son of God, and when we reached the zoo I did." After publishing works such as *The Problem of Pain* (1940) and *The Screwtape Letters* (1942), he became one of the most well-known Christians in England. In the early 1940s, with Britain deep in the throes of World War II, the BBC invited him to give a series of live radio broadcasts about the Christian faith. These popular talks were first published as three different books, then collected into the book we know as *Mere Christianity*.

Lewis's reasoning powers are on display from the book's outset, where he begins by offering evidence for a Moral Law, or Law of

Human Nature, by which all people measure their actions. The very existence of this law implies that there must be a creator who made the world and this law by which it is governed. Yet our world is currently territory occupied by the rebel (Satan). This sad state of affairs is due to our free will. To truly be joined to God, we must be free to choose otherwise. And just as was the case when Eve yielded to Satan's temptation in the book of Genesis, we still want to be the center of things, to make ourselves more important than we are, and that desire is the root of all that has gone wrong in human history. As Lewis writes, "What Satan put into the heads of our remote ancestors was the idea that they could 'be like gods'—could set up on their own as if they had created themselves—be their own masters—invent some sort of happiness for themselves outside God, apart from God. And out of that hopeless attempt has come nearly all that we call human history—money, poverty, ambition, war, prostitution, classes, empires, slavery—the long terrible story of man trying to find something other than God which will make him happy."[1]

According to Lewis, God has helped to guide us in various ways: with our consciences, by choosing the Jews and teaching them, and, finally, through Jesus. In one of the book's most well-known passages, Lewis points out how preposterous it was for Jesus to claim that he could forgive other people's sins. Because of the sheer outrageousness of Jesus' claims, Lewis writes, we must classify Jesus one of three ways: Liar, Lunatic, or Lord. Once we do believe, Lewis asserts that how exactly Christ's death put us right with God is less important than the fact that it did and does. Christ's "perfect surrender and humiliation" and his conquest of death enable us to reach new life in him. This new life, this "Christ-life" means Christ quite literally operates through us, "that we are His fingers and muscles, the cells of His body."[2]

Lewis rejects the notion of morality as a set of restraints that prevents us from having fun and instead suggests that morality keeps the human machine running smoothly, preventing unnecessary strain and tension that may lead to breakdown. Morality has three parts: fair play between individuals, harmonization within each individual, and the general purpose or direction of human life as a whole. Since we are promised eternal life, all three are vital. Any disharmonies or problems we have with others and most especially within ourselves will only become exacerbated over time.

Lewis points out that all of us have different starting points; therefore, we are not to judge each other. For God judges us not on our raw material but on what we choose to do with it, and our outward results do not always indicate how far we have progressed. According to Lewis, all our lives we are making little choices that are turning us into either heavenly creatures in harmony with God or hellish creatures at war with God. Christian morality points us toward the former. Knowledge is an essential part of this transformation. The closer we get to becoming heavenly creatures, the more aware we are of the evil still in us. Lewis goes on to discuss several specific virtues, including forgiveness. He suggests that it is indeed possible to love the sinner and hate the sin—we do it all the time for ourselves. The worst sin, for Lewis, is pride.

Lewis advocates a kind of bold pretending as a method of progressing in the spiritual life. To him the first step in many different aspects of Christian life and belief is to act as if we are there already—for example, to act as if we are children of God, to act as if we love our neighbors, to act as if we love God—because this very pretending leads us to the reality. As he puts it, "Now, at the moment you realize 'Here I am, dressing up as Christ,' it is extremely likely that you will see at once some way in which at that very moment the pretence could be made less of a pretence and more of a reality. . . . The Christ Himself, the Son of God who is man (just like you) and God (just like His Father) is actually at your side and is already at that moment beginning to turn your pretence into a reality."[3] This process is all-consuming, for Christ calls us to "be perfect." He will not be satisfied with changing one part of us; he will change every part, as painful a process as that may be, until we have become the creatures he intended us to be. Lewis writes, "If we let Him—for we can prevent Him, if we choose—He will make the feeblest and filthiest of us into a god or goddess, a dazzling, radiant, immortal creature, pulsating all through with such energy and joy

Lewis seeks in *Mere Christianity* to help us see religion with fresh eyes, as a radical faith whose adherents might be likened to an underground group gathering in a war zone, a place where evil seems to have the upper hand, to hear messages of hope from the other side.

—Kathleen Norris

and wisdom and love as we cannot now imagine, a bright stainless mirror which reflects back to God perfectly (though, of course, on a smaller scale) His own boundless power and delight and goodness. The process will be long and in parts very painful, but that is what we are in for."[4]

Why *Mere Christianity* Is Essential

C. S. Lewis is one of the most recognized names in Christian history. Because of his academic background and his history as a former atheist, Lewis gained a reputation for presenting a "thinking man's Christianity." *Mere Christianity* is known as the most succinct description of his theology and the foundation for all of his other works. It has been hugely influential in twentieth- and twenty-first-century Christianity. The success of these collected broadcast talks and of Lewis himself stem at least in part from his distinctive story and voice. As a former atheist and a recent convert, he conveyed a sense of excitement and urgency. As an Oxford don and respected intellectual and author, he was at the same time a compelling voice of authority. Even in written form, Lewis's voice is no less distinctive and resounding, forceful and thought provoking. The reader can almost hear him emphatically build his case and dismiss rival views with his characteristic clear logic, vivid analogies, and good humor.

Mere Christianity is considered a classic of Christian apologetics—in other words, a passionate defense of Christianity. Apologetics is not always considered prime material for spiritual formation. Instead, it is often viewed as material for Christians to recommend to *non*-Christians or those who are new to the faith or as something for Christians to read in order to buttress their attempts at evangelism. *Mere Christianity* is indeed an excellent resource for anyone seeking to learn the basics of the faith or for someone who has doubts about the reasonableness of Christian belief. Lewis's background as a committed atheist who became a

Christian in midlife makes his perspective very helpful to anyone who struggles intellectually with faith.

But it is important to understand one's faith critically for more than just evangelizing or justifying one's beliefs to another. Right understanding is critical to true belief. How can we be confident in our beliefs without being sure of their foundation? Lewis himself argues both for theology and for experience. He writes, "Doctrines are not God: they are only a kind of map. But that map is based on the experience of hundreds of people who really were in touch with God—experiences compared with which any thrills or pious feelings you and I are likely to get on our own are very elementary and very confused. And secondly, if you want to get any further, you must use the map. . . . In other words Theology is practical: especially now. In the old days, when there was less education and discussion, perhaps it was possible to get on with a very few simple ideas about God. But it is not so now. Everyone reads, everyone hears things discussed. Consequently, if you do not listen to Theology, that will not mean that you have no ideas about God. It will mean that you have a lot of wrong ones—bad, muddled, out-of-date ideas."[5]

Finally, few authors describe spiritual transformation in such vivid and creative terms. As editorial board member Emilie Griffin says, "Lewis's treatment of spiritual transformation in *Mere Christianity* is very imaginative and compelling. You really can't do it without religion, grace, God." Among other analogies, he describes us as houses that God is renovating and as obstinate tin soldiers that Christ wants to transform into people. With a relentless and tough-minded tone, Lewis lays out just how dire our situation is and how hard it is to get better without the help of Christ. What we're doing isn't working; nothing will, except complete submission to Christ. Lewis's words provide a colorful reminder of the transformative work Christ is doing in us. As we read, we can reflect on where we started and how far we've come. And, of course, how much further we have yet to go.

How to Read *Mere Christianity*

Mere Christianity is not a long or particularly difficult book. Lewis's distinctive and compelling tone, characterized by his creative analogies and general good humor, make for enjoyable reading. Book 1, Lewis's discussion of moral law, probably contains the most difficult and dry material in the book, so do not be discouraged if you find Book 1 slow going. The rest is a bit easier and will certainly feel familiar to anyone with a Christian background. One strategy for reading might be that which Lewis himself recommends in the text. If you come across material that does not seem useful or helpful to you, skip it and move on.

EXCERPTS FROM

Mere Christianity

God created things which had free will. That means creatures which can go either wrong or right. Some people think they can imagine a creature which was free but had no possibility of going wrong; I cannot. If a thing is free to be good it is also free to be bad. And free will is what has made evil possible. Why, then, did God give them free will? Because free will, though it makes evil possible, is also the only thing that makes possible any love or goodness or joy worth having. A world of automata—of creatures that worked like machines—would hardly be worth creating. The happiness which God designs for His higher creatures is the happiness of being freely, voluntarily united to Him and to each other in an ecstasy of love and delight compared with which the most rapturous love between a man and a woman on this earth is mere milk and water. And for that they must be free.

Of course God knew what would happen if they used their freedom the wrong way: apparently He thought it worth the risk. . . .

When we have understood about free will, we shall see how silly it is to ask, as somebody once asked me: 'Why did God make a creature of such rotten stuff that it went wrong?' The better stuff a creature is made of—the cleverer and stronger and freer it is—then the better it will be if it goes right, then also the worse it will be if it goes wrong. A cow cannot be very good or very bad; a dog can be both better and worse; a child better and worse still; an ordinary man, still more so; a man of genius, still more so; a superhuman spirit best—or worst—of all.

How did the Dark Power go wrong? Here, no doubt, we ask a question to which human beings cannot give an answer with any certainty. A reasonable (and traditional) guess, based on our own experiences of going wrong, can, however, be offered. The moment you have a self at all, there is a possibility of putting yourself first—wanting to be the centre—wanting to be God, in fact. That was the sin of Satan: and that was all the sin he taught the human race. Some people think the fall of man had something to do with sex, but that is a mistake. (The story in the Book of Genesis rather suggests that some corruption in our sexual nature followed the fall and was its result, not its cause.) What Satan put into the heads of our remote ancestors was the idea that they could 'be like gods'—could set up on their own as if they had created themselves—be their own masters—invent some sort of happiness for themselves outside God, apart from God. And out of that hopeless attempt has come nearly all that we call human history—money, poverty, ambition, war, prostitution, classes, empire, slavery—the long terrible story of man trying to find something other than God which will make him happy.

The reason why it can never succeed is this. God made us: invented us as a man invents an engine. A car is made to run on petrol, and it would not run properly on anything else. Now

God designed the human machine to run on Himself. He Himself is the fuel our spirits were designed to burn, or the food our spirits were designed to feed on. There is no other. That is why it is just no good asking God to make us happy in our own way without bothering about religion. God cannot give us a happiness and peace apart from Himself, because it is not there. There is no such thing.

That is the key to history. Terrific energy is expended—civilisations are built up—excellent institutions devised; but each time something goes wrong. Some fatal flaw always brings back the selfish and cruel people to the top and it all slides back into misery and ruin. In fact, the machine conks. It seems to start up all right and runs a few yards, and then it breaks down. They are trying to run it on the wrong juice. That is what Satan has done to us humans.

And what did God do? First of all He left us conscience, the sense of right and wrong: and all through history there have been people trying (some of them very hard) to obey it. None of them ever quite succeeded. Secondly, He sent the human race what I call good dreams: I mean those queer stories scattered all through the heathen religions about a god who dies and comes to life again and, by his death, has somehow given new life to men. Thirdly, He selected one particular people and spent several centuries hammering into their heads the sort of God He was—that there was only one of Him and that He cared about right conduct. Those people were the Jews, and the Old Testament gives an account of the hammering process.

Then comes the real shock. Among these Jews there suddenly turns up a man who goes about talking as if He was God. He claims to forgive sins. He says He has always existed. He says He is coming to judge the world at the end of time. Now let us get this clear. Among Pantheists, like the Indians, anyone might say that he was a part of God, or one with God: there would be nothing very odd about it. But this man, since He was a Jew, could not mean that kind of God. God, in their language, meant the Being outside the world, who had made it and was infinitely different from anything else. And when you have grasped that, you will see that what this man said was, quite simply, the most shocking thing that has ever been uttered by human lips.

One part of the claim tends to slip past us unnoticed because we have heard it so often that we no longer see what it amounts to. I mean the claim to forgive sins: any sins. Now unless the speaker is God, this is really so preposterous as to be comic. We can all understand how a man forgives offences against himself. You tread on my toes and I forgive you, you steal my money and I forgive you. But what should we make of a man, himself unrobed and untrodden on, who announced that he forgave you for treading on other men's toes and stealing other men's money? Asinine fatuity is the kindest description we should give of his conduct. Yet this is what Jesus did. He told people that their sins were forgiven, and never waited to consult all the other people who their sins had undoubtedly injured. He unhesitatingly behaved as if He was the party chiefly concerned, the person chiefly offended in all offences. This makes sense only if He really was the God whose laws are broken and whose love is wounded in every sin. In the mouth of any speaker who is not God, these words would imply what I can only regard as a silliness and conceit unrivalled by any other character in history.

Yet (and this is the strange, significant thing) even His enemies, when they read the Gospels, do not usually get the impression of silliness and conceit. Still less do unprejudiced readers. Christ says that He is 'humble and meek' and we believe Him; not noticing that, if He were merely a man, humility and meekness are the very last characteristics we could attribute to some of His sayings.

I am trying here to prevent anyone saying the really foolish thing that people often say about Him: 'I'm ready to accept Jesus as a great moral teacher, but I don't accept His claim to be God.' That is the one thing we must not say. A man who was merely a man and said the sort of things Jesus said would not be a great moral teacher. He would either be a lunatic—on a level with the man who says he is a poached egg—or else he would be the Devil of Hell. You must make your choice. Either this man was, and is, the Son of God: or else a madman or something worse. You can shut Him up for a fool, you can spit at Him and kill Him as a demon; or you can fall at His feet and call Him Lord and God. But let us not come with any patronizing nonsense about His being a great human teacher. He has not left that open to us. He did not intend to.

IS CHRISTIANITY HARD OR EASY?

The Christian way is different: harder, and easier. Christ says 'Give me All. I don't want so much of your time and so much of your money and so much of your work. I want You. I have not come to torment your natural self, but to kill it. No half-measures are any good. I don't want to cut off a branch here and a branch there, I want to have the whole tree down. I don't want to drill the tooth, or crown it, or stop it, but to have it out. Hand over the whole natural self, all the desires which you think innocent as well as the ones you think wicked—the whole outfit. I will give you a new self instead. In fact, I will give you Myself: my own will shall become yours.'

Both harder and easier than what we are all trying to do. You have noticed, I expect, that Christ himself sometimes describes the Christian way as very hard, sometimes as very easy. He says, 'Take up your Cross'—in other words, it is like going to be beaten to death in a concentration camp. Next minute he says, 'My yoke is easy and my burden light.' He means both. And one can see just why both are true.

Teachers will tell you that the laziest boy in the class is the one who works hardest in the end. They mean this. If you give two boys, say, a proposition in geometry to do, the one who is prepared to take trouble will try to understand it. The lazy boy will try to learn it by heart because, for the moment, that needs less effort. But six months later, when they are preparing for an exam, that lazy boy is doing hours and hours of miserable

My Personal Top 5

BRENDA QUINN

1 ***He Cares for You***, Corrie ten Boom. I share Dutch heritage with Corrie and have been moved by her story since first hearing it. The way she met God during her stay in Ravensbrook concentration camp and the forgiveness she exhibited afterward have inspired me as I encounter life's challenges. She is one, for me, in that "cloud of witnesses," who encourages me to overcome through the power of Christ.

2 ***Life Together***, Dietrich Bonhoeffer. I first read *Life Together* in my early post-college years. I was hungry for Christian fellowship done well, was living far from family, and had entered three unique groups of believers through a position in ministry and a commitment to two church groups. I became fascinated with Bonhoeffer's proposition that it is only through Christ-filled life in both solitude and fellowship that we experience life-giving Christian community.

3 ***Renovation of the Heart***, Dallas Willard. I was drawn to Willard's thesis in the book that all the parts of the self need to be transformed by Christ. I have seen this truth in my own life and felt that I needed continuing help in opening all of me to Jesus' free work within. Indeed, every part suffers when one part is not surrendered. Willard offers expert teaching and guidance in understanding the facets of our being and in yielding them to Christ's refining.

4 ***The Practice of the Presence of God***, Brother Lawrence. I discovered this book shortly after getting married and beginning to experience the reality of the "daily." I realized that I needed to make a way for encountering God in so many of my activities that weren't overtly spiritual. Brother Lawrence soon became my hero and I began viewing my daily routines as opportunities for experiencing God's presence. I had a horrible time with housekeeping, but, indeed, Brother Lawrence literally seemed to sit with me in the washing of the pans!

5 ***What's So Amazing About Grace?***, Philip Yancey. I have worked closely with Philip in writing several small group study guides for his books, cowriting a one-year devotional book, and editing a reader filled with his writing. *What's So Amazing About Grace?* became the second study guide I wrote. The book reached into my core and stunned me with the truth of its message, which, of course, is the amazing message of the gospel. Each time I go back it has the same effect. I need the message over and over again.

BRENDA QUINN is a writer and editor who works at home in Colorado. She continues to appreciate each of the books above as she and her husband raise three sons and enjoy ministry through their church and with Renovaré.

drudgery over things the other boy understands and positively enjoys, in a few minutes. Laziness means more work in the long run. Or look at it this way. In a battle, or in mountain climbing, there is often one thing which it takes a lot of pluck to do; but it is also, in the long run, the safest thing to do. If you funk it, you will find yourself, hours later, in far worse danger. The cowardly thing is also the most dangerous thing.

It is like that here. The terrible thing, the almost impossible thing, is to hand over your whole self—all your wishes and precautions—to Christ. But it is far easier than what we are all trying to do instead. For what we are trying to do is to remain what we call 'ourselves,' to keep personal happiness as our great aim in life, and yet at the same time to be 'good.' We are all trying to let our mind and heart go their own way—centred on money or pleasure or ambition—and hoping, in spite of this, to behave honestly and chastely and humbly. And that is exactly what Christ warned us you could not do. As He said, a thistle cannot produce figs. If I am a field that contains nothing but grass-seed, I cannot produce wheat. Cutting the grass may keep it short: but I shall still produce grass and no wheat. If I want to produce wheat, the change must go deeper than the surface. I must be ploughed up and re-sown.

That is why the real problem of the Christian life comes where people do not usually look for it. It comes the very moment you wake up each morning. All your wishes and hopes for the day rush at you like wild animals. And the first job each morning consists simply in shoving them all back; in listening to that other voice, taking that other point of view, letting that other larger, stronger, quieter life come flowing in. And so on, all day. Standing back from all your natural fussings and frettings; coming in out of the wind.

We can only do it for moments at first. But from those moments the new sort of life will be spreading through our system: because now we are letting Him work at the right part of us. It is the difference between paint, which is merely laid on the surface, and a dye or stain which soaks right through. He never talked vague, idealistic gas. When he said, 'Be perfect,' He meant it. He meant that we must go in for the full treatment. It is hard; but the sort of compromise we are all hankering after is harder—in fact, it is impossible. It may be hard for an egg to turn into a bird: it would be a jolly sight harder for it to learn to fly while remaining an egg. We are like eggs at present. And you cannot go on indefinitely being just an ordinary, decent egg. We must be hatched or go bad.[6]

A Study Guide for *Mere Christianity*

1. What, if anything, about Lewis's writing reflects the fact that it was meant to be read aloud? How might the message strike you differently if you were listening to it rather than reading it?

2. How do you think the fact that Lewis wrote and delivered these addresses during World War II and its immediate aftermath affected its tone? How might Lewis's experiences as a soldier have influenced his writing and perspective?

3. Lewis's "Liar, Lunatic, or Lord" argument is one of the most famous passages in the book. Do you think people today continue to view Jesus as just an enlightened teacher? Do you find Lewis's argument convincing? Why or why not?

4. Lewis describes us as machines meant to run on God, with morality as the instruction book to keep us running as smoothly as possible. How does this analogy help your understanding? What other analogies of his stand out to you as particularly colorful or helpful?

5. What is hard about Christianity? Why is it ultimately the easiest choice? Was becoming a Christian hard or easy for you? Why?

6. Lewis realized it was indeed possible to love the sinner and hate the sin because he felt this way about himself, and in fact the love he felt for himself made him hate the sin all the more. How might this way of looking at things help you to love others better? How have you experienced this feeling of hating a sin you have committed because of the love you feel for yourself?

7. Lewis advises that if we are having trouble loving God or each other, we should just act as if we do. What is his reasoning? How has this principle worked or not worked for you?

8. Lewis describes us as being like tin soldiers that Christ is trying to turn into live people like himself, with his *zoe* (spiritual life) running through them. Yet we fight and resist because we don't like the tin part of ourselves being destroyed. How have you experienced this transformation? What parts of you resist the life that is in Christ or, as Lewis puts it, want to stay tin?

The Return of the Prodigal Son

HENRI J. M. NOUWEN

Although claiming my true identity as a child of God, I still live as though the God to whom I am returning demands an explanation. I still think about his love as conditional and about home as a place I am not yet fully sure of. While walking home, I keep entertaining doubts about whether I will be truly welcome when I get there.

H ENRI J. M. NOUWEN was born in 1932 in the Netherlands. He always knew he wanted to become a priest and fulfilled this desire at a young age. A prolific author, he wrote many popular books about spirituality, including *The Wounded Healer* (1979), but his hectic schedule as an author and professor at Harvard took a toll on him. In 1986 he left Harvard to be the pastor of L'Arche Daybreak community in Toronto, a place in which those with intellectual disabilities and those who work as their assistants live together in Christian community and where Nouwen remained for the last ten years of his life. He wrote *The Return of the Prodigal Son* at this pivotal time of transition.

Nouwen's story begins with a painting. When he sees a reproduction of Rembrandt's *The Return of the Prodigal Son* in a friend's office, the intensity of his reaction shocks him. He is particularly touched by the depiction of the father's large hands on the boy's shoulders and longs to spend more time with the painting, eventually finding a way to view the original in St. Petersburg, Russia. After returning

Henri J. M. Nouwen's *The Return of the Prodigal Son* is an extended meditation on Jesus' parable of the son who asks for his inheritance, squanders it, and returns home defeated, only to be welcomed and forgiven.

from his trip, he begins his new job at L'Arche Daybreak. He hangs his print of Rembrandt's painting in his office there, and as he gazes upon it, reflecting on the people in the background and looking at the father and son, Nouwen realizes that, even after spending years teaching the spiritual life, he has remained an observer and never actually entered that central space with God as depicted by the father and son in the painting to ask and receive forgiveness. He hopes moving from Harvard to L'Arche is a step in this direction, and the painting soon becomes a window through which he can step into God's kingdom. Through the images in the painting along with the physical realities of his life at L'Arche, he is able to enter and remain in the place of God's indwelling in a way he never was able to do with his former intellectually focused life.

Nouwen begins his exploration of his spiritual life by meditating on the painting's image of the younger son. Nouwen sees himself in the younger son in his search for a home. After teaching and traveling for many years, Nouwen felt exhausted and homeless and longed for a homecoming such as the one experienced by the younger son. Leaving home, for the prodigal and for us, means more than just physically packing up and going. Nouwen describes leaving home as denying how we belong to God, denying that we are God's beloved and that God is our home. Why would any of us do such a thing? As Nouwen explains, we fall prey to the siren song of other voices that tell us we need success, fame, popularity, and power. We are too quick to believe that we will only be loved *if* we do this or don't do that. So we leave our home and our Father who loves us and gives us the freedom to leave, even though he never ceases calling back his beloved.

In the parable, when the younger son reaches the very bottom, when he is lonely and so disconnected to those around him that he is no longer considered human, only then does he remember his sonship and seek to return. For Nouwen, too, it was when he experienced a devastating low of a lost friendship that God called him home, reminding him that no friendship or community could ever meet his needs. And just as the son prepares a speech for his father to explain why he has come home, so, too, does Nouwen realize that he harbors doubts about God's truly welcoming him home, that he still views God as someone who demands an explanation.

He also realizes that the prodigal's plan to accept the role of a hired hand is not a true repentance. It does not show a true willingness to accept God's forgiveness. For Nouwen this reluctance is based again on a desire to be in charge of our own lives. He writes, "Do I want to break away from my deep-rooted rebellion against God and surrender myself so absolutely to God's love that a new person can emerge? Receiving forgiveness requires a total willingness to let God be God and do all the healing, restoring, and renewing. As long as I want to do even a part of that myself, I end up with partial solutions, such as becoming a hired servant."[1] Nouwen sees Jesus as the true prodigal, who gave away all that the Father had given him in order that we could return to the Father with him.

A better symbol of the Incarnation, I can hardly imagine.

—Philip Yancey (referring to Henri Nouwen and his life at L'Arche)

Nouwen then turns to the elder son, he who expressed anger because he felt his father was rewarding his brother's behavior over his own steadfastness. Nouwen also sees qualities of the elder brother in himself. He never openly rebelled or disobeyed and even felt at times envious of those who did. His obedience at times felt like a burden. In reflecting on the elder son, he points out the resentment, judgment, and condemnation that so often resides in those who are considered just or righteous. But it is also clear that the Father's love is offered as equally and freely to the elder son. The elder son is also lost, and he, too, is invited to return. In accepting that he is loved just the same as his younger brother, he must change his view of both father-son relationships. We must recognize that we, too, are lost and that we must trust the Father in order to be found. Nouwen calls us to replace our resentment with its opposite, gratitude. Dwelling in gratitude rather than resentment is a conscious choice, but the more we make it, the easier it will become. Here, too, we find Jesus, offering God's love to all the resentful, obedient children as well as to the sinners.

Finally, Nouwen turns to the father. Both the parable and the painting are more about the father than about either son. Nouwen finds great significance in Rembrandt's portrayal of the father as nearly blind. To Nouwen that physical blindness conveys the deep inner sight; the father recognizes his son by using his heart. To be a true father, he must allow his children to be free to reject his love. He cannot force himself on his children but instead waits for them with love, in order to bless them. This Father, God, does not care to punish. We have already been punished enough by our own waywardness. Instead he just wants to love and bless us. To God, we are all favorites.

Nouwen writes that he has spent most of his life trying to find God, to know God, and to love God, but that he did not sufficiently realize that God was trying to find him, know him, and love him. Like the father in the parable who runs halfway to meet his son, God, too, heedless of dignity, rushes to welcome us. Nouwen writes that he has trouble accepting this because of his own low self-esteem, because he does not see himself as worthy. He realizes he has seen his low self-esteem as a kind of virtue, a way to guard against pride and conceit, instead of a rejection of his own goodness. Our God is a God who rejoices, even when what is worthy of celebration seems overshadowed by that which is dark in the world. Nouwen writes, "People who have come to know the joy of God do not deny the darkness, but they choose not to live in it."[2]

Finally, Nouwen comes to the realization that the Father is not only his final resting place, but that he, too, is called to be the Father. To do so, he has to let go of all his fear of God's power, his fear of being punished. Only then is he free to live out God's compassion. Jesus called us to "Be compassionate as your Father is compassionate." We must seek to progress until we see the world through the Father's eyes. Nouwen writes of the difficulties he faces in fighting his longings for power, recognition, and affection in order to achieve spiritual fatherhood. He describes three steps to compassionate fatherhood: grief, forgiveness, and generosity. We grieve prayerfully at the sinfulness and subsequent suffering of God's children in order to prepare ourselves to receive anyone, no matter what his or her journey has been. We seek to forgive unconditionally, without pride or the need to feel recognized for doing so. And we pour ourselves out for our brothers and sisters. Living out these three steps creates a kind of sacred emptiness within ourselves, where we can be nonjudgmental and open ourselves to God's unconditional love.

Why *The Return of the Prodigal Son* Is Essential

Henri Nouwen was one of the most prolific Christian writers of the twentieth century. One of Nouwen's books, *The Wounded Healer,* touched on some of the same subjects Nouwen touches on here. Yet *The Return of the Prodigal Son,* threaded through as it is with Nouwen's personal story, has touched people in a way that few books do. Many have experienced healing and reconciliation through its pages. Editorial board member Richard Rohr describes *The Return of the Prodigal Son* as "a masterpiece of good theology that is applied to the healing of relationships in a way that really touches people."

Nouwen's message of the forgiveness and welcome that God offers to all of us, both our prodigal and our elder selves, is a powerful lesson. How have we allowed our own lack of self-worth and, at the same time, our overweening pride to talk us into rejecting God's welcome? Nouwen gives us an important tool to reflect on this question. With his very personal reflections, he models for us the spiritual discipline of meditation on Scripture, putting ourselves in the place of each character. Just as he puts himself in the role of first the younger son, then the elder son, and finally the father, we can experience the truth and wisdom of the Bible in a new way by seeking to, as much as possible, place ourselves into the biblical story. As the prodigal, how did we leave God? How can we allow ourselves to accept God's welcome and forgiveness? As the elder son, how do we resent others? How do we treat the sinners in our midst? And how are we called to be the father in our lives?

The healing Nouwen received through his extended meditation on the parable and the painting also represents an important lesson for our spiritual journeys. Like Nouwen, we come to our Christian faith carrying the various wounds the world and sin have inflicted on us. Some say that the first years of being a Christian are the years of healing. As we travel with Nouwen through his personal journey, we can reflect on where we need healing and reconciliation.

How to Read *The Return of the Prodigal Son*

The Return of the Prodigal Son is an intensely personal book, more of a memoir of spiritual healing than a work of theology. For many this focus on Nouwen's personal feelings and experiences will make the book easier to read, but others may have trouble relating to his insights for the very same reason. We strongly encourage you to try Nouwen's method of putting yourself in the place of the various characters of the parable.

Another helpful strategy might be to find a print of the Rembrandt painting that inspired Nouwen and try reflecting on the painting as he did.

The Return of the Prodigal Son

During the year after I first saw the *Prodigal Son,* my spiritual journey was marked by three phases which helped me to find the structure of my story.

The first phase was my experience of being the younger son. The long years of university teaching and the intense involvement in South and Central American affairs had left me feeling quite lost. I had wandered far and wide, met people with all sorts of life-styles and convictions, and become part of many movements. But at the end of it all, I felt homeless and very tired. When I saw the tender way in which the father touched the shoulders of his young son and held him close to his heart, I felt very deeply that I was that lost son and wanted to return, as he did, to be embraced as he was. For a long time I thought of myself as the prodigal son on his way home, anticipating the moment of being welcomed by my Father.

Then, quite unexpectedly, something in my perspective shifted. After my year in France and my visit to the Hermitage in Saint Petersburg, the feelings of desperation that had made me identify so strongly with the younger son moved to the background of my consciousness. I had made up my mind to go to Daybreak in Toronto and, as a result, felt more self-confident than before.

The second phase in my spiritual journey was initiated one evening while talking about Rembrandt's journey to Bart Gavigan, a friend from England who had come to know me quite intimately during the past year. While I explained to Bart how strongly I had been able to identify with the younger son, he looked at me quite intently and said, "I wonder if you are not more like the elder son." With these words he opened up a new space within me.

Frankly, I had never thought of myself as the elder son, but once Bart confronted me with the possibility, countless ideas started running through my head. Beginning with the simple fact that I am, indeed, the eldest child in my own family, I came to see how I had lived a quite dutiful life. When I was six years old, I already wanted to become a priest and never changed my mind. I was born, baptized, confirmed, and ordained in the same church and had always been obedient to my parents, my teachers, my bishops, and my God. I had never run away from home, never wasted my time and money on sensual pursuits, and had never gotten lost in "debauchery and drunkenness." For my entire life I had been quite responsible, traditional, and homebound. But, with all of that, I may, in fact, have been just as lost as the younger son. I suddenly saw myself in a completely new way. I saw my jealousy, my anger, my touchiness, doggedness and sullenness, and, most of all, my subtle self-righteousness. I saw how much of a complainer I was and how much of my thinking and feeling was ridden with resentment. For a time it became impossible to see how I could ever have thought of myself as his younger son. I was the elder son for sure, but just as lost as his younger brother, even though I had stayed "home" all my life.

I had been working very hard on my father's farm, but had never fully tasted the joy of being at home. Instead of being grateful for all the privileges I had received, I had become a very resentful person: jealous of my younger brothers and sisters who had taken so many risks and were so warmly welcomed back. During my first year and a half at Daybreak, Bart's insightful remark continued to guide my inner life.

There was more to come. In the months following the celebration of the thirtieth anniversary of my ordination to the priesthood, I gradually entered into very dark interior places and began to experience immense inner anguish. I came to a point where I could no longer feel safe in my own community and had to leave to seek help in my struggle and to work directly on my inner healing. The few books I could take with me were all about Rembrandt and the parable of the prodigal son. While living in a rather isolated place, far away from my friends and community, I found great consolation in reading about the tormented life of the great Dutch painter and learning more about the agonizing journey that ultimately had enabled him to paint this magnificent work.

For hours I looked at the splendid drawings and paintings he created in the midst of all his setbacks, disillusionment, and grief, and I came to understand how from his brush there emerged the figure of a nearly blind old man holding his son in a gesture of all-forgiving compassion. One must have died many deaths and cried many tears to have painted a portrait of God in such humility.

It was during this period of immense inner pain that another friend spoke the word that I most needed to hear and opened up the third phase of my spiritual journey. Sue Mosteller, who had been with the Daybreak community from the early seventies and had played an important role in bringing me there, had given me indispensable support when things had become difficult, and had encouraged me to struggle through whatever needed to be suffered to reach true inner freedom. When she visited me in my "hermitage" and spoke with me about the *Prodigal Son,* she said, "Whether you are the younger son or the

My Personal Top 5

DAVID NEFF

1 ***The Common Ventures of Life***, D. Elton Trueblood. Trueblood wrote these essays in the midst of post-nuclear angst, when young Christians were questioning whether they had any future and really ought to invest themselves in family and work—the "common ventures of life." Trueblood showed that these things had a deep spiritual meaning that could shine through the shadow of a nuclear cloud. I read these essays under a different cloud—the one cast by the Vietnam war. But they were just as encouraging for me as they had been for an earlier generation.

2 ***The Earth Is the Lord's*** and ***The Sabbath***, Abraham Joshua Heschel. Before reading Heschel's essay on the Sabbath, I gave God grudging obedience. Heschel helped me glimpse God's law as his gift to us—and a vehicle for his presence in our midst.

3 ***The Meaning of Persons***, Paul Tournier. I read this Swiss psychologist when psychology was dominated by behaviorism and faith was cowering before empiricism. He reawakened my appreciation for the human person as a unique individual, with a God-given value and psychic dynamics that could not be accounted for in purely empirical terms.

4 ***The Prophets***, Abraham Joshua Heschel. This book helped me understand that although God's wrath is real, it is God's passionate love for his creatures that drives his judgment against those who harm them.

5 ***The Seven Storey Mountain***, Thomas Merton. Reading Merton's conversion narrative confirmed for me the truth that radical personal reorientation is possible and that the Christian tradition could be a beacon for that reorientation—even in an age of relevance. It could have just as easily been a book by Chuck Colson or C. S. Lewis that did this for me, but in fact, it was Merton's memoir.

DAVID NEFF is the editor in chief and vice president of *Christianity Today International.*

elder son, you have to realize that you are called to become the father."

Her words struck me like a thunderbolt because, after all my years of living with the painting and looking at the old man holding his son, it had never occurred to me that the father was the one who expressed most fully my vocation in life.

Sue did not give me much chance to protest: "You have been looking for friends all your life; you have been craving for affection as long as I've known you; you have been interested in thousands of things; you have been begging for attention, appreciation, and affirmation left and right. The time has come to claim your true vocation—to be a father who can welcome his children home without asking them any questions and without wanting anything from them in return. Look at the father in your painting and you will know who you are called to be. We, at Daybreak, and most people around you don't need you to be a good friend or even a kind brother. We need you to be a father who can claim for himself the authority of true compassion."

Looking at the bearded old man with his full red cloak, I felt deep resistance to thinking about myself in that way. I felt quite ready to identify myself with the spendthrift younger son or the resentful elder son, but the idea of being like the old man who had nothing to lose because he had lost all, and only to give, overwhelmed me with fear. Nevertheless, Rembrandt died when he was sixty-three years old and I am a lot closer to that age than to the age of either of the two sons. Rembrandt was willing to put himself in the father's place; why not I?

The year and a half since Sue Mosteller's challenge has been a time to begin claiming my spiritual fatherhood. It has been a slow and arduous struggle, and sometimes I still feel the desire to remain the son and never to grow old. But I also have tasted the immense joy of children coming home and of laying hands on them in a gesture of forgiveness and blessing. I have come to know in a small way what it means to be a father who asks no questions, wanting only to welcome his children home. . . .

For, indeed, I am the younger son; I am the elder son; and I am on my way to becoming the father. And for you who will make this spiritual journey with me, I hope and pray that you too will discover within yourselves not only the lost children of God, but also the compassionate mother and father that is God.[3]

A Study Guide for *The Return of the Prodigal Son*

1. Nouwen realizes that he has spent too much of his life as a bystander or observer, mostly because of his reluctance to relinquish control. How have you remained the bystander in your spiritual life? What keeps you from asking and receiving forgiveness?

2. Which of the three characters have you most identified with in the past? Did your thoughts change after reading this book? How could you see yourself in all three?

3. In what ways have you "left home," i.e., moved away from God in your life?

4. Nouwen writes about his constant doubts about being truly welcomed home by God. "Although claiming my true identity as a child of God, I still live as though the God to whom I am returning demands an explanation. I still think about his love as conditional and about home as a place I am not yet fully sure of. While walking home, I keep entertaining doubts about whether I will be truly welcome when I get there."[4] How have you fallen prey to such doubts?

5. Nouwen writes that receiving God's forgiveness is one of the greatest challenges of the spiritual life. Do you agree? Why or why not? What might prevent us from welcoming forgiveness?

6. What do you think of Nouwen's interpretation of Jesus as the prodigal son? Have you ever thought of Jesus this way? If not, what new ways of thinking about Jesus does it open up for you?

7. Is it hard for you to see God as one who wants only to love and bless you, not punish? If so, why?

8. When have you struggled with accepting that God loves each of us equally? Have you ever, like Nouwen, mistaken low self-esteem for a virtue rather than a rejection of your goodness?

9. When, if ever, have you experienced the sacred emptiness of which Nouwen writes, that of unconditional love and forgiveness?

10. How have you, like Nouwen, felt the desire to remain a dependent, a spiritual child? How have you felt a call to be the father or mother?

Best Contemporary Authors

Although we decided that the authors and books for our list of twenty-five were to be chosen from proven works from past authors, that does not mean wisdom for our life with God ended with the early Church or the Middle Ages or the Reformation or the year 2000. While it may be too soon to determine which contemporary books will rise above this age and become perennial classics for the Church, it is not as difficult to discern contemporary authors who consistently share that spiritual wisdom for our time and our place and who we feel confident in pointing others to as the best contemporary teachers.

The *25 Books* editorial board decided not to overcomplicate the process. Each selected their top five choices. After adding together the nominations and after minimal debate and discussion, nine authors naturally emerged. This list, therefore, provides a sample of the best contemporary voices who can provide us an eternal perspective on how to make our way in the culture today. Each has something deep and fundamental to teach us about our discipleship to Jesus. For each author we have added a brief introduction and descriptions of their best work published so far in their career.

—Julia L. Roller and Lyle SmithGraybeal

Wendell Berry

Writer, activist, farmer, and lifelong Baptist, Wendell Berry has written more than forty books, including novels, short stories, poems, and essays. Best known for his strong endorsement of an agrarian lifestyle, Berry has farmed land in his native Kentucky for more than forty years. Some of his most prominent themes are the interconnectedness of life and our responsibility to care for creation.

These themes are borne out in his essays and poetry, but also in his novels and short fiction set in a fictional Kentucky small town named Port William.

Selected Books

The Unsettling of America

Berry's groundbreaking work describes farming as a spiritual discipline, as well as an answer to many of the problems within our culture, such as loss of community, lack of connection to nature, lack of meaningful work, and environmental destruction. He reminds us that we must take responsibility for our actions, recognizing that what we eat, for example, affects the world around us. Berry was one of the earliest prophets of the practice of buying food locally, but he also urges readers to learn about food and gardening and produce as much of their own food as possible. Sierra Club, 1977, rev. 1996, 234 pages.

A Place on Earth

In this and the other Port William novels, Berry describes a community much like the one for which he advocates in his non-fiction, based on individual household farms, centered around the rhythms of the harvest. *A Place on Earth* describes the Port William community at the end of WWII as the members of the town deal with issues of loss and redemption. Berry's prose writing is as lyrical as his poetry, making his novels as worthy of savoring for their beauty as for their ideas. Crosspoint, 1983, rev. 2001, 320 pages.

Sex, Economy, Freedom & Community

In this collection of eight essays, Berry again advocates for small communities based on individual households that take responsibility for more of their own farming, education, etc. Includes the powerful essay "Christianity and the Survival of Creation," in which Berry affirms the goodness of all creation, even that which we might not find particularly helpful, such as stinging insects or microorganisms, and indicts Christians for participating in the destruction of creation by colluding with government, economic forces, and technology. Pantheon, 1994, 208 pages.

That Distant Land: The Collected Stories

This collection of all of Berry's Port William short stories chronicles the small town's journey through the twentieth century. Characterized by a leisurely pace, plain speech, and an emphasis on the very human characters of the townspeople, these stories illustrate not only the beauty of a small self-supporting community but also its decline in the modern world. Counterpoint, 2005, 408 pages.

A Timbered Choir: The Sabbath Poems 1979–1997

"I go among the trees and sit still." Written after his Sunday walks through the forests and field surrounding his Port Royal, Kentucky, farm, Berry's poems describe the beauty of nature, although often with a recognition of the damage inflicted on it by the modern world. Through this poetry, which is mainly traditional blank verse, Berry calls us to take practical steps to arrest environmental degradation. Counterpoint, 1999, 240 pages.

Richard J. Foster

A Quaker minister, professor, and founder of a number of ministry and other structures that have promoted thoughtful writing and intentional reflection, Foster is a pastor's pastor, always listening for the daily step of the Spirit in our lives and yet not afraid to found structures that have helped shape the vision of the modern Church. Through his writing and speaking, Foster has helped many to reconnect with classic Church tradition, from spiritual disciplines to essential devotional writings. A notable achievement is founding Renovaré, a ministry that through writings and events on spiritual practices and the history of the Church has promoted and resourced a modern vision of intentional Christian formation and lifelong discipleship.

Selected Books

Celebration of Discipline: The Path to Spiritual Growth

Providing a biblical and historical foundation and numerous windows onto the life of spiritual practice, *Celebration* introduces and makes the case for engagement in twelve classical spiritual disciplines: meditation, prayer, fasting, study, simplicity, solitude, submission, service, confession, worship, guidance, and celebration. It is a groundbreaking book for modern Christian spiritual practice because of its accessibility and practicality and because it draws on the roots of the Church without regard to creed, class, or communion. HarperOne, 25th anniversary edition, 2003, 256 pages.

Streams of Living Water: Essential Practices from the Six Great Traditions of Christian Faith

God's Spirit has been at work in the life of the Church—with individuals and the institution—for over two thousand years. At times various themes of the with-God life have fallen into disuse and need renewed attention. This is essentially the message of *Streams* as Foster highlights six traditions of Christian life and faith—Contemplative, Holiness, Charismatic, Social Justice, Evangelical, and Incarnational—that God has worked with throughout our common Christian history and are available to us as we seek a balanced practice of discipleship to Jesus. HarperOne, 1998, 448 pages.

Freedom of Simplicity: Finding Harmony in a Complex World

"Seek first God's kingdom and his righteousness"—this is the foundation and point of departure for Christian simplicity, the motivational measure by which all of our choices for living life in the world are made. While simplicity is only one Christian discipline among others, it is foundational to a life of discipleship to Jesus. Choosing cumbersome possessions and activities over simplicity too often will lead to lives weighed down by the cares of the world, unavailable to little more than lifestyle maintenance. The work considers the complexity of simplicity, looks at its biblical roots, and discusses its practice in our personal, family, church, and world arenas. HarperOne, 1981, rev. 2005, 272 pages.

Prayer: Finding the Heart's True Home

At the same time a primer on prayer and a catalog of twenty-one different types of prayer, Foster mines the history of the Church for helping us with our own spiritual practice. Dividing these types of prayer into three sections—Inward, Upward, and Outward—the book casts a vision for the life of prayer and provides guidance in each of these ways of praying. No modern book has done more to share the height and breadth and depth of our contemplative life with God. HarperOne, 10th anniversary edition, 2003, 288 pages.

Anne Lamott

Northern California writer Anne Lamott's roots are in fiction, but her first-person memoirs are the works that have made her a household name. She first found a large audience with *Operating Instructions,* her account of her first year as the single mother of her son, Sam. Next came her story about coming to faith, *Traveling Mercies,* followed by several others. Although passionate about political causes—Lamott calls herself a left-wing Christian—much of her writing centers on her daily life and her family, making her journey easy to relate to. Her uncommon and unflinching honesty, combined with humor and a passion for the craft of writing, feels all too rare among contemporary Christian writers.

Selected Books

Traveling Mercies: Some Thoughts on Faith

Lamott's first book on faith issues, *Traveling Mercies* is a series of autobiographical essays spanning her troubled childhood, her addictions to food, pills, and alcohol, and her powerful encounter with Jesus and subsequent decision to become a Christian and join St. Andrew Presbyterian Church, a move that surprised no one more than Lamott herself. Anchor, 1999, rev. 2000, 275 pages.

Grace (Eventually): Thoughts on Faith

Lamott's third collection of thoughts on faith includes her reflections on subjects as varied as parenting, church life, and the mellowing of her attitude toward George W. Bush. By turns zany, irreverent, funny, and heartbreaking, her continuing faith journey is described with grace and a refreshing humility. Riverhead, 2008, 253 pages.

Bird by Bird: Some Instructions on Writing and Life

Lamott's guide to the craft of writing combines her quirky, self-deprecating tone with practical and indispensable advice for anyone who has ever thought about writing. Illustrating every point with humor and stories from her own writing experience and classes, Lamott proves herself the teacher you always wished you had. Anchor, 1994, 240 pages.

Brian McLaren

At one time an English teacher and later a pastor, Brian McLaren is a synthesizer of ideas from seemingly disparate sources. Part journalist, priest, theologian, entrepreneur, and networker, McLaren's writing is (at the least):

- inter-confessional—introducing ideas and practices from most every tradition of the Church

- inter-disciplinary—seeing a variety of subjects through various lenses of academia: sociology, psychology, theology, and more
- inter-millennial—considering outlooks and faith formation practices from the early and contemporary Church, and everything in-between
- inter-jectory—questioning dominant views of discipleship and theology for the sake of a redeemed world

All in all, his writing helps us see the Church as it is and as it could be, now and in the future.

Selected Books

A Generous Orthodoxy

The subtitle of this book says it all: "Why I Am a Missional, Evangelical, Post/Protestant, Liberal/Conservative, Mystical/Poetic, Biblical, Charismatic/Contemplative, Fundamentalist/Calvinist, Anabaptist/Anglican, Methodist, Catholic, Green, Incarnational, Depressed-yet-Hopeful, Emergent, Unfinished CHRISTIAN." Both a confession and a manifesto, McLaren calls for a vision of life in Christ that transcends the human-defined differences that we create for the sake of the love of Jesus in the world. We are helped to see that there is no "us" nor "them," only "we." Zondervan, 2006, 352 pages.

A New Kind of Christian

The first of a fiction triology, *A New Kind of Christian* is set as a conversation between Dan, an any-pastor from suburban U.S.A., and Neo, a high school science teacher originally from Jamaica. Through the two men's discussions, McLaren considers a variety of topics—view of God, role of the Christian in the world, nationalism, and others—as we move from a modernist to a post-modern culture. Highly accessible and yet full of theory and application from a variety of academic disciplines, *A New Kind of Christian* is quite valuable for reconsidering Christian faith and practice for men and women in today's culture. Jossey-Bass, 2001, 192 pages.

Everything Must Change

With the eyes of a global journalist and the heart of a local pastor, McLaren considers the many global crises we face today—economic, environmental, military, and more—and the difference the world-affirming and world-transforming message of Jesus makes. For the life Jesus describes to become real on a wide scale we must reconsider and repent of the ways that we live. We can dream and act on a new vision for humanity and all of God's creation. Thomas Nelson, 2007, 336 pages.

A New Kind of Christianity

A foundations book, in this title McLaren provides the thinking behind *A New Kind of Christian* and many of his other books via ten questions that he feels the Church must answer for our day. For instance, question #5 is, "What Is the Gospel?" An essential for all of McLaren's readers (sympathizers and detractors), the book addresses a wide and varied range of topics from a Jesus-motivated and Church-centered perspective. HarperOne, 2010, 336 pages.

Eugene H. Peterson

The founding pastor of Christ Our King Presbyterian Church in Bel Air, Maryland, and for many years the James M. Houston Professor of Spiritual Theology at Regent College, Vancouver, Eugene Peterson has perhaps done more than anyone in the last fifty years for helping clergy develop a pastoral vocation. Intentionally striving to keep his own church to a smaller membership of 300 to 500 persons, Peterson sees himself primarily as a spiritual director as opposed to a preacher or chief executive. In each of his books there shines through the heart of a pastor and prophet who cares for the souls of his readers, comforting those afflicted by life in the modern world and also afflicting those overly comfortable with the ways and means of American culture.

Selected Books

The Message: The Bible in Contemporary Language

A paraphrase of the Bible written while consulting the original Hebrew and Greek texts, *The Message* takes the often difficult to work with language of strict translations and puts these most-important writings in the language of the common vernacular of everyday life. Available and helpful to both those new to the Bible and longtime users, it provides a fresh perspective on passages both familiar and inaccessible. NavPress, various editions and years of publication.

Spiritual Theology series

This five-book series considers a variety of aspects of our life with God fundamental to intentional Christian formation. Eerdmans, published between 2005 and 2010.

Christ Plays in Ten Thousand Places: A Conversation in Spiritual Theology—Recasts the vision and practice of spirituality for daily living, grounding it in the life of the Trinity and common experience.

Eat This Book: A Conversation in the Art of Spiritual Reading—Introducing the *lectio divina* method of Scripture reflection, reminds us that the Bible is to be read for both information and formation.

The Jesus Way: A Conversation on the Ways That Jesus Is the Way—Looking at the lives of Abraham, Moses, David, Elijah, Isaiah of Jerusalem, and Isaiah of the Exile, considers the ways that Jesus is the Way of life for us in contradistinction to the ways of American culture.

Tell It Slant: A Conversation on the Language of Jesus in His Stories and Prayers—Peterson reminds us that all language is God language, as Jesus in the earthiness of his parables, prayers, teachings, and admonishments makes clear.

Practice Resurrection: A Conversation on Growing Up in Christ—A study of the book of Ephesians, the book reminds us that resurrection is for living out now.

The Pastor: A Memoir

While not his *magnum opus,* the memoir *The Pastor* may end up being the capstone of Peterson's fruitful pastoring and writing career. In it he lays down many of the inspirations and directions for the culturally contrarian and yet ultimately satisfying ways that his pastoral guidance would lead us. HarperOne, 2011, 336 pages.

A Long Obedience in the Same Direction: Discipleship in an Instant Society

Working with the Psalms of Ascent (Psalms 120–134), Peterson makes the case that discipleship to Jesus is not a plan or program but a lifetime of commitment, recommitment, and commitment again. Following the Savior is a lifelong process that is new every day and at the same time firmly founded by the wisdom of years and experience. InterVarsity Press, 20th anniversary edition, 2000, 216 pages.

Five Smooth Stones for Pastoral Work

Written out of his experience with a group of pastors during his years at Christ Our King in Bel Air, here we are reminded that while management training and techniques can be helpful for pastoral work, ultimately it is a life of intentional formation in Christlikeness that will help us become pastors of depth and insight. Five books of the Hebrew Scriptures—Song of Songs, Ruth, Lamentations, Ecclesiastes, and Esther—form the intellectual backbone for this countercultural work. Eerdmans, 1992, 251 pages.

John Stott

An Anglican priest, speaker, evangelist, and writer, John R. W. Stott served as the rector of All Souls Church in London for twenty-five years and is now rector emeritus. Named by *Time* magazine in 2005 as one of the 100 most influential people in the world and described by David Edwards as "the most influential clergyman in the Church of England during the twentieth century," Stott is known for his careful biblical exposition, intellectually rigorous yet accessible teaching, and a relentless focus on the need for daily discipleship to Jesus.

Selected Books

Basic Christianity

In his best-known book, Stott lays out the basic tenets of Christian faith and discusses how these beliefs should play out in daily life. This handbook to the fundamentals of the faith is useful for new and longtime Christians or people just seeking to learn more about Christianity. After explaining the significance of Jesus' identity, teachings, and resurrections, Stott calls his readers to action in the world through Jesus' body, the Church. InterVarsity Press, 1971, 180 pages.

The Bible Speaks Today New Testament series

Stott's greatest contribution to Bible exposition, this series addresses several key New Testament books, such as Acts, Romans, Galatians, and Ephesians, as well as a book on the Sermon on the Mount subtitled "Christian Counter-Culture." InterVarsity Press, 1968–1996.

Why I Am a Christian

Stott's highly personal and persuasive story of the theological basis of his own faith, complete with stories from the lives of other famous Christians. His reasons include that he was raised to be a Christian and that he believes Christ pursued him, in addition to characteristically logical explanations of why he believes Christ is the key to freedom and the answer to his own personal aspirations. InterVarsity Press, 2003, 140 pages.

The Cross of Christ

In this book, considered by some to be his masterpiece, Stott explains what the cross means for Christians today. InterVarsity Press, 20th anniversary edition, 2006, 380 pages.

Walter Wangerin Jr.

Lutheran pastor and author of more than thirty books, Wangerin currently holds the Jochum chair at Valparaiso University in Indiana, where he teaches literature and creative writing. His boundless imagination has helped so many to see Christ, the Bible, and their role in the world in new ways. His allegories and images are often simple but never simplistic, instead shaded with many layers of meaning.

Selected Books

The Book of the Dun Cow

In this fable, Chauntecleer the rooster and those in his animal kingdom must keep evil Wyrm imprisoned beneath the earth. Wangerin's first novel, *The Book of the Dun Cow* won both the National Book Award and *The New York Times* Best Children's Book of the Year. The animals rise above their own petty natures to fight Wyrm, and the dog Mundo Cani becomes a most unlikely Christ figure. HarperOne, 25th anniversary edition, 2003, 256 pages.

The Book of God

Wangerin's novelization captures the whole of the Bible as one magnificent sweeping story. Zondervan, 1996, 850 pages.

Ragman and Other Cries of Faith

This collection of stories, allegories, and meditations are powerful reflections on the life of faith. The title story has touched many with its depiction of a Christ figure who takes on the afflictions of those to whom he sells rags. HarperOne, 1994, rev. 2004, 224 pages.

As for Me & My House: Crafting Your Marriage to Last

By turns relationship guide and memoir, Wangerin's grittiness and honesty come through as he not only presents principles for thriving in this most important of relationships but elucidates them with personal stories that are, at times, written confessions. Thomas Nelson, 2001, 288 pages.

Dallas Willard

An ordained Southern Baptist minister, a professor of philosophy at the University of Southern California and other schools, and a one-time worship leader of a small Quaker church in southern California, Willard is an interdisciplinary thinker who draws on psychology, sociology, philosophy, and other perspectives to describe and encourage human transformation into Christlikeness. Willard has the ability to challenge readers intellectually while at the same time inspiring them to change their inner lives. Perhaps the greatest value of his writing is the ability to quickly and creatively cause his readers or hearers to step back and question their assumptions while, at the same time, cast a vision for life with God and describe the milieu of the inner life in which each person lives.

Selected Books

The Divine Conspiracy: Rediscovering Our Hidden Life in God

Willard's *magnum opus,* this book from its very beginning unsettles us by causing us to consider whether or not we are actually heading in the correct direction with our lives and then offering a call to repentance, or "turning." Before moving into an exposition of Jesus' "Sermon on the Mount," a sermon of Jesus by which we can daily live, Willard paints a very clear and clever image of the "God-bathed World" in which Jesus lived and to which we are invited to open our eyes. HarperOne, 1998, 448 pages.

The Spirit of the Disciplines: Understanding How God Changes Lives

As God founded an order of creation based on matter and the physical, so the life of the Spirit and our spirits in this life are embodied. The physical participation of the body in the classical spiritual disciplines is a primary way to influence and transform each of our spirits. In *The Spirit of the Disciplines* Willard makes the case for our participation in a variety of spiritual practices and provides beginning guidance for this way of engagement. HarperOne, 1999, 288 pages.

Renovation of the Heart: Putting on the Character of Christ

Thought. Feeling. Will. Body. Social context. Soul. These are the six elements of a person that need transformation by God. *Renovation of the Heart* describes this process of change from a philosophical and psychological perspective, explaining that everything that we see on the outside of a person is determined by the life of the heart. Especially helpful is Willard's "VIM" acronym—Vision, Intention, Means—which helps us think about the necessary ingredients if a person is to move further along the path to salvation in this and the next life. NavPress, 2002, 272 pages.

Hearing God: Developing a Conversational Relationship with God

Speaking to God is only one part of a conversation. The other is listening and doing so in a way that honors the unique nature of God, a being who now as well as throughout history speaks in a wide variety of ways—through dreams and visions, angels, audible words, Holy Scripture, the created order, and much more. Here Willard casts a broad vision and presents first steps for spending time with and listening to God in ways that are authentically biblical yet often overlooked. InterVarsity Press, 1999, 228 pages.

N. T. Wright

The former Anglican Bishop of Durham, England, for twenty years a professor of New Testament studies at Cambridge, McGill, and Oxford universities, and now chair of New Testament and Early Christianity at University of St. Andrews's School of Divinity, Wright's greatest contribution has been making complicated theological ideas and propositions available to an everyday audience. Much like C. S. Lewis before him, Wright has creatively and winsomely presented complex ideas in a fashion that informs and enhances daily living.

Selected Books

Simply Christian: Why Christianity Makes Sense

At the same time a warm welcome to those outside of the Christian faith and a challenge to those who think they have their faith and practice all figured out, *Simply Christian* provides a bracing introduction to faith in Jesus. Assuming a skeptical audience, Wright connects our everyday and yet often unrecognized philosophical musings—for instance, the ability to discern some things as beautiful and beyond average, the nature of and need for justice, etc.—with a simple and accessible description of what it means to be a follower of Jesus in today's world. HarperOne, 2010, 256 pages.

Surprised by Hope: Rethinking Heaven, the Resurrection, and the Mission of the Church

As we all know, the Christian life is not only about what happens when we die, but what we do with our lives before we die. What we believe about life after death is a guiding factor in what we do with life before death. Wright argues that Jesus' resurrection was the first step in the renewal of the whole of creation. As such, Christians and the larger Church are called to bring this new life, this new and renewed order of resurrected being, into the common life of the world today. HarperOne, 2008, 352 pages.

The Challenge of Jesus: Rediscovering Who Jesus Was and Is

A reduction and at the same time an expansion of Wright's earlier work *Jesus and the Victory of God,* this volume addresses many of the core questions of the historical Jesus discussions in a way that considers them both as scholarly propositions and as ontological sustenance for our daily living. For instance, was the resurrection real and, assuming so, what does this mean for our daily lives? InterVarsity Press, 1999, 202 pages.

Scripture and the Authority of God: How to Read the Bible Today

All of us—liberals, conservatives, and all shades in between—are guilty of misreading Scripture and of using it for our own purposes. Here Wright points out this obvious truth and presents a more authentic, historic, and commonsense understanding of biblical authority. HarperOne, 2011, 224 pages.

Editorial Board

Gayle D. Beebe is the current president of Westmont College in Santa Barbara, California. He has been a professor and administrator in higher education for twenty years. He is the author or editor of ten books, including *Longing for God: Seven Paths of Christian Devotion* (coauthored with Richard J. Foster), *The Shaping of an Effective Leader: Eight Formative Principles of Leadership,* and a general editor of *The Life with God Bible.*

James Catford is vice-chair of Renovaré USA and chair of Renovaré Britain and Ireland. He is group chief executive of Bible Society, England and Wales (BFBS), and was formerly publishing director at HodderHeadline and HarperCollins.

Richard J. Foster is the founder of Renovaré. He has authored or coauthored seven books, including *Celebration of Discipline, Prayer: Finding the Heart's True Home, Freedom of Simplicity, The Challenge of the Disciplined Life, Streams of Living Water, Life with God: Reading the Bible for Spiritual Transformation* (with Kathryn A. Helmers), and *Longing for God* (with Gayle Beebe). He is also the lead editor of *The Life with God Bible.*

Emilie Griffin is the author of *Souls in Full Sail: Christian Spirituality for the Later Years* and *Wonderful and Dark Is This Road,* a brief introduction to Christian mystics. The author of sixteen books on the spiritual life, she edited the *HarperCollins Spiritual Classics* series and contributed to *The Life with God Bible* and Zondervan's *History of Christian Spirituality.*

Frederica Mathewes-Green is the *khouria* (spiritual mother) of Holy Cross Orthodox Church in Baltimore, Maryland. She is the author of many books about ancient Eastern Christianity, including *Facing East* and *The Illumined Heart,* a popular speaker, and contributor to *Christianity Today, First Things,* and many other publications.

Michael G. Maudlin (Mickey) is a senior vice president, executive editor, and director of Bible Publishing for HarperOne, the religion and spirituality imprint of HarperCollins. He works with bestselling authors such as Rob Bell, N. T. Wright, Dallas Willard, Brian McLaren, the C. S. Lewis Estate, and many others. Maudlin is also responsible for developing new Bible products for the New Revised Standard Version (NRSV). Before coming to Harper, he served as both editorial vice president and managing editor of the flagship evangelical magazine *Christianity Today* and earlier as general books editor with InterVarsity Press.

Fr. Richard Rohr is a Franciscan priest of the New Mexico Province. He was ordained in 1970, founded the New Jerusalem Community in Cincinnati in 1971 and the Center for Action and Contemplation in Albuquerque in 1987. He is most known for his many recorded conferences and his latest books, *Everything Belongs, The Naked Now,* and *Falling Upward.*

Julia L. Roller is a writer and editor whose books include *A Year with God* (coedited with Richard J. Foster), *A Year with Aslan,* and *Learning from Jesus* (coauthored with Lynda L. Graybeal). She was also the project editor for *The Life with God Bible.*

Lyle SmithGraybeal comes from a background in retail business and inner-city ministry and has been involved with Renovaré in one aspect or another for more than twenty years. He is currently the Renovaré Coordinator, where he works on print and electronic publishing, event planning, and international projects, and is a contributor to *The Life with God Bible.*

Phyllis Tickle is the compiler of *The Divine Hours* series of manuals for observing fixed-hour prayer and the author of some two dozen books in the field of religion, including the bestselling *The Great Emergence—How Christianity Is Changing and Why.* She lectures widely, both in this country and abroad, on Emergence Christianity and the role of the institutional Church today.

Chris Webb is president of Renovaré USA, a Christian ministry dedicated to helping people experience a richer life with God through spiritual formation. A former Anglican priest in Wales, he has ministered in a wide variety of contexts, from farming communities to blue-collar steelworking towns; he also spent a year with a church for the homeless.

Dallas Willard is a professor in the School of Philosophy at the University of Southern California and an ordained minister. He is the author of several books including *The Divine Conspiracy,* which was selected as *Christianity Today*'s Book of the Year for 1999. He displays a scholarly acumen and a pastor's heart, seeking to integrate philosophy, theology, and ethics with practical discipleship and Christian day-to-day living.

John Wilson is the founding editor of *Books & Culture,* a bimonthly review. He has edited five volumes in the *Best Christian Writing* series. His essays and reviews appear in the *New York Times Book Review,* the *Wall Street Journal,* the *Boston Globe, Commonweal, First Things, National Review, The Weekly Standard, Christianity Today,* and other publications.

Notes

Introduction

1. C. S. Lewis, Introduction to Athanasius's *On the Incarnation,* www.spurgeon .org/~phil/history/ath-inc.htm#ch_o.

2. Lewis, www.spurgeon.org/~phil/history/ath-inc.htm#ch_o.

3. Richard J. Foster, *Life with God* (San Francisco: HarperOne, 2008), 3.

Chapter 1

Epigraph: St. Athanasius, *On the Incarnation,* Christian Classics Ethereal Library, www .ccel.org/ccel/athanasius/incarnation.ii.html.

1. Athanasius, *Incarnation,* www.ccel.org/ccel/athanasius/incarnation.iii.html.

2. Athanasius, *Incarnation,* www.ccel.org/ccel/athanasius/incarnation.iii.html.

3. Athanasius, *Incarnation,* www.ccel.org/ccel/athanasius/incarnation.iv.html.

4. Athanasius, *Incarnation,* www.ccel.org/ccel/athanasius/incarnation.iv.html.

5. Athanasius, *Incarnation,* www.ccel.org/ccel/athanasius/incarnation.v.html.

6. Athanasius, *Incarnation,* www.ccel.org/ccel/athanasius/incarnation.v.html.

7. Encyclopaedia Britannica, 9th ed., vol. 2 (New York: Charles Scribner's Sons, 1878), quoted in the introduction to *On the Incarnation,* www.amazon.com/ Incarnation-Saint-Athanasius/dp/1434811247/ref=sr_1_1?s=books&ie=UTF8&qid=12 95915972&sr=1-1#reader_1434811247.

8. Richard J. Foster, *Celebration of Discipline* (San Francisco: HarperOne, 1998), 66.

9. Athanasius, *Incarnation,* www.ccel.org/ccel/athanasius/incarnation.iii.html.

10. Athanasius, *Incarnation,* www.ccel.org/ccel/athanasius/incarnation.iv.html.

11. Athanasius, *Incarnation,* www.ccel.org/ccel/athanasius/incarnation.iv.html.

12. Athanasius, *Incarnation,* www.ccel.org/ccel/athanasius/incarnation.vi.html.

13. Athanasius, *Incarnation,* www.ccel.org/ccel/athanasius/incarnation.ix.html.

Chapter 2

Epigraph: Saint Augustine, *Confessions,* trans. R. S. Pine-Coffin (London: Penguin, 1961), 21.

1. Augustine, *Confessions,* 32.

2. Augustine, *Confessions,* 75.

3. Augustine, *Confessions,* 82.

4. Augustine, *Confessions,* 82.

5. Augustine, *Confessions,* 89.

6. Augustine, *Confessions,* 116.

7. Augustine, *Confessions,* 175.

8. Augustine, *Confessions,* 178.

9. Augustine, *Confessions,* 243.

10. Augustine, *Confessions,* 47–48, 49–53.

11. Augustine, *Confessions,* 60.

12. Augustine, *Confessions,* 79.

13. Augustine, *Confessions,* 169.

Chapter 3

Epigraph: The Sayings of the Desert Fathers, trans. Benedicta Ward, SLG (Kalamazoo, MI: Cistercian, 1975), 44.

1. Ward, *Desert Fathers,* 3.

2. Ward, *Desert Fathers,* 13.

3. Ward, *Desert Fathers,* 50.

4. Ward, *Desert Fathers,* 27.

5. Ward, *Desert Fathers,* 42.

6. Ward, *Desert Fathers,* 3.

7. Ward, *Desert Fathers,* 143.

8. Ward, *Desert Fathers,* 141.

9. Metropolitan Anthony of Sourozh, preface to Ward, *Desert Fathers,* xvi.

10. Ward, *Desert Fathers,* 21, 24, 42–43, 87–88, 91–92, 98, 103, 138–39, 164–65, 169–70, 171, 172, 175, 178, 179–80, 185, 189, 191, 224–25, 230–31.

11. Ward, *Desert Fathers,* 8.

12. Ward, *Desert Fathers,* 52.

13. Ward, *Desert Fathers,* 107.

Chapter 4

Epigraph: Timothy Fry, ed., *The Rule of St. Benedict in English* (Collegeville, MN: Liturgical Press, 1980), 95–96.

1. Fry, *Rule,* 18.

2. Fry, *Rule,* 26.

3. Fry, *Rule,* 42–43.

4. Fry, *Rule,* 47.

5. Fry, *Rule,* 49.

6. Fry, *Rule,* 61.

7. Fry, *Rule,* 64.

8. Fry, *Rule,* 65.

9. Fry, *Rule,* 26.

10. Fry, *Rule,* 27–31, 42–43, 52–53, 54–55, 92, 95–96.

11. Fry, *Rule,* 30.

12. Fry, *Rule,* 56.

Chapter 5

Epigraph: Dante Alighieri, *The Inferno,* trans. Allen Mandelbaum (New York: Random House, 1980), World of Dante, www.worldofdante.org/comedy/dante/inferno.xml/1.1.

1. Dante, *Inferno,* www.worldofdante.org/comedy/dante/inferno.xml/1.7.
2. Dante Alighieri, *Purgatorio,* trans. Allen Mandelbaum (New York: Random House, 1982), World of Dante, www.worldofdante.org/comedy/dante/purgatory.xml/2.16.
3. Dante, *Purgatorio,* www.worldofdante.org/comedy/dante/purgatory.xml/2.23.
4. Dante Alighieri, *Paradiso,* trans. Allen Mandelbaum (New York: Random House, 1984), World of Dante, www.worldofdante.org/comedy/dante/paradise.xml/3.14.
5. Dante, *Paradiso,* www.worldofdante.org/comedy/dante/paradise.xml/3.6.
6. Dante, *Paradiso,* www.worldofdante.org/comedy/dante/paradise.xml/3.7.
7. Dante, *Inferno* and *Purgatorio*, www.divinecomedy.org/divine_comedy.html.
8. Dante, *Purgatorio,* www.worldofdante.org/comedy/dante/purgatory.xml/2.3.
9. Dante, *Paradiso,* www.worldofdante.org/comedy/dante/paradise.xml/3.22.

Chapter 6

Epigraph: Unknown author, *The Cloud of Unknowing,* trans. Carmen Acevedo Butcher (Boston: Shambhala, 2009), 22.

1. Butcher, *Cloud,* 14.
2. Butcher, *Cloud,* 16.
3. Butcher, *Cloud,* 12.
4. Butcher, *Cloud,* 24.
5. Butcher, *Cloud,* 93.
6. Butcher, *Cloud,* 97.
7. Butcher, *Cloud,* 165–66.
8. Butcher, *Cloud,* 151.
9. Butcher, *Cloud,* 21.
10. Butcher, *Cloud,* 163.
11. Butcher, *Cloud,* 11–18, 21–22.
12. Butcher, *Cloud,* 74–75.

Chapter 7

Epigraph: Julian of Norwich, *All Shall Be Well: Revelations of Divine Love,* written in modern language by Ellyn Sanna (Vestal, NY: Anamchara Books, 2011), 264.

1. Julian, *All Shall Be Well,* 22.
2. Julian, *All Shall Be Well,* 53.
3. Julian, *All Shall Be Well,* 105.
4. Julian, *All Shall Be Well,* 54.

5. Julian, *All Shall Be Well,* 54.

6. Julian, *All Shall Be Well,* 123.

7. Julian, *All Shall Be Well,* 134.

8. Julian, *All Shall Be Well,* 134.

9. Julian, *All Shall Be Well,* 160.

10. Julian, *All Shall Be Well,* 165.

11. Julian, *All Shall Be Well,* 252.

12. Julian, *All Shall Be Well,* 311.

13. Ellyn Sanna, introduction to Julian, *All Shall Be Well,* 21.

14. Julian, *All Shall Be Well,* 33–35, 160–62, 229–31.

15. Julian, *All Shall Be Well,* 60.

16. Julian, *All Shall Be Well,* 117.

Chapter 8

Epigraph: Thomas à Kempis, *The Imitation of Christ,* trans. William C. Creasy (Notre Dame, IN: Ave Maria, 1989, 2004), 32.

1. Creasy, *Imitation,* 60–61.

2. Creasy, *Imitation,* 33.

3. Creasy, *Imitation,* 53.

4. Creasy, *Imitation,* 81.

5. Creasy, *Imitation,* 100–1.

6. Creasy, *Imitation,* 112–13.

7. Creasy, *Imitation,* 172.

8. Creasy, *Imitation,* 184.

9. Richard J. Foster, Renovare *Perspective* 11, no.1 (January 2001), www.renovare .us/Portals/0/documents/perspective_11_1.pdf.

10. Creasy, *Imitation,* 75.

11. Luke 17:21.

12. Creasy, *Imitation,* 30–31, 64–66.

13. Creasy, *Imitation,* 51.

14. Creasy, *Imitation,* 73.

Chapter 9

Epigraph: Philokalia: The Eastern Christian Spiritual Texts. Selections Annotated & Explained, trans. G. E. H. Palmer, Philip Sherrard, and Bishop Kallistos Ware, annotated by Allyne Smith (Woodstock, VT: Skylight, 1995), 169.

1. Introduction to vol. 1 of *The Philokalia: The Complete Text,* compiled by St. Nikodimos of the Holy Mountain and St. Makarios of Corinth, trans. G. E. H. Palmer, Philip Sherrard, and Bishop Kallistos Ware, www.scribd.com/doc/22006204/ Philokalia-Complete-Text, 13.

2. Palmer, et al, introduction to vol. 1 of *Philokalia,* 14.

3. *Philokalia: Selections,* 203.

4. *Philokalia: Selections,* 201.

5. *Philokalia: Selections,* 205.

6. *Philokalia: Selections,* 71.

7. *Philokalia: Selections,* 97.

8. *Philokalia: Selections,* 109.

9. *Philokalia: Selections,* 177.

10. *Philokalia: Selections,* 173.

11. *Philokalia: Selections,* 173.

12. *Philokalia,* trans. G. E. H. Palmer, Philip Sherrard, and Bishop Kallistos Ware, www.scribd.com/doc/22006204/Philokalia-Complete-Text.

Chapter 10

Epigraph: John Calvin, *Institutes of the Christian Religion,* trans. Henry Beveridge, www.ccel.org/ccel/calvin/institutes.iii.ii.html.

1. Calvin, *Institutes,* www.ccel.org/ccel/calvin/institutes.iii.iii.html.

2. Calvin, *Institutes,* www.ccel.org/ccel/calvin/institutes.iii.ii.html and www.ccel .org/ccel/calvin/institutes.v.vii.html.

Chapter 11

Epigraph: Teresa of Ávila, *The Interior Castle,* trans. The Benedictines of Stanbrook, rev. Very Rev. Fr. Benedict Zimmerman, O.C.D. (London: Thomas Baker, 1921), www.ccel.org/ccel/teresa/castle2.v.i.html.

1. Teresa, *Interior Castle,* www.ccel.org/ccel/teresa/castle2.v.i.html.

2. Teresa, *Interior Castle,* www.ccel.org/ccel/teresa/castle2.vii.ii.html.

3. Teresa, *Interior Castle,* www.ccel.org/ccel/teresa/castle2.viii.iii.html.

4. Teresa, *Interior Castle,* www.ccel.org/ccel/teresa/castle2.viii.i.html.

5. Teresa, *Interior Castle,* www.ccel.org/ccel/teresa/castle2.vi.i.html.

6. Teresa, *Interior Castle,* www.ccel.org/ccel/teresa/castle2.v.ii.html.

7. Teresa, *Interior Castle,* www.ccel.org/ccel/teresa/castle2.viii.iii.html.

8. Dallas Willard, introduction to Teresa of Ávila, *The Interior Castle* (San Francisco: HarperOne, 2004), xvi.

9. Teresa, *Interior Castle,* www.ccel.org/ccel/teresa/castle2.v.i.html and www .ccel.org/ccel/teresa/castle2.ix.ii.html.

10. Teresa, *Interior Castle,* www.ccel.org/ccel/teresa/castle2.vi.i.html.

Chapter 12

Epigraph: John of the Cross, *Dark Night of the Soul,* trans. E. Allison Peers, www.ccel .org/ccel/john_cross/dark_night.vii.viii.html.

1. John, *Dark Night,* www.ccel.org/ccel/john_cross/dark_night.viii.i.html.

2. John, *Dark Night,* www.ccel.org/ccel/john_cross/dark_night.viii.iii.html.

3. John, *Dark Night,* www.ccel.org/ccel/john_cross/dark_night.viii.v.html.

4. John, *Dark Night,* www.ccel.org/ccel/john_cross/dark_night.viii.vi.html.

5. John, *Dark Night,* www.ccel.org/ccel/john_cross/dark_night.vi.html; www.ccel.org/ccel/john_cross/dark_night.vii.viii.html; www.ccel.org/ccel/john_cross/dark_night.viii.v.html.

Chapter 13

Epigraph: Blaise Pascal, *Pensées,* trans. A. J. Krailsheimer (New York: Penguin, 1966, 1995), 141.

1. Pascal, *Pensées,* 38.

2. Pascal, *Pensées,* 4, 6, 46–49, 95–97, 285–86.

3. Pascal, *Pensées,* 123.

Chapter 14

Epigraph: John Bunyan, *The Pilgrim's Progress,* www.ccel.org/ccel/bunyan/pilgrim.iii.html.

1. Bunyan, *Pilgrim's Progress,* www.ccel.org/ccel/bunyan/pilgrim.iv.x.html.

2. Bunyan, *Pilgrim's Progress,* www.ccel.org/ccel/bunyan/pilgrim.iv.x.html.

3. Bunyan, *Pilgrim's Progress,* www.ccel.org/ccel/bunyan/pilgrim.iv.xi.html.

4. Bunyan, *Pilgrim's Progress,* www.ccel.org/ccel/bunyan/pilgrim.iv.i.html and www.ccel.org/ccel/bunyan/pilgrim.iv.ii.html.

Chapter 15

Epigraph: Brother Lawrence, *The Practice of the Presence of God* (London: Epworth, n.d.), www.ccel.org/ccel/lawrence/practice.iii.iv.html.

1. Lawrence, *Practice,* www.ccel.org/ccel/lawrence/practice.iii.iv.html.

2. Lawrence, *Practice,* www.ccel.org/ccel/lawrence/practice.iii.ii.html.

3. Lawrence, *Practice,* www.ccel.org/ccel/lawrence/practice.iii.iv.html.

4. Richard J. Foster, *Prayers from the Heart* (San Francisco: HarperOne, 1994), xi.

5. Lawrence, *Practice,* www.ccel.org/ccel/lawrence/practice.iv.ix.html.

6. Brother Lawrence and Frank Laubach, *Practicing His Presence* (Jacksonville, FL: Seedsowers, 1973), 45–49, 75–78.

7. Lawrence and Laubach, *Practicing His Presence,* 42.

8. Lawrence and Laubach, *Practicing His Presence,* 88.

9. Lawrence and Laubach, *Practicing His Presence,* 105.

10. Lawrence and Laubach, *Practicing His Presence,* 52.

Chapter 16

Epigraph: William Law, *A Serious Call to a Devout and Holy Life,* Christian Classics Ethereal Library, www.ccel.org/ccel/law/serious_call.iii.html.

1. Law, *Serious Call,* www.ccel.org/ccel/law/serious_call.ii.html.
2. Law, *Serious Call,* www.ccel.org/ccel/law/serious_call.ii.html.
3. Law, *Serious Call,* www.ccel.org/ccel/law/serious_call.v.html.
4. Law, *Serious Call,* www.ccel.org/ccel/law/serious_call.vii.html.
5. Law, *Serious Call,* www.ccel.org/ccel/law/serious_call.xvi.html.
6. Richard J. Foster and James Bryan Smith, eds., *Devotional Classics* (San Francisco: HarperOne, 2005), 162.
7. Law, *Serious Call,* www.ccel.org/ccel/law/serious_call.ii.html.
8. Law, *Serious Call,* www.ccel.org/ccel/law/serious_call.iii.html.
9. Law, *Serious Call,* www.ccel.org/ccel/law/serious_call.iii.html.
10. Law, *Serious Call,* www.ccel.org/ccel/law/serious_call.x.html.

Chapter 17

Epigraph: Unknown author, *The Way of a Pilgrim,* trans. Helen Bacovcin (New York: Image/Doubleday, 1978), 3.

1. Bacovcin, *Way of a Pilgrim,* 112.
2. Bacovcin, *Way of a Pilgrim,* 66.
3. Bacovcin, *Way of a Pilgrim,* 3–4, 6–9.
4. Bacovcin, *Way of a Pilgrim,* 13.

Chapter 18

Epigraph: Fyodor Dostoevsky, *The Brothers Karamazov,* www.ccel.org/ccel/dostoevsky/brothers.iii_3.html.

1. Dostoevsky, *Brothers,* www.ccel.org/ccel/dostoevsky/brothers.iii_7.html.
2. Dostoevsky, *Brothers,* www.ccel.org/ccel/dostoevsky/brothers.v_4.html.
3. Dostoevsky, *Brothers,* www.ccel.org/ccel/dostoevsky/brothers.v.html.

Chapter 19

Epigraph: G. K. Chesterton, *Orthodoxy* (San Francisco: Ignatius, 1908), 107.

1. Chesterton, *Orthodoxy,* 32, 33.
2. Chesterton, *Orthodoxy,* 52–53.
3. Chesterton, *Orthodoxy,* 59.
4. Chesterton, *Orthodoxy,* 60.
5. Chesterton, *Orthodoxy,* 154.
6. Chesterton, *Orthodoxy,* 156.
7. Chesterton, *Orthodoxy,* 167.
8. Chesterton, *Orthodoxy,* 167.

9. Chesterton, *Orthodoxy,* 114.

10. Chesterton, *Orthodoxy,* 65.

11. Chesterton, *Orthodoxy,* 69.

12. Chesterton, *Orthodoxy,* 13–16, 161–62, 163–65.

13. Chesterton, *Orthodoxy,* 64.

14. Chesterton, *Orthodoxy,* 161, 162.

15. Chesterton, *Orthodoxy,* 163.

Chapter 20

Epigraph: Gerard Manley Hopkins, *Poems* (London: Humphrey Milford, 1918), www.bartleby.com/122/52.html.

1. Foster, *Celebration of Discipline,* 29, 30.

2. John E. Keating, *The Wreck of the Deutschland: An Essay and Commentary* (Bulletin Kent, OH: Kent State University, 1963), 9.

3. Keating, *Wreck,* 9.

4. Hopkins, *Poems,* www.bartleby.com/122/4.html.

5. Hopkins, *Poems,* www.bartleby.com/122/13.html.

6. Hopkins, *Poems,* www.bartleby.com/122/7.html.

7. Hopkins, *Poems,* www.bartleby.com/122/34.html.

Chapter 21

Epigraph: Dietrich Bonhoeffer, *The Cost of Discipleship* (Touchstone: New York, 1959), 44–45.

1. Bonhoeffer, *Discipleship,* 44–45.

2. Bonhoeffer, *Discipleship,* 37.

3. Bonhoeffer, *Discipleship,* 54.

4. Bonhoeffer, *Discipleship,* 55.

5. Bonhoeffer, *Discipleship,* 92.

6. Bonhoeffer, *Discipleship,* 227.

7. Bonhoeffer, *Discipleship,* 159.

8. Bonhoeffer, *Discipleship,* 43–45, 301–4.

9. Bonhoeffer, *Discipleship,* 43.

10. Bonhoeffer, *Discipleship,* 92.

Chapter 22

Epigraph: Thomas R. Kelly, *A Testament of Devotion* (San Francisco: HarperOne, 1941), 97.

1. Kelly, *Testament,* 12.

2. Kelly, *Testament,* 27.

3. Kelly, *Testament,* 39.

4. Kelly, *Testament,* 57.

5. Kelly, *Testament,* 60.

6. Kelly, *Testament,* 70–71.

7. Kelly, *Testament,* 83.

8. Kelly, *Testament,* 100.

9. Richard J. Foster, introduction to Kelly, *Testament,* x.

10. Kelly, *Testament,* 9–14, 98–100.

11. Kelly, *Testament,* 27.

12. Kelly, *Testament,* 54.

13. Kelly, *Testament,* 100.

Chapter 23

Epigraph: Thomas Merton, *The Seven Storey Mountain* (San Diego: Harvest/Harcourt Brace, 1948, 1976), 280.

1. Merton, *Seven Storey Mountain,* 94.

2. Merton, *Seven Storey Mountain,* 123.

3. Merton, *Seven Storey Mountain,* 127.

4. Merton, *Seven Storey Mountain,* 231.

5. Merton, *Seven Storey Mountain,* 250–51.

6. Merton, *Seven Storey Mountain,* 320.

7. Merton, *Seven Storey Mountain,* 406.

8. Merton, *Seven Storey Mountain,* 410.

9. *A Year with Thomas Merton: Daily Meditations from His Journals,* comp. and ed. Jonathan Montaldo (San Francisco: HarperOne, 2004), 81.

10. Merton, *Seven Storey Mountain,* 122–25, 346–48.

11. Merton, *Seven Storey Mountain,* 72.

12. Merton, *Seven Storey Mountain,* 92.

13. Merton, *Seven Storey Mountain,* 136.

14. Merton, *Seven Storey Mountain,* 250–51.

15. Merton, *Seven Storey Mountain,* 323.

16. Merton, *Seven Storey Mountain,* 419.

Chapter 24

Epigraph: C. S. Lewis, *Mere Christianity,* rev. ed. (San Francisco, HarperOne, 1980), 189.

1. Lewis, *Mere Christianity,* 49.

2. Lewis, *Mere Christianity,* 64.

3. Lewis, *Mere Christianity,* 188–89.

4. Lewis, *Mere Christianity,* 205–6.

5. Lewis, *Mere Christianity,* 154–55.

6. Lewis, *Mere Christianity,* 47–52, 196–99.

7. Lewis, *Mere Christianity,* 84.

Chapter 25

Epigraph: Henri J. M. Nouwen, *The Return of the Prodigal Son* (New York: Image Doubleday, 1992), 52.

1. Nouwen, *Prodigal Son,* 53.
2. Nouwen, *Prodigal Son,* 117.
3. Nouwen, *Prodigal Son,* 19–23.
4. Nouwen, *Prodigal Son,* 52.

Permissions

Acknowledgments

First, we are grateful to all the people who submitted their personal top five lists. You allowed the project to start strong and your selections and comments were of great help to us in preparing the final list and the additional material in this book. For a list of these folks please visit www.renovare.us/25books.

We owe a great debt of gratitude to all the members of the editorial board: Gayle Beebe, James Catford, Richard J. Foster, Emilie Griffin, Frederica Mathewes-Green, Mickey Maudlin, Richard Rohr, Phyllis Tickle, Dallas Willard, Chris Webb, and John Wilson. Their enthusiastic advocacy and insight into the twenty-five books highlighted herein made the list not only noteworthy but informed.

Special thanks also go to Lynda Graybeal, who helped to locate many of the quotations used in the book, and to Mickey Maudlin, Cynthia DiTiberio, Kathryn Renz, and Carolyn Holland at HarperOne for their hard work to make this book a reality. We want to recognize Lisa Zuniga in particular, for her expert guidance through a complicated production process.

Julia thanks her husband, Ryan Waterman, whose support makes her writing possible, and her sons, Ben and Luke, who provide all kinds of inspiration and who are so understanding when Mommy has to work. Lyle thanks the staff, Board, and Ministry Team of Renovaré USA and Felicia, his spouse, for support in this and many other ministry projects, aspired and actual.

—Julia L. Roller and Lyle SmithGraybeal

What Is Renovaré?

Renovaré USA is a nonprofit Christian organization that models, resources, and advocates fullness of life with God experienced, by grace, through the spiritual practices of Jesus and of the historical Church. We imagine a world in which people's lives flourish as they increasingly become like Jesus.

Through personal relationships, conferences and retreats, written and web-based resources, church consultations, and other means, Renovaré USA pursues these core ideas:

Life with God—The aim of God in history is the creation of an all-inclusive community of loving persons with God himself at the center of this community as its prime Sustainer and most glorious Inhabitant.

The Availability of God's Kingdom—Salvation is life in the kingdom of God through Jesus Christ. We can experience genuine, substantive life in this kingdom, beginning now and continuing through all eternity.

The Necessity of Grace—We are utterly dependent upon Jesus Christ, our ever-living Savior, Teacher, Lord, and Friend for genuine spiritual transformation.

The Means of Grace—Amongst the variety of ways God has given for us to be open to his transforming grace, we recognize the crucial importance of intentional spiritual practices and disciplines (such as prayer, service, or fasting).

A Balanced Vision of Life in Christ—We seek to embrace the abundant life of Jesus in all its fullness: contemplative, holiness, charismatic, social justice, evangelical, and incarnational.

A Practical Strategy for Spiritual Formation—Spiritual friendship is an essential part of our growth in Christlikeness. We encourage the creation of Spiritual Formation Groups as a solid foundation for mutual support and nurture.

The Centrality of Scripture—We immerse ourselves in the Bible: it is the great revelation of God's purposes in history, a sure guide for growth into Christlikeness, and an ever rich resource for our spiritual formation.

The Value of the Christian Tradition—We are engaged in the historical "Great Conversation" on spiritual formation developed from Scripture by the Church's classical spiritual writings.

Christian in commitment, ecumenical in breadth, and international in scope, Renovaré USA helps us in becoming like Jesus. The Renovaré Covenant succinctly communicates our hope for all those who look to him for life:

In utter dependence upon Jesus Christ as my ever-living Savior, Teacher, Lord, and Friend, I will seek continual renewal through:
> • spiritual exercises • spiritual gifts • acts of service

RENOVARÉ

Renovaré USA
8 Inverness Drive East, Suite 102
Englewood, CO, 80112 USA
303-792-0152   www.renovare.us

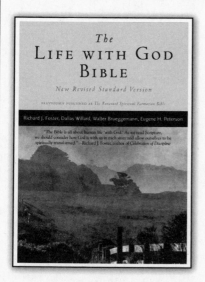

THE BIBLE
for
LIFELONG CHRISTIAN SPIRITUAL FORMATION

With General Editors Richard J. Foster, Dallas Willard, Gayle Beebe, Tom Oden, and Lynda L. Graybeal and 50+ other contributors, *The Life with God Bible* features:

- Fifteen progressive essays on living life with God

- Introductions and notes for each book of the Bible

- Personal spiritual practices integrated into the text

- Spiritual Disciplines Index of eighteen spiritual disciplines in Scripture

- Profiles of key biblical characters highlighting their growth

- Bibliography of key spiritual formation books

- Suggested plans for Scripture engagement

- Maps and a concordance

- The New Revised Standard Version translation

*Combining the depth of
a study Bible with the
warmth of a devotional Bible,*
The Life with God Bible
*is a revolutionary resource that
brings Scripture alive
for daily life.*

Available in leather-like, paper, or hard cover with or without the Deuterocanonical Books.

Purchase *The Life With God Bible* from your favorite bookseller.

RENOVARÉ

HARPER BIBLES